FILMMAKERS SERIES
edited by
ANTHONY SLIDE

Order in the Universe

The Films of John Carpenter

Second Edition

Robert C. Cumbow

Filmmakers Series, No. 70

The Scarecrow Press, Inc.
Lanham, Maryland, and London
2000

SCARECROW PRESS, INC.

Published in the United States of America
by Scarecrow Press, Inc.
4720 Boston Way, Lanham, Maryland 20706
http://www.scarecrowpress.com

4 Pleydell Gardens, Folkestone
Kent CT20 2DN, England

British Library Cataloguing in Publication Information Available

Library of Congress Cataloging-in-Publication Data
Cumbow, Robert C., 1946-
    Order in the universe : the films of John Carpenter / Robert C. Cumbow.— 2nd ed.
      p. cm. — (Filmmakers series ; no. 70)
    Includes bibliographical references and index.
    ISBN 0-8108-3719-6 ISBN: 978-0-8108-3719-5
    1. Carpenter, John, 1948—Criticism and interpretation. I. Title. II. Series.
PN1998.3.C38 C8 2000
791.43'0233'092—dc21   00-025592
First edition / 1990 / 0-8108-2344-6

♾™ The paper used in this publication meets the minimum requirements of
American National Standard for Information Sciences—Permanence of
Paper for Printed Library Materials, ANSI/NISO Z39.48-1992.
Manufactured in the United States of America.

For

Rachel Elizabeth Cumbow

who let me see *Big Trouble in Little China* with the eyes of a child

and

Irena Alexis Cumbow

who knows why *Vampires* is a pretty cool movie

Contents

Acknowledgments

Throughout this book, all comments attributed to John Carpenter but not footnoted or otherwise documented are from a personal interview I conducted with him on June 19, 1989, and are excerpted for use here with Mr. Carpenter's kind permission.

My deepest thanks to Mr. Carpenter and to his associate, Sandy King, who gave more than generously of their time—and to these people, without whose help, inspiration, and sometimes just good conversation, the job would have been a lot tougher: Nazir Ali, Betty Werblun, Charles Nishida, Julie Springer, Stephanie Ogle, Jeff Shannon, Sean Axmaker, Jim Revius, Keith Simanton, Chris Stephens, Linda Leahy, Robin Ray, Tim Wright, Marc Bright, Mark Steensland, Tony Williams, and Richard T. Jameson.

For help in locating needed photos and videotapes, I am grateful again to the wonderful staffs of Jerry Ohlinger's Movie Material Store, New York, and of Larry Edmunds Bookshop, Hollywood; Stephanie Ogle at Cinema Books, Seattle; the Museum of Modern Art Film Stills Archive, New York; the Film Distribution Center at the University of Southern California School of Cinema and TV, Los Angeles; Don Bartholomew at the University of Washington Media Center, Seattle; John Black and Fred Hopkins of Backtrack Video, Seattle; and Bruce McElwain, film collector, of Bellingham, Washington.

And as always my love and thanks to Grace, Rachel, and Irena.

1

Stirrings

Introduction

> Besides being complicated, reality, in my experience, is usually odd. It is not neat, not obvious, not what you expect. ... Reality, in fact, is usually something you could not have guessed.
>
> —C. S. Lewis
> *Mere Christianity*

> While order *does* exist in the universe, it is not at all what we had in mind.
>
> —Professor Howard Birack
> The Doppler Institute of Physics

The auteur theory—which was never a theory at all but merely a policy defining the approach of certain film critics—has been out of fashion now for a couple of decades. But that has not changed the fact that there remain film directors who, every time out, evince a consistent and recognizable stylistic and thematic vision and whose films may thus be regarded as a body of work. John Carpenter is such a director, and I make no apology for taking such an approach to his work.

Auteurism had already gone into a period of decadent excess when Carpenter emerged in the late Seventies. People like Arthur Hiller, Franklin J. Schaffner, and Jack Smight were insisting on, and receiving, possessory credit for films of no distinguishing personal character. Die-hard auteurist critics were claiming to have found a new personal genius in every unknown director whose name appeared on a passably interesting film. It was tough to spot the real thing.

I might not have rushed to see a film called *Halloween* had it not been for Richard T. Jameson's review in *Movietone News*, which took note of a meticulous approach to framing and an attention to cinematic order that made a minor masterpiece out of what might have been just another low-budget remake of *Psycho*.

Jameson's review notes that in *Halloween* John Carpenter "appears to have set out to reinstate scrupulous, meaningful framing all by himself ... Carpenter's *direction* has undercut the idea of a world with any secure breathing-room ... we feel a desperate need to keep an eye on every sector of screenspace ... no periphery is accidentally arrived at; the directorial eye never loses control. Virtually every shot contains corners, apertures, fillable black holes fraught with ghastly potentiality ... John Carpenter doesn't want this kind of cinematically invigorating evil to end; it's intrinsic to a classical order he believes in."[1] Two decades later, these remain among the most perceptive words to have been written about John Carpenter.

A belief in the ordering power of the frame as a stabilizing force in an increasingly chaotic world is, of course, basic to the idea of making movies, but all too few moviemakers seem to embrace it. Contemporary Hollywood movies are mostly indistinguishable from television, in John Carpenter's view: "They go on videotape really well because they are all shot a certain way—dead center."[2] Not only the lack of a visual sense but also the production process itself has contributed to what might be termed the televization of the movies: "In Hollywood, movies have turned into television. ... What they do with a picture is they take it out and they test it with several audiences and they get demographics on the film. They alter the film to play to the audience. It's like computer-done movies. There's no humanity in them."[3]

Films, for John Carpenter (who has made them for both the big screen and the small one), are a search for—and a confrontation with—new order, in the same sense that all art is an effort to reorder the universe, or at least one's vision of it. Not only the director but also his characters pursue the phantom Order. Carpenter's films are populated by seekers whose quest for meaning is usually rewarded, but who often discover an order quite different from the reassuring one they set out to find.

Understand: This is not the common horror motif of finding one's ordered existence invaded by some other force, collapsing into chaos. This is the far deeper, more devastating (and sometimes transfiguring) experience of finding that the order in accord with which one has lived one's life is *not the right one*; that some *other* order altogether controls—and perhaps has always controlled. It is the horror of Job discovering that you can't avoid evil merely by living righteously; of Oedipus learning that terrible limits are imposed upon free will and intelligence; of Ivan Ilich recognizing that the agony of disease is nothing compared to the agony of knowing that the life you have lived has not been the right one.

This is no chance encounter with evil. It is the ultimate horror announced in the discovery that Michael Myers is, after all, the Bogey Man (*Halloween*), or that the end and purpose of all of our existence are the very opposite of what we have been taught (*Prince of Darkness*), or that everything we see is wrong (*They Live*), or that our complacent lives are mere masks for the terrible order right next door, waiting to ooze in through the slightest crack and destroy us utterly (*In the Mouth of Madness*).

As a metaphor for this unexpected order, Carpenter's films have often arrived at neurosis, psychosis, or some other mental aberration, recognizing—as Stanley Kubrick did in his film of Stephen King's *The Shining*—that the truly mad do not suffer from a jumbled, confused view of the world around them, but from a tendency to see things all too simply and clearly. In Kubrick's film, the labyrinth provides the perfect emblem of a vision of the world that is both twisted and pre-eminently orderly—a terrifying emblem of the complex and entrapping power of structure. It's as if the filmmaker were looking with irony at the darker side of his own devotion to structural perfection. The condition in which Kubrick's (not necessarily King's) Jack Torrance finds himself is like that of Kurtz in both Conrad's *Heart of Darkness* and Coppola's *Apocalypse Now*: "He's clear in his mind, but his soul is mad."

This is exactly the condition that Carpenter's searchers and would be saviors must confront. "All my films are basically morality plays," he has said.[4] From the Academy Award winning live-action short *The Resurrection of Broncho Billy*, which may be legitimately considered the first "John Carpenter Film," right up through *Vampires*, the anxieties of contemporary urban life form a subtext to the writer-director's tales of fantasy, horror and science fiction. The psychosis of crowding is seen in microcosm in the claustrophobic *Dark Star* and in macrocosm in the street schizos of *Prince of Darkness* and the bleak cityscapes of *They Live*. As has always been true of the horror genre, the monsters of John Carpenter's films are literal on the narrative level only. On the moral level, they are objective correlates for the suppressed fears and desires of contemporary human beings.

Carpenter has often been accused of being a manipulative filmmaker. But of course all filmmaking is manipulative. Hitchcock was a master of manipulation. Carpenter's manipulation of his medium does not go for the easy, knee-jerk effect that is associated with accusations of manipulation. "You need to have certain charisma and power, to be able to lead people and control them," Carpenter says of the role of the film director—and he means controlling not only the cast and crew on the set, but the audience as well, as evidenced in his definition of the film director as "someone who can express a point of view of the world on film and hopefully move people."[5] Elsewhere he has said, "This idea, of the audience projecting their fantasy, is to me the secret of movies. And the secret for me is that I get emotionally involved with the characters I'm dealing with. How I feel about them is how I make them out on the screen, and how I want the audience to feel."[6]

Filmmaking isn't all art, and one sees in John Carpenter's career more dramatically than in most the tensions between the relative freedom of independent filmmaking and the more authoritarian—but more lucratively budgeted—atmosphere of studio production. Carpenter speaks of "the endless confrontation between management and creativity. They want it great, but they want it cheap."[7] Of his four-picture deal with "Les Mougins," the partnership of Andre Blay and Alive Pictures Chairman Shep Gordon, he has said, "I do them for a lower budget than most films can be done, to get creative control."[8] His frequent collaborator, producer Larry Franco, told *Cinefantastique*: "I think John will continue doing independent films for a while and see what happens. I think it would be very difficult for him after this picture [*Prince of Darkness*] to give up some of the creative control he's gotten."[9] It remains something of a truism to say that Carpenter's independent films are better, more personal, more defining. But the style and artistry of studio projects like *Starman* belie the glib simplicity of that observation.

By his own account, John Carpenter has always wanted to direct movies. It was Jack Arnold's 1953 film *It Came from Outer Space* that made him want to direct scary ones. At the University of Southern California, he created a series of short films in the horror and mock-horror vein with such titles as *Revenge of the Colossal Beasts, Gorgo vs. Godzilla, Terror from Space, The Warrior and the Demon, Sorcerer from Outer Space,* and *Gorgon the Space Monster*. And despite the love of westerns that permeates his films, and his sortie into the musical biopic with *Elvis*, he remains firmly implanted in the horror and science fiction genres.

In the popular consciousness, his name is still associated most with *Halloween*—the film that made his name more than a decade ago; the film that garnered the highest proportional return on investment of any independent film until that time (and for several years thereafter); the film that he wouldn't shake off until association with two inferior sequels finally led him to sell altogether his rights to the series.

Carpenter has said, "In France I'm an auteur, in Germany I'm a filmmaker, in the U.K. I'm a horror director, in the U.S. I'm a bum."[10]

Yet he enjoys a growing and rabid cult following that spawned numerous fan magazines and later Web sites in the United States, England,[11] and Japan. He stays close to his fans, possibly because he rose to filmmaking from the ranks of fandom himself, having edited his own fanzine, *Fantastic Films Illustrated*, during the mid-Sixties, and written for several others. He is highly respected among a coterie of critics and film enthusiasts who appreciate his genre-consciousness and his reverent, classical approach to filmmaking.

He continues to sustain a vibrantly active career, moving back and forth between more personal independent projects and big-studio jobs, occasionally as a hired gun. Whatever turns—new or familiar—he makes in his career, each new John Carpenter film surprises, presenting a new order even as it gives us the comfort of the by now familiar vision I attempt to trace in the pages that follow.

"I try," says John Carpenter, "to do things that I haven't done before."[12]

Notes

1. Jameson, Richard T., review of *Halloween*, in *Movietone News*, 60-61, February 1979, pp. 40-41.
2. In Fischer, Dennis, "John Carpenter's *They Live*," *Cinefantastique* 19:1/2, January 1989, p. 124.
3. *Ibid.*
4. In Fischer, *op. cit.*, p. 13.
5. In Taub, Eric, *Gaffers, Grips, and Best Boys*, New York: St. Martin's Press, 1987, p. 70.
6. McCarthy, Todd, "Trick and Treat" [John Carpenter interviewed by Todd McCarthy], *Film Comment* 16:1, Jan/Feb 1980, p. 23.
7. In Taub, *op. cit.*, p. 68.
8. In Fischer, *op. cit.*, p. 12.
9. In Fischer, Dennis, "*Prince of Darkness*," *Cinefantastique* 18:1, December 1987, p. 7.
10. Attributed to Carpenter in a Radio Canada interview in 1998 Canada, transcribed at: *http://radio-canada.ca/infoculture/speciale/fantasia/carpenter.html* and cited in an article by Sean Axmaker on Film.com, *http://www.film.com*.
11. *The John Carpenter File*, published by the John Carpenter Information Club, is no longer in publication.
12. In Taub, *op. cit.*, p. 69.

John Carpenter
1983

2

Sunrise

The Resurrection of Broncho Billy

Some cowboys can't afford their own horses. And a lot of film-makers can't afford to make westerns.

No genre looms larger in film history than the western, and no student of film fails to develop an appreciation, even a passion, for the western myth. But few of them ever get to make a western, because of the combined effect of financial and logistical difficulty and the self-fulfilling prophecy of the Death of the Western.

Although he didn't direct it, and shares screenplay credit with four other people, I want to think of *The Resurrection of Broncho Billy* as the first John Carpenter film, because it contains in seminal form four key elements that characterize all of his work: an atmosphere of contemporary urban neurosis that creates, in his characters, a yearning for a different kind of order; the search for that order in a pattern of mythic experience; transcendence of time, and the collision of different eras; and a reverence for the conventions of genre filmmaking.

The hero of *The Resurrection of Broncho Billy* inhabits a world that is already out of joint—a disjunction he has tried to put right, in his own little corner, by means of his devotion to classic western films. Like any hobby, it helps him make sense of his life; it gives him a defense against the assaults of the modern world. But his absorption in the western is more than a hobby. It is his salvation.

Just as contemporary urban neurosis is built upon a sense of disunity in one's life, the discovery of meaning depends upon a rediscovery of unity. In Billy's case, that means a bridge across time, a meeting of the old and the new in a way that makes sense of both.

The Resurrection of Broncho Billy offers the first instance of that blending of old and new that overhangs all of Carpenter's films. The opening montage, backed by Carpenter's original music (American folk-based themes), presents us with images not from the West but from *westerns* ... movie posters. This is absorption not in the past, but in the eternal present of myth.

"You'll be late for work!" comes a screech, modern time encroaching on the timelessness of myth.

Old Timer, born April 11, 1892, recounts for Billy tales of the West—the litany of who shot whom—and these too are not history but myth, out of time, filtered through the embellished memory of the Homeric artist-narrator. Significantly, Old Timer has given the boy an antique pocket watch. "One thing I told ya when I gave ya this watch, Billy—ya got ta wind it every once in a while." Billy doesn't wind the watch because he isn't interested in modern time, and it is not the watch's time-recording function that he cares about: It's the watch itself, as relic, as emblem of time. Billy himself is out of time—in the good sense of that expression.

Similarly, the fantasy that brings order and meaning to Billy's life, and helps him cope with adversity, is a fantasy not of the Old West, but of the *movie* West. It is not the dream of frontier glory but the conventions of a film genre that bring order—and, of course, that's what genre conventions are: an ordering device that sets individual experience into a framework of myth.

Billy's fantasies are heard in the sounds that he not so much imagines as imposes upon his contemporary world: hoofbeats, guitar music, saloon ambience. The roar of rush hour traffic becomes the sound of a thundering herd of cattle. His fantasies are heard in the conversation he introduces into an unsuspecting urban environment: "Yup," he says, and "Waal, if it's ... good enough fer you, it's ... good enough fer me" (pausing in the wrong places for John Wayne effect), and "I just been in one hell of a fight," he tells the waitress at the Orange Julius, putting a surprisingly upbeat spin on his mugging in an alleyway by street toughs.

Gesture, too, gives Billy a means by which to layer the western myth over his quotidian experience. He leans an elbow on the bar, spins over a silver piece, and orders up Red Eye. He eyes an unsuspecting (and increasingly troubled) businessman across a busy street and (with accelerated cross-tracking) crosses the street to face him, approaches him with confidence and an air of finality, pulls back his coat, ready for the draw ... and walks past. Bewildered, the businessman looks back, but Billy is already moving on.

The film's look reflects the same genre conventions in which its hero recasts his drab, stressful life: a ruddy-tinted monochrome like that of some of the old programmers. The role of Billy is played by Johnny Crawford, himself a western icon after a few seasons as Lucas McCain's young son on television's *The Rifleman.*

The Resurrection of Broncho Billy was edited by John Carpenter. Parodying a genre helped Carpenter learn pace and rhythm, the language of film editing. It also helped him discover what was great in classic Hollywood filmmaking, learning by mimicking, lovingly imitating.

Art meets—and overcomes—life repeatedly in *The Resurrection of Broncho Billy*, but nowhere so powerfully as in the film's climax, when art meets *art*. Billy encounters a young woman making sketches in the park. They are attracted to each other, and she begins to sketch him as a cowboy. Billy insists on authenticity ... but his criteria for authenticity are not history, nor the works of Russell or Remington. His touchstones are Gary Cooper and John Wayne. He rhapsodizes eloquently (and touchingly) on the hats worn by Cooper and Wayne, and this is what finally comes between them, boring the sketch artist into packing up and heading off across the field, cutting short what might have developed into a contemporary Relationship.

But now Billy's fantasy wins the day altogether. As if the hat soliloquy has wrought some magic in him—and as if the artist's choice of an open field as her environment has allowed the utter banishment of the cityscape that dominates most of the film—Billy *becomes* his fantasy. Color, albeit faded, bleeds into the image, and he pursues—on horseback, at last—the retreating artist, scooping her up and heading out across open country.

"Spendin' all that money on the movies—that's ridiculous," spouts Billy's landlady at the beginning of the film. But the guys who made *The Resurrection of Broncho Billy* clearly didn't think so. The film is, finally, something we will see again in the work of John Carpenter: an affirmation of the order of movies over the disorder of contemporary life. No wonder it won an Academy Award.

3

Let There Be Light

Dark Star

There's an almost deliberate lack of rehearsal and polish in *Dark Star*, a look like that of many student films—and that, indeed, is how *Dark Star* began. Initially titled *The Electric Dutchman*, then *Planetfall*, *Dark Star* was begun at the University of Southern California in 1970 and completed—for the first time—in 1972, a 50-minute student film with an investment of about $6,000 behind it—most of that Carpenter's own money. Too long to be a short, too short to be a feature, the film was reworked with the backing of Jack Murphy, a Canadian producer introduced to John Carpenter and Dan O'Bannon by fellow USC student Jonathan Kaplan—soon to build his own directorial reputation through his work for Roger Corman's New World Pictures. But it wasn't until 1974 that *Dark Star* got a theatrical release, after one more reworking and the outright sale of the film to independent distributor Jack H. Harris. The film didn't grow legs until the late Seventies, after *Star Wars* created a new science fiction boom and *Halloween* had made John Carpenter's name a household word.

The Carpenter–O'Bannon partnership, for which both men had high hopes, broke down after *Dark Star*, and in the years since, various stories about the circumstances of the breakdown have surfaced. The most heated point of variance between Carpenter and O'Bannon is over the question of credit for specific contributions to *Dark Star*, but all accounts agree generally that the talking bomb, the cryogenically frozen captain, and the Phoenix Asteroids were Dan O'Bannon's; the surfer motif and the observation dome chat between Talby and Doolittle were Carpenter's; and the rest was collaborative.

There was also a dispute between Carpenter and USC over ownership of the film, though Carpenter readily acknowledges that the film was made using USC equipment and facilities, much of it after he and O'Bannon were no longer enrolled at the school. The point of difference here focuses on the school's de facto custom of looking the other way in such arrangements and allowing students to take credit (and, occasionally, profit) from their work. "Nobody got paid a dime to work on *Dark Star*," O'Bannon has pointed out. "It was a student film, a labor of love."[1]

"Attention," reads the legend on the screen as *Dark Star* opens: "Incoming Communication." The film's situation and tone are introduced to us in a transmission from earth to the scout ship Dark Star, in a grainy, monochrome video image that recalls the somewhat slicker communications from home in *2001: A Space Odyssey*. The opening, with incoming messages accompanied by musical beeps, signals that *Dark Star* is built on satirical variations on themes from the two major sources of science fiction imagery from the Sixties: *2001* and the television series *Star Trek*.

Dark Star emerges as an offbeat science fiction comedy that runs something like Stanley Kubrick Meets Wile E. Coyote. References to Kubrick abound—*Dr. Strangelove* (the failure of a fail-safe system, and a recalcitrant bomb) and *2001* (the claustrophobia of space travel, man against machine, and the sense of a super-human destiny awaiting characters who undergo a star-change)—and they are not so much elbow nudges as good-hearted nods. "I'm no great fan of *Star Wars* or *Alien*," Carpenter has said. "What these films have mainly accomplished is to perfect the technique of showing ships moving around in outer space. ... *2001* eclipses them all."[2] One of the *2001* connections in *Dark Star* is the film's treatment of the inherent boredom of space travel, replacing *2001*'s vision of slick, dehumanized, commercial dullness with a sweaty, lived-in cabin fever. This is a comic treatment of an idea that had been previously treated as serious. Many of the ideas that *Dark Star* treated comically would, however, not be treated seriously until O'Bannon's screenplay for another claustrophobic trapped-in-a-spaceship movie saw light as *Alien*. That film shares much of *Dark Star*'s vision: the space crew as common working stiffs, the linkage of space-time with aging, the motherly female computer, the runaway alien on board. (Although the final credits for *Alien* give screenplay credit only to Walter Hill and David Giler, Carpenter joins O'Bannon in insisting that *Alien* was, from the beginning, O'Bannon's vision, and that most of what is on the screen in *Alien* is O'Bannon's work.)

In the notes to the 1974 Los Angeles Filmex, Carpenter is quoted as calling *Dark Star* a "*Waiting for Godot*" in space."[3] It is informed by the same kind of offbeat humor, pseudophilosophical musing, claustrophobic ennui, and overriding sense of futility. The laid-back, natural, almost improvisational dialogue delivery adds to the doomed indifference of the situation. Shots held a little too long underscore the languor. Such marks of student filmmaking as reliance on close-ups, voiceovers, and actors talking into the camera here become effective indices of the claustrophobia and boredom of life on the spacecraft. The ship's computer provides improbable wallpaper music, such as the science fiction, country-western tune "Benson, Arizona," and the big band instrumental "When Twilight Falls on NGC-891."

In command of the cramped, sweaty ship is Lt. Doolittle, whose response to most information is "Who cares?" Doolittle only occasionally alleviates his boredom by pursuing the mission of the scout ship Dark Star—to find uninhabited, "unstable" planets and destroy them, for reasons that are never very clear. "Don't give me any of that 'intelligent life' stuff," he says, when confronted by a vestigial glimmer of the wonder of space exploration. "Find me something I can blow up." It's a parody of the attitude of a particular type of filmmaker, reminding us of the film's origins in a film school project. But it's also a parody of the typically Howard Hawksian exchange between the man of action and the man of dreams, a character pattern that informs most of Carpenter's films. The crewmen themselves—long-haired, sweaty fallout of the hippie generation—are like a Hawksian team gone terribly awry.

Doolittle's efficacy as a commander is compared unfavorably with that of the mission's real commander, Powell, who has been killed by a radiation leak:

"A new star. What are you going to name it?"

"Who cares? Don't bother me."

"Commander Powell would have named it."

Any framework of guidance, control, or moral authority has been withdrawn: An uncaring Earth won't help the Dark Star's crew against the radiation leak that's already killed its commander, and is singularly unsympathetic when the Dark Star crew announces that the ship's entire supply of toilet paper has been destroyed.

The ship isn't only cramped, she's messy. It's in the crewmen's bunk bay that cabin fever most takes its toll: The men get on one another's nerves with solitaire, smoking, and an offbeat practical joke involving a rubber chicken. Petulant Boiler's response to every situation is violent. The rubber chicken drives Doolittle out of the bay to the relative sanity of making soothing music on the can-and-bottle synthesizer he's assembled in a semiprivate area of the ship.

In the observation dome, the dreamer Talby gazes at the stars. "I like it up here ... I can *watch* things up here." He talks of the proximity of the Phoenix Asteroids, which pass this way only once every 1.23 trillion years, and how he dreams of seeing them. Doolittle reveals that he's a frustrated surfer who desperately misses the freedom and openness of the beach. Into this stultifying atmosphere comes a little excitement: the combat of the sweet-voiced female computer vs. the testy male computer-bomb, Bomb Number 20; an asteroid storm animated in the style of the Id-Monster from *Forbidden Planet*; and an escaped alien who resembles a beachball with claws.

The alien is a delight, mocking the poverty-row special effects that characterized the earliest progenitors of the s.f.–horror film. Though the alien most resembles the title creature from *The Blob*, the clearest target for its mockery is another 1958 film, *It! The Terror from Beyond Space*. In *It!*, an obscure low-budget programmer, a relief mission sent to Mars to discover the fate of an earlier mission finds only one survivor, and arrests him for the murder of the others, despite his protests that "something" killed the members of his crew. On the return trip to earth, people on the ship start disappearing. When bodies turn up, drained of fluid, the accused murderer is exonerated, his story believed, and the crew must face combat with an intelligent, humanoid life form at large on the spacecraft. The creature inhabits the lower levels of the ship, trapping the crew on the upper levels, and all efforts to stop it with conventional weapons and electric shock fail. Finally, the survivors manage to suffocate the creature by pumping all the oxygen out of the ship (having first donned their own oxygenated suits).

Without sufficient imagination (or budget) to create a credibly alien creature, *It!* anthropomorphizes its Martian, against all evolutionary logic, into a vampire in a crusty-skinned, clawed, zip-up monster suit. It wasn't until the success of *Alien* that Dan O'Bannon, co-screenwriter on both *Dark Star* and *Alien*, was accused of stealing heavily from *It!* But *Dark Star*'s debt to *It!* is clear.

The image of Sgt. Pinback seeking the beachball creature out with only a broom for a weapon and coaxing the alien with a rubber mouse was, at the film's first appearance, an extension of *It!* and a cute play on a typical *Star Trek* TV episode situation. Seen from the post-*Alien* vantage, however, it points toward the memorable "Here, Kitty" sequence that highlighted the later film and has become a masterpiece of cinematic suspense.

Sergeant Pinback is the closest thing *Dark Star* has to a hero. He is a kind of Everyman, a schmo for whom everything goes wrong. Like all of us, he is at war with machines. Nothing works right for him: elevators, airlocks, bombs. He makes videotapes of all his complaints about Doolittle's mismanagement of the mission, about the other crewmen's inconsiderate treatment of him, about his lot in life. Someday someone will play these back, he earnestly believes.

Climactically, he has an intimate revelation: He's not really Pinback. He's not even an astronaut. He's a fuel maintenance technician

Granddaddy of *Dark Star*:
It! The Terror from Beyond Space

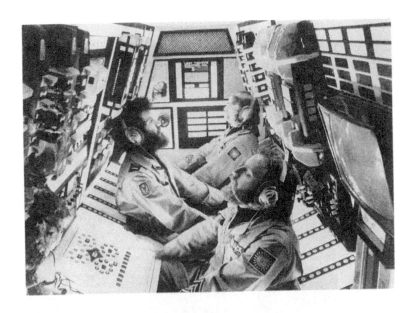

Above: Cabin Fever
The crew of the Dark Star: (front to back) Pinback (Dan O'Bannon), Doolittle (Brian Narelle), Boiler (Carl Kuniholm)
[Photo courtesy of Museum of Modern Art Film Stills Archive]
Below: Here, Kitty
Harry Dean Stanton and friend in *Alien*

named Bill Frug who's in this by mistake. He was wearing someone else's uniform. The real Pinback drowned himself in a vat of liquid fuel.

Pinback's identity crisis brings on an identity crisis in the other crewmen as well: Boiler wonders, "What's Talby's first name?" Doolittle, after some thought, asks, "What's *my* first name?"

Things come to a head when Bomb 20 determines to blow itself up despite the fact that the bomb-bay doors have jammed and the bomb can't be ejected from the ship. Neither the mother computer nor Pinback can successfully order the bomb to withdraw.

Commander Powell, killed by a radiation leak, is frozen in the ship's cryogenic chamber, but his still-active brainwaves are now tapped electronically by Doolittle for guidance (an idea that recurs in William Gibson's 1984 cyberpunk novel *Neuromancer*). Powell's brain advises Doolittle to talk the bomb out of exploding itself by confusing it. This leads to another bit of *Star Trek* parody—the climactic set piece in which a human being tries to foil a computer's programming. In this case Doolittle argues the computer-bomb to a position of skepticism, in the hope that the bomb will override its own corrupted program. It both does and doesn't work: The bomb retreats to its bomb bay to think things through, only to emerge having adopted the centrist position that it is God. The new Big Bang that climaxes the film is heralded by the computer's declaration, "Let there be light."

Left outside the ship, and so not killed in the explosion, Doolittle and Talby face a more spectacular fate: The Phoenix Asteroids pass by, and Talby joins them, *becomes* one of them. Doolittle ends the film by surfing on a piece of space debris into the atmosphere, where he burns up. "What a beautiful way to die," says Talby, seconds before each embraces his meteoric end: "— as a falling star!" And on this meta-phoric swan song of the psychedelic era, *Dark Star* comes to a close. The appropriate, even wished-for, end to which Talby and Doolittle each come suggests a kind of order to the universe, a kind of rightness to it all. The creation and re-creation images that bracketed *2001: A Space Odyssey* are echoed here with a more outrageous imagery. People become stars. Not ashes to ashes, but energy to energy—with only the briefest respite in between for something called life.

Notes

1. Information in this and the preceding paragraph is summmarized from John Carpenter's comments in Jordan Fox's interview in *Cinefantastique* 10:1, Summer 1980, and from O'Bannon, Dan, "The Remaking of *Dark Star*," in Peary, Danny, ed., *Omni's Screen Flights/Screen Fantasies*, New York: Doubleday, 1984, pp. 147-51, the best available statement of O'Bannon's account.

2. Fox, Jordan R., Interview, "Riding High on Horror," *Cinefantastique* 10:1, Summer 1980, p. 9.

3. Cited in Sobchak, Vivian Carol, *The Limits of Infinity: The American Science Fiction Film*, New York: A. S. Barnes & Co., 1980, p. 165.

4

<u>There Are No Heroes Any More</u>

Assault on Precinct 13

> *Assault on Precinct 13* came up very quickly. An investor
> from Philadelphia had some money and said, "Let's make a
> movie." And so, I said, "Let's go," and I wrote the script in eight
> days. I wanted to do a western, but wasn't able to do a western,
> and it was the closest thing to it. Of course, a lot of movies I made
> *are* westerns.
>
> —John Carpenter

After the light-hearted (although dark-sided) whimsy of *The Resurrection of Broncho Billy* and *Dark Star*, *Assault on Precinct 13* comes as a shock. Though its dialogue is often witty, there is nothing whimsical or comical about it. Its horrifying situations, compelling rhythms, and haunting set pieces have earned it a deserved reputation as one of Carpenter's finest films. There is nothing of the student or amateur in *Assault on Precinct 13*. It announces itself as the work of an assured professional with an uncompromising vision and a steady stylistic hand. Though released in 1976, it was limited mostly to festival play in its first three years of life, and it wasn't until 1979, after *Halloween*, that *Assault on Precinct 13* was first reviewed by the *New York Times.* Had it been more widely seen, undoubtedly *this* film, not *Halloween*, would have been the one that proclaimed the arrival of John Carpenter.

Vaunted in many circles as a remake of *Rio Bravo*, the film is undeniably an urban western like *The Resurrection of Broncho Billy*, in which the complexities of the modern world are recast in the mythic simplicity of the law of the gun. A plethora of references to *The Searchers*, *Red River*, *Once Upon a Time in the West* and *The Wild Bunch* call attention to the film's generic identity as a western, and to its aesthetic significance as a *commentary* on the western. But for all that, it's finally a remake more of *Night of the Living Dead* than of *Rio Bravo*.

Monsters Rising

In fact, one might trace the ancestry of *Assault on Precinct 13* along a direct line from *Forbidden Planet* through Alfred Hitchcock's *The Birds* through *Night of the Living Dead*. In each of these films, a small group of trapped individuals attempt to defend themselves against the attacks of a motiveless, irrational enemy intent on brute destruction. In each film, the characters and their relationships are developed in terms of their response to the crisis. Each film includes at least one "blocked" sexual relationship, and in each film the monster arguably arises as a correlate for the brutal defenses of a threatened psyche.

Forbidden Planet is a colorful science fiction fantasy based on Shakespeare's *The Tempest*. In the film, a crew of astronauts from Earth visit the planet Altair-4 and find there the only survivors of an Earth colony: Dr. Morbius and his daughter, Altura. They are besieged by a monster who proves to be the objectification of Morbius's own Id, as he subconsciously lashes out against the visitors and the threat they represent to the idyllic existence he shares with his daughter.

The Birds is a psychological suspense thriller built around the visit to Bodega Bay of Melanie Daniels, a vivacious, high-living play-girl with a Reputation and an eye for Bodegan Mitch Brenner, who lives in the coast town with his widowed mother and his much younger sister. With Melanie's arrival begins a series of unprovoked, deadly attacks on humans by birds. The attacks are at one point attributed to Melanie, but are finally more plausibly seen as a metaphor for the fiercely protective psyche of Lydia Brenner, the jealous mother. Her fear of losing her son repeatedly blocks the burgeoning relationship between Mitch and Melanie, but only because Melanie's arrival has disrupted her own crypto-incestuous relationship with Mitch, cloaked in terms of respectable domesticity. As she sleeps, the birds exact a terrible vengeance on Melanie, just as the sleep of Morbius's reason brought forth monsters against Commander Addams, Doc Ostrow, and Lieutenant Farman, all of whom took a more than passing interest in Altura.[1]

Night of the Living Dead is, of course, an outright horror film, and still one of the most skillfully made cheapies ever to hit the big market. In the film, the reanimation of the unburied dead into flesh-eating zombies is attributed to radiation released by a satellite that is exploded as it returns from a space mission. But the attacks that begin when Johnny teases his sister Barbara in a rural Pennsylvania cemetery serve as a handy correlate for a sexual relationship desired by both siblings but blocked by the incest taboo. This perspective becomes all the more compelling in light of the fact that, at the film's psychosexual climax, the traumatized Barbara is carried off by her zombified brother, while in the basement a reanimated child kills and eats her own parents. The film's hero, Ben, a loner (and the only black man in a house full of white defenders), is discarded ignominiously at the end, shot by deputies who mistake him for one of the zombies.

The attack on the police station in *Assault on Precinct 13* is motivated by the gang Street Thunder's oath of vengeance against police who have mowed down six of their members. It is also whimsically attributed to sunspot activity in a throwaway reference to *The Texas Chainsaw Massacre*. But the attack on the station is actually precipitated when Lawson, having shot the gang member who killed his daughter, runs into the station for protection and promptly goes catatonic (as, interestingly, do Melanie Daniels in *The Birds* and Barbara in *Night of the Living Dead*). The moral foundation for the defense of the precinct house becomes the determination of three characters—Lt. Bishop, Leigh, and Napoleon Wilson—to protect Lawson. Those who profess an interest in protecting only themselves—Wells, Julie—are "not good enough" in the Hawksian sense, and end up being killed by the attackers.

The pattern of similarity in the four films is enhanced by the recognition that, in each, a repressed incestuous relationship is informed by a death: Morbius, a widower, lives a domestic life with his daughter, just as widowed Lydia Brenner does with her son. In *Night of the Living Dead*, much is made of the fact that Johnny and Barbara have come many miles to place flowers on the grave of a dead father, at the behest of an invalid mother. In *Assault on Precinct 13*, Lawson and his daughter are on their way to persuade Kathy's nanny to come and live with them, someone named Fred—presumably the nanny's husband—having died and left her with no reason for not making the move. The pattern would be even more compelling if Kathy's mother were dead and Lawson a widower, which would signal a Morbius-like incestuousness in Lawson's relationship with his daughter; and, while nothing specific in the film's action or dialogue suggests this, nothing denies it either. There is no mention of nor reference to Kathy's mother, and Lawson's sense of urgency about having the nanny move in with them, and his reference to an empty room waiting for her, suggest the desperation of the single parent.

In any case, the situations that, in all four of these films, attend the summoning up of monsters call to mind the fury of what Robin Wood, in *American Nightmare*, has called the Return of the Repressed.[2] A self-professed social and sexual radical, Wood argues that American family life is the product of the repression of natural instincts and desires leading in other directions, and that the American horror film typically presents monsters that function as images of what has been repressed returning to claim its own, reasserting itself over uneasy, artificial domestication. The achievement of *Assault on Precinct 13* is to layer this horror film metaphor over the mythic pattern of the western—and specifically the Howard Hawks western.

The Politics of Disorder

What strikes one first about the film, though, before codes and subtexts shape a matrix of meaning, is its disarmingly off-balance atmosphere. To some degree, it's an atmosphere characteristic of the low-budget horror film, and fueled at least in part by the use of unknown actors.

In the original *Star Trek* television series, whenever Captain Kirk mounted a landing party and said something like, "Mr. Spock, Dr. McCoy, Ensign Purvis, prepare to beam down," well, you just knew it was curtains for Purvis. The guy you never heard of is always cannon fodder. But in independent films cast with unknown actors, you've never heard of *any* of them. You're not even sure who the hero is, who you're supposed to be rooting for. So you know that all bets are off. Anything could happen to anybody. That atmosphere is part of what made the early independent horror films of Tobe Hooper and George Romero so intense. That same ambience informs *Assault on Precinct 13*: You never know who the expendables are—a suspense-building technique supported not only by the absence of an identifiable "star," but also by the director's willingness, à la Hitchcock in *Psycho*, to blithely bump off an apparent lead player.

The film's only remotely familiar actor is Henry Brandon, who played the villainous Scar in John Ford's *The Searchers* (one of many iconographic western connections in the film). Charles Cyphers, who plays Starker, the cop assigned to escort three convicts from Los Cruces penitentiary to Sonora's Death Row, would later become a familiar character actor in the films of Carpenter and others, but when *Assault on Precinct 13* was new to the screen, so was he. These two actors, together with the specially billed Kim Richards, who plays Lawson's daughter Kathy, are among the first to disappear from the screen as the gang begins its murderous rampage. Austin Stoker's Ethan Bishop finally shapes up to be the film's hero, but Laurie Zimmer's Leigh, Darwin Joston's Napoleon Wilson, and Tony Burton's Wells are equally important. The film's pattern of random, unexpected death keeps us off-balance throughout, expecting that at any time any of these characters could also be eliminated.

Disorder is represented by more than the omnipresence of the possibility of random death and the uncertainty of a central heroic icon. The environment itself is one of disorder. The film's opening title, "Anderson, California—a Los Angeles ghetto," identifies an area initially indistinct because glimpsed by night, a jumble of blue-lit concrete shot in medium-close as gang members creep along walls and scramble up a flight of stairs and down a corridor before being halted and summarily gunned down by police. This opening is recorded with a hand held camera, moving along with the gang members in the confusion and the dark, in a single take that doesn't end until a disembodied voice of authority yells, "Freeze!" and a hell of gunfire is unleashed.

Next we are introduced to the only four members of the street gang we ever get a close look at. Over a slow pan of a section of Anderson in the yellow light of day, we hear a radio news report of the killing of the six gang members, and a statement from a public official justifying the extreme tactics of law enforcement officers on the grounds that sophisticated automatic weapons are in the hands of the youth gangs, heightening the danger to all. The exterior pan is echoed by an interior pan, beginning as a shot of the weapons in question, then sweeping across a room that apparently functions as a sort of communal headquarters for the gang. The four warlords—one black, one Hispanic, one white, one Asian—swear vengeance "for The Six," and draw and commingle their own blood to seal the oath. "Cholo," one of them mutters.

At this point, two scenes into the film, disorientation is at its peak. It's hard for us not to sympathize with young men shot down before they have a chance to resist, and with the loyalty with which their brothers swear vengeance. On the other hand, it's hard to identify with gang members who tote automatic weapons and readily carve their own arms with knives. Further, we don't know what "cholo" is or what it means.

Desperately needing a center, a point of order, and unable to identify with either the police on one extreme or the gang on the other, we are introduced to Ethan Bishop. He leaves his West Los Angeles home for his "first night out" as a police officer on the streets of L.A. We have no reason at this point to know that Bishop will become one of the film's three heroes, but we have every reason to want to identify with him and depend on him. He's a cop, and as such represents a force of order; but he's black, and so we assume he does *not* represent the reactionary police action symbolized by the disembodied shotgun barrels in the opening scene, and not so easily opposed to the inner city ethnic youths we saw in the second. Whatever his alliances, Bishop seems likeable, and we are drawn to him.

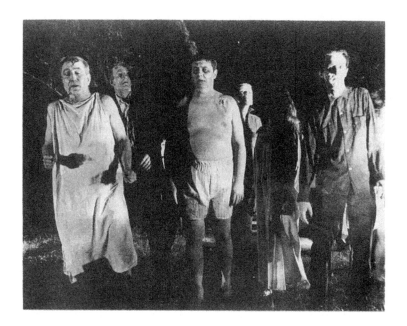

Progenitors of *Assault on Precinct 13*
Facing page: Above: *Forbidden Planet*: Morbius (Walter Pidgeon) introduces his daughter Altura (Anne Francis) to Starship Commander Addams (Leslie Nielsen). Below: The Fall of the House of Brenner in *The Birds*: Mitch Brenner (Rod Taylor), Cathy Brenner (Angela Cartwright), Melanie Daniels (Tippi Hedren), Lydia Brenner (Jessica Tandy). This page: The onset of the zombie ghouls in *Night of the Living Dead*.

As Bishop talks on his car radio, a car slides up alongside him, drops back, slides up again ... and each time, the driver looks over at Bishop (and directly toward the camera). Whether this is a calculated directorial event, or an accident of independent film production, the feeling of menace it creates—though never materially connecting with the film's action—forms part of the fabric of threat that Carpenter, in film after film, weaves into unexpected areas of his frame.

And now we get another of those jarring bits of independent horror movie atmosphere: Finished with his official business on the two-way radio, Bishop is now listening to the news. He hears a report on the previous night's violent gang incident, identifying the gang as the interracial "Street Thunder," and suggesting that the upsurge of violence may be related to sunspots—a phenomenon that Bishop will later cite (tongue in cheek?) to a skeptical precinct captain—causing "pressure on the atmosphere." This throwaway "explanation" is a sidewise jab at *The Texas Chainsaw Massacre*, which used a similar premise to "explain" the outbreak of senseless violence in its back-country cannibals, and at *Night of the Living Dead*, which invoked radiation to explain the resurrection of the unburied dead to roam the countryside seeking living flesh. It is as if Carpenter is dismissing the frivolity of B-film horror, even while using its trappings to enhance a more realistic tale of modern urban life.

Images from *Night of the Living Dead* abound in *Assault on Precinct 13*, announcing the film's real debt to the horror genre: A small group trapped inside a building; night-time attacks; compositions of half a dozen or so attackers lurching through the darkness toward the building; hands groping through windows ("That's just what happens when you're trapped," said Carpenter, when asked about the similarities); barricading windows and doors; wholesale killing as a means of self-preservation; a catatonic victim; the besiegers "taking the bodies away" so things look normal (invoking the invaders' *eating* of the bodies in *Night of the Living Dead*); discussing whether or not to take refuge in the basement ("We'd be trapped down there"); a plan to get away in a car and get help, and the failure of that plan; the last stand occurring in the long-avoided basement; the dusk-to-dawn structure of the film.

A more direct, less fantastic kind of horror is also called into play: As the gang members cruise through Anderson in a big, lumbering old car, one of them, the white one, depicted as more intensely psychopathic than the rest, takes out a rifle and casually aims it at bystanders, focusing on them through the rifle's scope. The horror of the crosshairs stresses how easily he could kill any of them, striking us with his completely arbitrary power over life and death, and calling to mind Peter

Bogdanovich's *Targets*, another film that eschewed mythic horrors for real ones. The white gang member pointedly aims at, but does not shoot, two people on the street, both emblematic of the black ghetto: a woman on her way home from the grocery store, and a man sitting on the sidewalk sucking at a bottle of wine. The fact that he doesn't shoot them may seem at first to suggest that he is looking for a more appropriate victim, that the gang stands for vengeance specifically against exemplars of the society that oppresses them and whose arbitrary law enforcement has wiped out six of their number. But we are soon to find that this is not the case.

Carpenter continues to enhance the ominous tone of the film. An "ice cream man" readies his gun, and takes notes: Is he an undercover surveillance man? Or is Anderson such a bad neighborhood that even the ice cream vendors pack rods and jot down the license plate numbers of suspicious vehicles? People move around in cars, moving toward an ultimate convergence with one another and with destiny: Ethan, Lawson and Kathy, the gang leaders, the ice cream man, the prison van.

The film has been quick-paced enough already, but as it reaches its first climax—the psychopath's casual point-blank shooting of a child—the action becomes frenetic. The killing of Kathy is for my money the most horrifying moment in all of Carpenter's films—certainly both more shocking and scarier than anything in his horror films. Topically, generically, and stylistically it blows the viewer's already uncertain expectations to smithereens. For rarely, even in anything-can-happen independent horror films, do we see a child murdered. Children are often jeopardized in such films: For example, the sustained possibility of a little girl's meeting a horrible death at the hands of either a psychopathic axe-murderer or his huge pet alligator makes Tobe Hooper's *Eaten Alive* (a.k.a. *Starlight Murders* or *Horror Hotel*) a tooth-grinding experience. But seldom does any filmmaker actually *depict* the slaughter of a child. The fact that Carpenter chooses to do so at this point reveals the tenacity with which he intends to depict Street Thunder not as some sympathetic sociopolitical force but as the embodiment of arbitrary, mindless evil.

The frenetic activity becomes unnerving as Lawson, the deranged father of the murdered girl, comes into the precinct house in a state of shock, babbling about someone outside chasing him, but unable to tell the story of his daughter's murder and of his subsequent killing of the psycho—leading Starker to quip, "A lot of action for a closed-down station."

Not until Lawson is inside the station do we see more of Street Thunder than the four warlords who swore the blood oath. Once the siege begins, their numbers swell to seeming hundreds, darting among trees and parked cars, emerging from the blue-lit night, flicking half-seen through shadows, zipping in from all parts of the Panavision frame. But now, following the killing of the child, they have become faceless attackers like Romero's zombies, emblematic of pure evil because they are conscienceless—and maybe even *un*conscious.

By the time the battle for the station begins, Carpenter has made sure that we know the layout. He's learned from Hawks, Ford, and Kurosawa that spatial relationships must be established during the calm, so that the viewer may better comprehend, and so emotionally surrender to, the mechanics and geography of the battle itself. Exposition, for Carpenter, is always as much a visual as a verbal process. He shows us around the station well enough in the early scenes that when the fury of combat is loosed, we don't need to wonder about the wheres and hows. We know where we are—and we know we're *stuck* there.

Being trapped is a critical motif in the Carpenter canon. Even in his earliest work it forms a subtext: Broncho Billy is "trapped" by the economic and social realities of contemporary urban life; the crew of the Dark Star are trapped in their tiny, claustrophobic ship. But in *Assault on Precinct 13* the image of people under siege becomes explicit and sets a tone that informs most of Carpenter's later films. The gang's use of silencers forms the basis for a set piece that is one of Carpenter's most frightening, a scene of claustrophobic horror rooted in Hitchcock's *The Birds*: Set upon by a faceless, soundless, motiveless enemy, trapped in the little precinct house—and in the confines of the motion picture frame—the defenders of the police station endure the horror of bullets smacking into windows and walls with no accompanying gunshots, peppering the station relentlessly, death and destruction meted out with an irrational arbitrariness that invites madness as the only possible response.

The atmosphere of threat and disorder is further sustained by Carpenter's music for the film. The main title, which recurs throughout the film and again as end title, lays down a five-note synthesizer motif that suggests menacing possibility, and that is used in the film proper for building suspense. Overlaying this is a series of high, organ-like chords evoking a Gothic mood. At some points in the film, Carpenter employs a long, high, nervewrackingly sustained synthesizer chord to enhance moments of quiet tension. Only one theme is orderly, melodic, and nonthreatening: a short, blue guitar melody used for tender moments such as an L.A. sunset and a dirge for Julie after she is killed in the gang's second assault. (Arguably, this little tune contains the roots of Carpenter's title theme for *Escape from New York* and the urban blues tunes of *They Live*.)

The stylistic elements of *Assault on Precinct 13*, then, contrive to sustain an atmosphere of disorder and threat, amplifying the out-of-joint world to which order must somehow be restored. Whence comes that order?

The Politics of Personal Heroism

Order will not be restored through the forces of economic power: A Coke machine is used to barricade a door—the most inventive use of a Coke machine since *Dr. Strangelove*. The exemplar of commercial power is reduced to humble, material utility.

The police won't restore order, either—at least not in their conventional presence. Lawson, the closest thing in the film to an average citizen, is open to his daughter about his distrust of—and contempt for—the police. When Kathy suggests that her father ask the police for directions, recalling how her teacher, Mrs. Seward, encourages the children to ask the police for help when they're lost, Lawson replies, "Obviously Mrs. Seward has never taken any big steps outside of the 6th grade. ... We're not in any trouble."

The institution of the police force as keepers of the public safety is dead: The prison warden brutalizes the prisoners; the escort, Starker, though he raises an eyebrow at the prison brutality, clearly holds the Death Row convicts in contempt, and harbors few if any humane feelings for them—only an idle curiosity that unnerves the enigmatic killer Napoleon Wilson. Trust in the police is placed in the mouths of naïve characters—Kathy and Julie. "Why would anybody want to shoot at a police station?" Julie asks at the beginning of the first assault. She never appreciates, as Bishop does, the irony of being trapped in the one place you'd consider the safest: "We're in the middle of a city, inside a police station! ... Someone's *bound* to come by!" In the climax of the film, Bishop will use a "Support Your Local Police" sign to cushion the explosion of acetylene he rigs to foil the gang's final assault: Cheap sentiment gives way to tough reality, as the film debunks easy, sloganeering politics in favor of the real politics of individual heroism.

And therein lies the restoration of order: individual behavior, on the personal level, conforming to a meaningful code of human relationships. This is to be found, to be sure, not so much in real life as in film. As in *The Resurrection of Broncho Billy*, Carpenter turns to film conventions—and the order they bestow—for his answer to the stresses of modern life. (And speaking of resurrections, with the gang members killed on Friday night, and the action of the film proper running from Saturday afternoon into Sunday morning, the film is structured not only as a cinematic dark night of the soul but also as a passion and resurrec-

tion.) *Assault on Precinct 13*'s unapologetic invocation of the world of
Howard Hawks suggests exactly where that new order is to be found.

The situation is a Hawksian one to begin with. The original title
of the film was *Anderson's Alamo*, and Street Thunder's dropping of
the blood-marked banner on the doorstep of the beleaguered station
house serves the same function as the playing of the mariachi tune
"*Deguello*" does in *Rio Bravo*: to invoke the call for No Quarter ordered by Santa Ana over the small band of defenders of the Alamo.
Leigh refers to it as a "cholo," the word we heard one of the four gang
members use in the blood-oath scene; Wells interprets its meaning: "To
the death."

References to *Rio Bravo* in the course of the film tend to run less
to plot than to codes of behavior, stylistic gesture, moments of grace.
Bishop's decisive acceptance (and trust) of Wilson comes when, having
released Wilson and Wells from their cells, Bishop tosses the convicted
killer a shotgun with which to mow down the Street Thunder detachment coming in the door. It's a specific echo of a gesture in *Rio Bravo*,
when Colorado gets Sheriff John T. Chance out of a scrape by engi-
neering a distraction and tossing him his rifle. Leigh's name seems a
tribute to the writer of *Rio Bravo*, Leigh Brackett, and her seemingly
fated kinship with Wilson, evident in the way they spontaneously and
electrically *connect* when she's "just passin' through," references the
similar connection between John T. Chance and Feathers in *Rio Bravo*.

Bishop's plan to lure Street Thunder into the basement, then en-
gineer an explosion using flares and a tank of gas, recalls Chance's
tactic of exploding sticks of dynamite with rifle fire to drive Nathan
Burdett's thugs out of their stronghold. And the means by which the
patrolmen in the rescuing prowl car find out something is amiss is the
sound of blood dripping onto the roof of their car from the bodies of the
utility linemen hanging above, shot by Street Thunder. This puts some
interesting spin on Dude's discovery of a runaway assassin in *Rio
Bravo*, because here it's the *sound*, not the sight, of the blood that's the
tipoff—a stylistic correlate to the gun battle with silencers, where we
have the *sight* of the damage done by bullets, without the usual attendant sound.

Carpenter's teams are a deliberate invocation of Hawksian professionals: Thrown together by fate, they are not always good teams, and
are often separated by distrust. Still, they do their best by one another,
each respecting the others as human beings, and each demanding from
the others the same courage and loyalty he expects of—and delivers—
himself. In *Dark Star* and later in *Big Trouble in Little China* we see
comic versions of such teams, but most Carpenter films are dominated

by serious Hawksian teams who test one another even as they are tested by their circumstances.

Carpenter even echoes Hawks's terms for the mettle of his characters: They are either good enough or not good enough. Napoleon Wilson applauds Leigh's handling of a tough situation in releasing the prisoners from their cells while staving off a Street Thunder attack, laying a victim low with a kick to the groin *and* sustaining a slug to her arm. "That was close timing in there ... you were good." Leigh remains self-critical, in true Hawksian fashion: Looking at Julie's body, she retorts, "If I had been any good in *here*, she might still be alive."

The two women in the station, Julie and Leigh, are the two types of Hawksian woman: one not good enough, the other monumentally good in every sense. Julie cracks under the pressure, and even espouses surrendering Lawson to the attackers to get them to go away—something Wilson, Bishop, and Leigh specifically and emphatically will not do, and this commitment is finally the moral center of the film. "He came in here for help," says Bishop, "and we're going to give him all the help we can," even though Lawson is catatonic, and Bishop doesn't even know what it was that brought Lawson to the station. Wilson echoes Bishop when he tells Leigh that there are two things he won't run from: a helpless man ... and the second is left unstated but fully understood. Leigh, catching the sexual signal from Wilson, remarks, "The very least of our problems is that we've run out of time." Wilson replies, "It's an old story with me. I was *born* out of time." These are consciously anachronistic heroes.

Julie and Wells, the two major characters who place self-interest above protection of the team, die before the end of the film. Interestingly, both Julie and Kathy—the two female characters killed in the film—wear yellow, and end up with coats over their faces. Leigh's sweater (like Bishop's uniform) is beige, its flesh tones tending to make her more human, both prettier and tougher than Julie. When Street Thunder cuts the power to the station, making the film's dominant color blue, Leigh comes off even stronger, while Julie pales to a greenish hue.

Lawson, who runs to the precinct house for safety and brings hell with him, goes catatonic, but not before he has killed the murderer of his child. He may not be good enough, but he has his Moment.

When Wells decides to use his gun against the team and make a break to save his own skin, Leigh grabs hold of his gun by the barrel and talks him out of it, then discovers that the gun is empty: "I go through all that and his gun isn't even loaded" (a sexual innuendo by which Leigh—and the film—reject Wells as not good enough). Wells notes that, with the silencer on his gun, "I been clickin' off empty shots all night and I didn't even know it."

Wells is untrusting and untrustworthy, because he stands for nothing. When he and Wilson must decide which of them is to go outside and hot-wire a car to make a run for help, he says, "I'll lose ... I always lose ... I've had bad luck all my life." He avoids the anticipated loss of a coin toss by insisting on doing "taters": grown men, hardened criminals, in the middle of a bloody siege, doing "one-potato, two-potato." Wells loses—and argues about the outcome. As he heads out, he says, "Ain't anybody gonna wish me luck?" Bishop and Leigh wish him luck in unison. Then, as if it hadn't been his own idea, he shakes his head. "Two cops wishin' me luck ... I'm doomed."

Wells is a whiner, low on the scale of professionalism that Carpenter borrows from Hawks. Unlike Groot and Stumpy, whose constant complaining serves as a check on the excesses of Tom Dunson and John T. Chance in *Red River* and *Rio Bravo* respectively, Wells really *isn't* good enough. He fires an empty pistol, feels sorry for himself, wears on his sleeve the "attitude problem" Wilson ascribes to him and, in the end, fails to help the besieged defenders.

Leigh, on the other hand, is good indeed. It is she who, as the team takes shape, announces, "We're all together." When she gets shot, both her dispassionate reaction and her subsequent regard of the wound as a minor nuisance recall *Red River*'s Tess Millay (same arm, too). Wilson, on a later occasion, reinforces his earlier compliment: "You *are* good." She replies, "*Some*times," suggesting Wilson's own repeated catch phrase, "I have my moments."

But the real heroes, and the focus of the film, we finally decide, are Ethan Bishop and Napoleon Wilson—brothers under the skin. Their characters are limned in much the same way. Each shares a memory from his youth that has left emotional scars: Bishop's recollection of his ghetto roots and the time his father sent him to the police to be terrified; Wilson's recounting of a preacher who had told him he had "something to do with death."

Each, too, is able to laugh at himself: Leigh, making coffee for Bishop, asks, "Black?" and Bishop replies with a grin, "For over 30 years!" Leigh doesn't appreciate the gag—perhaps she sees it as an inappropriate attempt to share intimacy—and Bishop quickly apologizes. Moments later she will warm to him as he shares his childhood memory—and he bests her when he corrects her assumption that his father got him out of Anderson by explaining that he walked out himself as a teenager. Similarly with Wilson: When the warden kicks the chair out from under Wilson, the convict dusts himself off and explains to Starker, "I don't sit on a chair as well as I used to." Besides being a joke at his own expense, the line may be an oblique reference to sodomy or other abuses inflicted on him in prison.

Ethan Bishop's name might well be made from John Wayne's Ethan Edwards in *The Searchers* and William Holden's Pike Bishop in *The Wild Bunch*—two exemplars of the dark-sided western hero in films that represent both the "golden age" of the Fifties western and the revisionism of the Sergio Leone–influenced Vietnam-era western. He certainly seems a western movie hero in the making. Riding out for his first patrol, he has a radio conversation with his commander, who scoffs at Bishop's eagerness: "You want to be a hero your first night out, Lieutenant?"

"Yes, sir," replies Bishop, with a smile. The answer crackles back: "There are no heroes any more, Bishop—only men who follow orders."

Bishop accommodatingly follows the order to report to the precinct to which he has been assigned—a deserted one, scheduled to be closed the next morning. Bishop has no chip on his shoulder; but he clearly has something to prove, if only to himself. When the radio news story identifies the gang as Street Thunder and makes a point of the "highly unusual interracial mixture of the gang," Bishop turns the radio off. The suggestion is one of uncomfortable familiarity. Are these his roots? The reminder of an ugliness he would rather not face? The encroachment of a threat he has rejected by getting himself out of Anderson (and onto the police force!), but has not fully expelled from his consciousness?

His story of how his father took him to jail with a note instructing the police to put him in a cell and teach him that "We lock up bad boys" is, interestingly, the story Alfred Hitchcock used to tell about his own youth and the roots of the fear of the police that haunts his own films. In Bishop it has, however, inspired the desired reaction: Bishop has been good, stayed out of trouble, and got himself out of Anderson—only to return as a police officer.

Wilson's youthful experience has, by contrast, placed him on the other side of the law. But to judge from the contrast between Wilson and his jailers, and later between Wilson and Street Thunder, the wrong guys seem to be in prison in this world. Carpenter is hardly sympathetic to Wilson's crimes, but he suggests that some legitimate sense of social or personal justice underlies the killings for which he is imprisoned, as opposed to the sadistic brutality of the warden's thugs and the mindless violence of the attackers outside the police station.

Asked on the prison bus why he killed two men, Napoleon Wilson, the convicted killer in chains who becomes one of the film's heroes, tells his guard, Starker, what a preacher told him once: "You've got something to do with death." The line is a direct quote from Sergio Leone's *Once Upon a Time in the West*. There it is used to plumb the mystery of the lone man with a harmonica, whose motives and identity remain opaque until the film's finale. Wilson preserves his mystery even longer than that: "Where'd you get a name like Napoleon?" Starker asks him. "I'll tell you sometime," says Wilson. "When?" "At the moment of dying," replies Wilson—another line from *Once Upon a Time in the West*. Starker doesn't live to get an answer from Wilson.

Bishop later asks Wilson the same question and gets the same answer. The real reason for Wilson's given name is never revealed in the film because Wilson never reaches the moment of dying. Maybe, like the heroes of Sergio Leone's western films, he is eternal. "[Leone is] one of my favorite directors," Carpenter has said. "I think *Once Upon a Time in the West* is a great movie. But I think Leone's work in his spaghetti westerns was both the ultimate and the death of westerns. It was great ... great stuff."

There is a strong sense in which *Assault on Precinct 13* is a post-Death of the Western western. Besides all the quotes from and references to classic westerns, the film also seems to be asking, and answering, a question: Now that the western is dead, what are we left with? *The Resurrection of Broncho Billy* tendered a bittersweet, comic answer; *Assault on Precinct 13* offers the same answer in a more serious and brutal vein: What we are left with is a system of values, not social but individual, interpersonal. They are serious values and real, even if they have been given to us by the Movies; and our only hope lies in those who are strong enough to adopt those values and live by them.

Wilson gets his own back from the warden who has brutalized him. Just before boarding the bus to Sonora he wangles a chance to take a breath of fresh air and uses his chains to trip up the warden. "He don't stand up as well as he used to," quips Wilson, as he is subdued by the guards. And when Wells obliquely compliments him on his gag, calling him "fancy," Wilson replies, "I have my moments."

Like the archetypal western hero of few words, Wilson favors conversation that runs to simple, repeated phrases. "Got a smoke?" he asks everyone he meets. (Wells and Starker are almost sadistic in denying him one; Bishop is apologetic; Wilson finally gets his smoke from Leigh, who even lights it for him, like Lauren Bacall's Marie for Humphrey Bogart's Harry Morgan in *To Have and Have Not*.) Late in the film, Wilson picks up a new phrase—"You can't argue with a confident man"—to measure his growing respect for Bishop, the man of action who is sure his plan will protect them long enough for rescuers to arrive. Wilson's trust is not misplaced.

In the final scene, Bishop angrily stops the rescuing cops from returning Wilson to his chains. The final crackling moments of dialogue
give us more Hawksian quippery:

Bishop: "It would be a privilege if you'd walk outside with me."
Wilson: "I know it would."
Bishop: "You're pretty fancy, Wilson."
Wilson: "I have my moments."

Moments are, finally, *all* he has—all *any* of them has—but that,
the film seems to be saying, is enough.

And with this echo of the early dialogue between Wilson and
Wells boarding the bus to Sonora, cop and criminal walk upstairs, out
of the basement and into the dawn, together. As they start up the short
flight of stairs from the basement—placing the film in a neat frame that
opened with gang members scuffling up a similar dark stairwell—
Carpenter cuts away to his end titles.

The Politics of Pure Evil

Tony Williams, writing in Robin Wood's *American Nightmare*,
affirms the film's recognition of the proximity of the western and horror genres, but consigns the film to the level of nothing more than
mythic artifact, based on his finding that Carpenter has not closely ex-
amined the radical implications of his imagery.

"Carpenter has made an unconsciously reactionary film whose
implications are highly disturbing," writes Williams.[3] But why disturbing? Because "reactionary"? Or because unconsciously so? A century
of film criticism and interviews with celebrated filmmakers has shown
us that the implications of their works are often unconscious to the artists themselves. Ford, Hawks, and Hitchcock repeatedly insisted (with,
I grant, varying degrees of slyness) on the technical and pedestrian
qualities of their work ("job of work" was a favorite phrase of Ford's)
to the exclusion of any psychological or mythical content.

Williams argues generally that *Assault on Precinct 13* ruins its
potency as sociopolitical comment by muddling its imagery. "Unlike
Rio Bravo, the film lacks an outside agency of acceptable law and order
to which both characters and audience can appeal. The choice is between anarchic violence and arbitrary legality."[4] But the tone in which
Williams brings this up seems to overlook the fact that this is precisely
Carpenter's point. The world of *Assault on Precinct 13* is one in which
the disorder represented by street crime has become at least as organized and powerful as the police, and neither the law and order nor the

crime and disorder end of the scale represents an acceptable moral alternative for citizens like Lawson (who decries the horribleness of the Anderson ghetto in almost the same breath as he resists his daughter's suggestion that they seek the help of the police).

In Carpenter's world, institutions have failed—a legitimate, and even fashionable, view of America during the post-Vietnam, post-Watergate years. An abandoned police station defended by criminals is as potent an image of the failure of institutional morality as the abandoned church inhabited by bandits in Sergio Leone's *For a Few Dollars More*. In the absence of an external moral order, a new order is created on the level of individual heroism, built on the ruins of institutional authority. Leone's films mourned the passing of titanic heroes in a world being taken over by a new order that had no room for them; Carpenter's films celebrate the reemergence of Hawksian heroes whose simple code of behavior fills the moral void left by the decay of that same order.

Part of Williams's problem is that he wants Street Thunder to be something Carpenter did not make them. Citing their interracial mix and the fact that they live commune-like in a ghetto, he says, "It is as if the non-violent sixties protest movement of flower power has changed tactics and turned into an uncontrollable revolutionary force which the American establishment can not ignore or attempt to recuperate into the system."[5] Flower power? Williams, it seems, wants Woodstock and can't forgive Carpenter for giving him Altamont.

Williams emphatically uses the word "inter-ethnic" four times in his short article to describe Street Thunder, yet never once to describe the besieged victims. The defenders of the precinct house are a more varied and valid cross section of society than the attackers: They comprise cops and killers, men and women, black, brown, and white. Williams only grudgingly acknowledges that Ethan Bishop's being black has something to do with the film, but suggests that it only "disrupts efforts to keep besieged and besiegers clearly separated,"[6] blurs the stark good vs. evil distinction Carpenter wants to preserve between Street Thunder and the station's defenders. This is a simplistic way of explaining away the fact that there are black characters on both sides of the good/evil line—a fact that shouldn't be troublesome in the first place, except to a viewer who is disappointed by the absence of the racial stereotyping he so eagerly expected.

The real message of the interracial mix on both sides of the line of siege is that no race has a monopoly on good or evil and that, institutionalized moral demarcations having failed, the distinctions must be drawn along new lines—lines that have nothing to do with race, sex, class (Bishop's roots are in the same Anderson ghetto that spawned

Street Thunder), or one's affiliation with law enforcement (Bishop, Leigh) or crime (Wilson, Wells). Heroes are where you find them.

Carpenter is not explicit about how the new heroism is to be defined, but on the film's own terms it has much to do with behavior according to a simple code of duty to other human beings, striking a delicate balance between authoritarian self-interest (the warden, Starker, Wells, Julie) and absorption of the will into the faceless and mindless mass represented by Street Thunder.

Williams fixes on the detail of a gang member's beret adorned with a red triangle to argue a political dimension to Street Thunder: "The attempt is to equate the Marxist alternative to American society with mindless violence. It belongs in the tradition of American right-wing movies where conservative individualism is opposed to unindividualized, violent totalitarianism."[7] One symbol doth not a message make, and Williams seems to be milking a lot out of an incidental costume detail glimpsed four times during the film and seen clearly only once. If the shoe fits, of course ... but Williams seems unaware that the celebration of conservative individualism is precisely a facet of *Rio Bravo* (and, of course, of another Hawks film that looms large in Carpenter's canon, *The Thing*).

There are two ways of interpreting Williams's argument: First, Street Thunder *could have* represented a sociopolitical alternative, so Carpenter should not have failed to exploit the inherent possibility. The answer to this is: That's not the film John Carpenter wanted to make. Discussing the film that might have been rather than the one that is can be a useful form of film criticism, but only if the critic resists the temptation to judge the filmmaker ill for having made his own film instead of the one the critic would prefer him to have made.

Second: Street Thunder *does* represent a sociopolitical alternative, and Carpenter's film finally doesn't work because he fails to see and respond to the sociopolitical implications inherent in his own characters. But nothing in *Assault on Precinct 13* suggests or invites a comparison of Street Thunder with flower power or political revolution. The gang members are painted not as ideologues but as their opposite. These guys are not the Fabian Society, the Wobblies, or the Black Panthers. They're the Crips and the Bloods. The beret worn by one of the gang leaders is hardly a compelling indicator of revolution, any more than the mock-Indian garb of one of the gang leaders suggests anything beyond an *hommage* to the western genre in which *Assault on Precinct 13* is rooted. Carpenter is at pains to make them an emblem of evil, not of some opposing, but valid, social force. That's because to him Street Thunder exemplifies not political change but the horrifying criminality born of urban psychosis.

Williams finds Carpenter to be playing unfairly in taking a group
of characters that *might* have been a symbol of some sociopolitical alternative, and portraying them instead—through the image of the killing of the little girl—as mindless evil. What he can't quite accept at this
point is the fact that Carpenter *believes* in evil, and in the fight against
it. Williams can be forgiven for not having the foresight to see in *Assault on Precinct 13* what becomes readily apparent in later Carpenter
films. It's hard to forgive him, though, for using only literary antece-
dents when he accuses Carpenter of attempting to blackwash the valid
social opposition that Street Thunder might have stood for.

Williams references several romance novels in which children are
kidnapped or killed by Indians, in an effort to make the Indians a simplistic image of pure evil instead of the real social and moral dilemma
they actually represent in American history and law. But the roots of
the child-killing image are more validly sought in the *film* tradition of
which *Assault on Precinct 13* is a part. It is the killing of a child that
justifies the communal uprising against the monster in the archetypal
horror film, the 1933 *Frankenstein*. *The Quatermass Experiment*, one
of Carpenter's favorite films, and one that has had a profound influence
on his work, evokes *Frankenstein*'s child-killing scene when an infected astronaut must literally stay his own hand from killing a little
girl. Children are killed by the bad guys of John Ford's *The Searchers*,
Samuel Fuller's *Underworld U.S.A.*, and Sergio Leone's *Once Upon a
Time in the West*. All of those films celebrate titanic individualism over
forces of threat and oppression, whether those forces are alien (the rac-
ist xenophobia of both Scar and Ethan in *The Searchers*), criminal (the
many-fingered criminal empire of *Underworld U.S.A.*), or economic
(the encroaching capitalist empire of *Once Upon a Time in the West*).

Williams makes much of the fact that the attackers in *Assault on
Precinct 13* are unapologetically based on the Indians of traditional
western films, and that one of the members of the gang wears a pseudo-
Indian costume. He sees this use of the image of the Indian as one that,
whether consciously or not, deals onto the table the card that suggests a
legitimate social alternative represented in the gang. There are two
things wrong with this approach. First, Williams's implication that the
portrayal of the Indian in the "classic western" is wholly negative and
insensitive betrays a failure to look with an unbiased eye at such films
as *She Wore a Yellow Ribbon* and many others, in which the Indian's
kinship with the white man is emphasized over simplistic images of
violent savagery.

Second, if the portrayal of Indians in some "classic westerns," and
neo-Indian Street Thunder in *Assault on Precinct 13*, reduces them to
images of pure evil, what of it? The portrayal of Polyphemus in *The*

Odyssey may be equally inaccurate and insulting to one-eyed giants. But neither the Homeric epic nor the Carpenter film make pretensions toward historical or cultural accuracy. Rather, they are seeking images of threat and terror with which to play out the age-old mythic battle of good vs. evil. The Indians of a John Ford—or a John Carpenter—film are no more supposed to represent "real" Indians than George Romero's zombies are supposed to represent real dead people.

It's more than a little shaky to accuse of negative stereotyping a film whose premises so scrupulously insist that not *all* cops are good, not *all* convicts are bad, not *all* women are weak. *Assault on Precinct 13* does not propose that social rebels are evil, any more than Ford's film proposes that Indians are savage, or than *Hansel and Gretel* proposes that stepmothers are wicked. Rather, the film is concerned with *these* social rebels, *these* cops, *these* cons—individual people responding to a situation, not a situation made allegorically to stand for *all* people. The film's uncompromising individualism—the very opposite of stereotyping—is precisely its message.

The most telling element in Williams's critical attack on *Assault on Precinct 13* is his insistence upon contrasting the film with *Rio Bravo*. The implication of his contrast is that it's all right to celebrate conservative individualism when it does battle against the fascism of a Nathan Burdett (the town-running rancher-villain of the Hawks film), but not when it goes up against what Williams sees as a valid radical alternative to the American way of life. So it is finally Carpenter's apparent politics, not his lack of politics, that raises Williams's hackles. These are the excesses of a critical approach that refuses to accept the film on its own terms.

Robin Wood, editor and coauthor of the volume in which Williams's analysis appears, is largely in agreement with Williams, ascribing Carpenter's purported failure to "examine the connotative level of his own work" to "false innocence,"[8] and taking the Carpenter of *Assault on Precinct 13* to task for a "film-buff innocence" that combines *Rio Bravo* and *Night of the Living Dead* "without any apparent awareness of the ideological consequences of converting Hawks's fascists (or Romero's ghouls, for that matter) into an army of revolutionaries."[9] If *Rio Bravo* is, as Wood suggests, an antifascist film, and there's no reason it shouldn't be, that fact still doesn't make Howard Hawks a liberal, nor does it impose on John Carpenter the burden of reproducing Hawksian politics in a film that is little more than an *hommage* to the Hawks film. Later, in Carpenter's *The Thing*, which is not just an *hommage* but a partial remake, Carpenter chooses not to echo the Howard Hawks–Christian Nyby original's militarist, anti-liberal stance. In *Starman* Carpenter even rejects that stance outright, celebrating the victory of

Assault on Precinct 13
Above: Napoleon Wilson (Darwin Joston) helps the wounded Leigh (Laurie Zimmer) escape from the cell block.
Below: The street punk as "radical alternative"? Gilbert de la Peña as one of the leaders of Street Thunder, against the blighted landscape of Anderson.
[Photos courtesy of Museum of Modern Art Film Stills Archive]

the gentle liberal over the rock-hard militarist. But Wood finally balances his "false innocence" argument with a telling blow for the other viewpoint: "Tony Williams's complaint ... that John Carpenter lacks intellectual awareness of the implications of his material seems to me (though not without validity) problematic. The richness of an artist's work often arises from the dramatization of tensions and contradictions that intellectual awareness may actually inhibit and impoverish."[10] This is a recognition that will have profound implications for the study of Carpenter's *Halloween*, though Wood is, finally, unable to convince himself.

Praising Larry Cohen's *Demon*, George Romero's *Night of the Living Dead*, and Tobe Hooper's *The Texas Chainsaw Massacre* at the expense of Carpenter's *Halloween*, Wood writes that the former films "reflect ideological disintegration and lay bare the possibility of social revolution."[11] Leaving the unrevolutionary aspects of *Halloween* aside until I come to that film, I am nevertheless struck by the phrase "ideological disintegration"—for what better term to denote the utter collapse of easy, artificial signals (cop/cowboy/white/good vs. crook/Indian/black/bad) that Tony Williams tries to find in *Assault on Precinct 13*?

Notes

1. I have argued this interpretation of *The Birds* in more detail in "Caliban in Bodega Bay," *Movietone News* 41 (May 11, 1975), 3-8.
2. Wood, Robin, "Introduction," *American Nightmare: Essays on the Horror Film*, Toronto: Festival of Festivals, 1979, *passim*, esp. pp. 13-22.
3. Williams, Tony, *"Assault on Precinct 13*: The Mechanics of Repression," in Wood, ed., *American Nightmare*, pp. 67-73; p. 68.
4. *Ibid.*
5. Williams, *op. cit.*, p. 70.
6. *Ibid.*
7. *Ibid.*
8. Wood, "Introduction," p. 26.
9. Wood, "Introduction," pp. 24-6.
10. Wood, "World of Gods & Monsters: The Films of Larry Cohen," *American Nightmare*, p. 85.
11. Wood, "Introduction," p. 28.

Intermission:

Zuma Beach and
Eyes of Laura Mars

The success of Robert Altman's *Nashville* spawned a host of low-budget imitations in which a day or two in the life of a dozen or so characters in some meaningful environment (a car wash, a high school, a beach) became—or threatened to become—a microcosm of contemporary American life. A little less successful than most was the made-for-television *Zuma Beach*, in which a recording star whose career has taken a downturn deals with momentary adversity by rejuvenating herself among high school students at the beach where she herself spent time during her high school years. John Carpenter cowrote the teleplay for this indifferent film, but little of the Carpenter Touch is apparent in the finished film. The theme of the film, however—a solitary woman coping with adversity, reaching out to others—is one that recurs in Carpenter's more accomplished work, both of this period (*Eyes of Laura Mars*, *Someone's Watching Me!*) and later (*Starman*). The film is also distinguished by the first significant performance of P. J. Soles, who would soon play an important role in Carpenter's breakthrough film, *Halloween*.

John Carpenter wrote a screenplay called *Eyes* before *Halloween* made him a household word and made the subjective camera murderer's-eye-view a commonplace of the new horror film. Jack H. Harris, *Dark Star*'s distributor, introduced Carpenter to Jon Peters, who was developing the film. Carpenter's script was ultimately completely rewritten as well as retitled, but the essential premise of *Eyes of Laura Mars* is still Carpenter's: A photographer finds herself at times inexplicably seeing with someone else's eyes—a murderer's eyes. When this happens, she cannot see the murderer, of course—but she can see the victim and the circumstances of the killing. Her special psychic knowledge, inaccessible to the police, makes it necessary for her to discover the murderer herself.

The film establishes some problems about observation and the observer that will haunt much of Carpenter's mature work, as seen in

Eyes of Laura Mars
Laura (Faye Dunaway) in black, with her models and camera.

the interaction between the watcher and the watched in *Someone's Watching Me!*, the invocation of the observer-altered reality of the Heisenberg Uncertainty Principle and the theory of Schrödinger's Cat[1] in *Prince of Darkness*, the alien-controlled perceptible reality of *They Live*, and the Lovecraftian books of evil in *In the Mouth of Madness* whose mere reading can break down the fragile wall between our perceived reality and the darker one waiting next door.

Eyes of Laura Mars tackles head-on the question of the dream or hallucination as a transmission of another view of reality—the central question of art, after all, and one that was already crucial in the work of the British science fiction scenarist Nigel Kneale, who had a profound influence on John Carpenter.

There is also an abundance of mirror imagery in *Eyes of Laura Mars*, suggesting the vision of self and the confusion of love with self-love. This is critical to the revised plot—not the one Carpenter conceived—for in it the psychic photographer, Laura Mars, has her hallucinations and the trauma of murder further complicated by falling in love with the investigating police detective, John Neville.

Laura's visions are, in effect, those of a subjective camera. In one scene she uses a video camera and monitor to show Detective Neville what she means, how she sees. She can't see the killer; instead, she sees with the killer's eyes. No explanation is ever offered for this shared vision. We have to take Laura's clairvoyance at face value.

Neville turns out to be the killer—presumably drawn to Laura both by love and by their uncannily shared vision. The film climaxes with Neville, like a possessed wolf man, begging his loved one to release him from his psychopathic curse by killing him.

Carpenter had something rather different in mind for the finale, which is only partly realized in the film: " ... she must defend herself, seeing only herself through his eyes as he comes at her."[2]

As a photographer, Laura Mars *is* a camera; as a fashion photographer who exploits violence, she epitomizes the artist who uses violence as metaphor, who "sees" real violence with other people's eyes, who puts herself—albeit involuntarily—in the place of the doer of violence. The question is raised (and allowed to hang in the air) that she may be guilty of *causing* violence, of fostering an atmosphere in which violence flourishes. That same accusation is frequently leveled against makers of horror and action films, a fact that clearly haunts Carpenter's consciousness as well as his films.

Notes

1. German physicist Werner Heisenberg (1901-76) discovered that instruments could accurately measure either the speed or the location of a subatomic particle but not both simultaneously, from which he extrapolated the principle that the act of observation unavoidably affects the reality that is observed. In a much-discussed thought experiment, Austrian physicist Erwin Schrödinger (1887-1961) postulated a box into which a cat is placed. A button outside the box is then depressed, an act that either does or does not release a deadly gas inside the box. Once the button is pushed, but *before* the box is opened and the results are observed, is the cat living or dead? Schrödinger proposed that, until the state of the cat is ascertained by observation, the correct answer is neither. This suggests that the act of observation not only validates reality but, in a sense, creates it.
2. Fox, Jordan R., Interview, "Riding High on Horror," *Cinefantastique* 10:1, Summer 1980, p. 8.

5

It *Was* the Bogey Man

Halloween

Yablans ... came to us and said, "Would you make us a movie about babysitters?"

—Debra Hill[1]

The opening of *Halloween* reprises the metaphor of *Eyes of Laura Mars*: the camera as peeping Tom ... and as killer. The motif is sustained throughout the film, as the subjective camera makes killers—albeit shocked, unwilling ones—of us all, the heavy breathing of Michael becoming our own as we wonder what he/we will do next. As in the opening shot of *Assault on Precinct 13*, the moving camera presence creates a sense of disorder, an unsettling feeling that grips the viewer throughout the film: fear of sudden, random violence.

Following the main title shot—a slow track-in on a leering jack-o'-lantern—the opening sequence of *Halloween* is a spectacular tour-de-force, a four-minute single take that builds up to the brutal murder of a teenage girl in a quiet home in a quiet neighborhood in quiet Haddonfield, Illinois, on Halloween, 1963. The take ends as the murderer's mask is removed and a shock cut reveals the clown-suited killer to be the victim's six-year-old brother. The camera stares, then backs off, becoming a 15-second crane shot up away from the silent, blank-faced boy holding the bloody knife as his parents look on, questioning.[2]

Thereafter, as in *Jaws*, the shift to subjective camera often deliberately signals the presence, or possible presence, of the beast. In addition to imputing guilt to the audience, the subjective camera also serves the purpose of concealing the killer's identity in the crucial opening scene. The subjective camera technique was taken up by *Friday the 13th* and the raft of *Halloween* imitators that followed and became such a convention that it was parodied in the opening to Brian De Palma's *Blowout*. But it became a convention for a purely utilitarian reason—

The Shape

preventing us from seeing the killer's face—and acquired the unfortunate side effect of creating a sadistic woman-killing persona as the point of audience identification, something many critics and viewers reacted against.

The Moving Camera Writes

Carpenter has described the genesis of his use of the subjective camera in *Halloween* in this way:

> This all comes from my idea about scary films. It seems to me that the subjective camera as monster has been used all the time. It's not any kind of new idea. I recall 1957, Bert Gordon made a movie called *Beginning of the End*—giant locusts. There's one shot when they first discover the giant locusts where there's a deaf ... or mute ... character who's out there, and he sees one, and it takes the locust's point of view. It just zooms in at him and he screams.
>
> I used to see that hundreds of times in old Fifties monster movies. Here it came ... waaaugghhhh! ... and you screamed. Then there was *Jaws*, which at the beginning of the film took the shark's point of view coming up, which I thought was odd, but it seemed to work for everybody. Then there was *Grizzly. Grizzly* was a ripoff of *Jaws*, and they didn't have the bear for a long time, so they used a hand held camera walking through the woods. And it was *so bad*. It was like, "Come on, there's nothing scary about this." There's nothing that gets you, because *you* know it's this jiggling camera.
>
> I got obsessed with the idea of doing a smooth camera for a subjective shot, but it wasn't one that was constricted by tracks. In other words, when you dolly with a camera, what you do is lay down tracks, like railroad tracks, put the camera on it—sometimes you put it on a dance floor or a big piece of plywood—and you smoothly move the camera in, but the mobility—because you're dragging along about four or five people on the camera—is very limited. And you really rarely can spin around and do the kind of things that you can do when you're walking along and looking with your eyes.
>
> So, along comes something called Steadicam—or, in the case of *Halloween*, the Panaglide—which is a gyroscopic camera that's mounted on one person and it has an arm that comes out from his waist, and the camera's just mounted and it floats. So it doesn't have the rock-steadiness of a dolly, but it also doesn't have the human jerky movements of hand held—it's somewhere in between. I felt it would be a perfect subjective camera because

it could float and kind of move through some places, then turn around and run and go up stairs, and so forth. [In] *Eyes of Laura Mars*, they used a hand held camera for the killer. I was immensely disappointed because, again, it was like *Grizzly*, there's nothing scary about it.

So I wanted to use this weird camera that would zoom around, and so it seemed somewhat successful in *Halloween*. And, it also seems successful when you have to do a scene that has a lot of movement to it. You can just kind of walk around with the actors and keep shooting. *Wall Street*'s an example of that, where they just keep dodging that Steadicam in and out. Probably the greatest example of subjective camera was *Dark Passage* with Humphrey Bogart. I'd love to do something like that; that's a great film.

The long take that begins *Halloween* works for several reasons: First, the unmounted camera, steady though it is, wavers just enough to keep us unsettled, off balance, vulnerable to shock even if slightly prepared for it. Second, the shot establishes the motif of the subjective camera as the killer's point of view. Third, and most important, the shot draws us into the action by a point of view that is *unedited*. Had the opening sequence been presented conventionally, as a mounted sequence of shots, the viewer's mind would become an editor's mind, classifying, comparing, and relating the shots to assemble the story—in other words, a mind participating in the creation of the work and therefore more conscious of it *as* a work. The single take suppresses the artistic detachment that comes from mental montage, creating instead a direct involvement that—like real life—we are unable to edit. The impact, in other words, is visceral, not intellectual.

The strongest precedent for Carpenter's long-take opening to *Halloween* is found not in the annals of horror film but in the spectacular single-shot opening credits sequence of Orson Welles's *Touch of Evil*—a crane shot that begins on an extreme close-up, then pulls back to a cityscape, tracks the movements of two different sets of characters, and culminates in one character's reaction to an offscreen explosion. Both of the opening two shots of *Halloween* are grounded in the same technique: The first shot concentrates on setting a scene, building suspense, and culminating in shock. The second shot, because it is a crane shot, is a more direct descendent of the Welles shot, but it is shorter, simpler than the Welles shot, beginning close and ending high and wide, without the comings and goings and focal changes of Welles's *Touch of Evil* opening. Moreover, it establishes the ground rules under which, for the remainder of the film, Carpenter will switch from subjective to objective point of view, from killer's eye to director's eye.

The crane shot up and away, dwarfing the characters in the context of their surroundings, is a shot potent with emotional impact, and most commonly used as an end title shot, as in such diverse films as Jacques Demy's *The Umbrellas of Cherbourg*, Michael Cacoyannis's *Zorba the Greek*, and Sergio Leone's *Once Upon a Time in the West*. It was also used to great effect by Alan Pakula in the mountain-of-work library research scene of *All the President's Men*. But the second shot of *Halloween*, though as powerful in its way as any of these, is most remarkable if seen as a reversal of Hitchcock's celebrated crane shot in *Young and Innocent*, moving from high and wide over an entire ballroom of dancing couples to come to rest on the extreme close-up detail of the twitching eyelid of an onstage musician—the killer, as it turns out, masked in blackface. Carpenter, by contrast, begins on the unmasked face of his killer and pulls away to set the boy with the knife in the anomalous context of his quiet middle-American neighborhood.

The Boy with the Knife

The idea of the juvenile murderer as psychotic adult was not a new theme in horror film when *Halloween* appeared: Nearly a decade earlier, Bernard Girard's *The Mad Room* had assayed the same idea; a decade before that, in Alfred Hitchcock's *Psycho*, Norman Bates's adult psychosis was revealed to have been manifest in a murder committed in adolescence. *Halloween*'s structure—opening with a hideous murder as prologue, then focusing on events that occur many years later—is observable in *Hush ... Hush, Sweet Charlotte*, *Strait Jacket*, and other *Psycho*-influenced thrillers of the Sixties. *Halloween*'s first, horrifying knifing itself owes as much to the stabbing of a plump justice of the peace by the bride during a marriage ceremony in William Castle's *Homicidal* as it does to the shower murder in *Psycho*. Note, too, that in all three films—*Psycho*, *Homicidal*, and *Halloween*—the knife-wielding killer wears a disguise.

There is a sort of "second introduction" before the film proper gets under way. This sequence—set in Smith's Grove, Illinois, on October 30, 1978—depicts the now-adult Michael's escape from an asylum.[3] His psychiatrist, Dr. Loomis—a name borrowed in homage to *Psycho*—and a nurse have come to transport Michael, under sedation, to a different facility. Loomis meditates on the strange case of Michael Myers ("He hasn't spoken a word in 15 years"), and suggests what he will later make explicit: that Michael is not conventionally, or even unconventionally, *sick*, but is the embodiment of pure evil:

Nurse: "You never want him to get out."
Loomis: "Never."

When, moments later, Michael leaps silently, unpredictably, and from an almost impossible angle onto—then *into*—the van, the confining order of the classical movie frame is violated, its borders no longer safe. This violation of visual order is a correlate to the way in which the quiet order of life in Haddonfield is also about to be changed utterly. Richard T. Jameson observed, "Virtually every shot contains corners, apertures, black holes potentially fillable by a white ghost of a face; and the ever-drifting camera eye ... may be just the neutral, conveniently mobile recorder of the scene, or an inhabited point of view, an indicator of the one direction the vulnerable characters ought not to proceed in."[4] ("The first time I used Panavision," says Carpenter, "I thought, 'This is like painting a picture. Look at the room you have, on the sides. You can *use* the space.'"[5])

The off-kilter atmosphere created by Carpenter's ambivalent use of the subjective camera carries into the film proper, suggesting an underlying disorder in the superficial order of small-town life in middle-American Haddonfield (cf. the Hadleyville of *High Noon*—itself evocative of Mark Twain's corruptible Hadleyburg). The idyllic calm of tree-lined residential streets and picturesque falling autumn leaves is set off balance by the camera's insistence upon sneaking around trees and peering at its subjects from behind bushes. When Laurie, having been told to leave the key to the Myers house under the mat for her realtor father, approaches the now-abandoned house of murder, the camera gives us a point of view *inside* the Myers house, so that even before a shoulder slides into view, we sense a presence watching her. With Carpenter, a camera position is never arbitrary—it always conveys the *presence* of a narrative or participating eye.

Now Carpenter begins to lace atmosphere-building technique with plot-defining words. When Laurie hears a dull teacher lecturing on the notion of fate in the writings of someone named Samuels, the idea of an inescapable, repeated destiny is planted. Little Tommy Doyle is tormented by his schoolmates: "The Bogey Man is going to get you!" As the boy heads home from school after this incident, Michael's stolen state car cruises the school, tracking Tommy, with us in the back seat. The camera presence, which sometimes is that of Michael Myers and sometimes not, is nudged by incidental dialogue into something conveying a supernatural intrusion into the world.

Laurie sees Michael go behind a bush, and Annie skeptically jokes when she doesn't find him there: "Laurie, dear ... he wants to talk to you ... he wants to take you out tonight." All Annie wants to do is to tease Laurie about her skittishness *and* about her datelessness, but she's also making an unintentional prophecy. The dialogue Carpenter puts into her mouth points the attentive viewer in the direction of the film's sub-surface psychodynamics.

He Comes Home

Laurie gets the shakes from seeing Michael turning up here and there. She's spooked by screams but then recognizes the source of the noise as only a group of trick-or-treaters. "I thought you outgrew superstition," she says to herself.

You don't.

A headstone is stolen—the headstone of the sister Michael murdered as a child.

We start to get glimpses—always in long shot and in dusky semi-darkness—of Michael's face, ghostly white, like a supernatural being. A closer look will reveal that The Face is a mask, but for now its paleness—possibly explainable as the result of spending 15 years inside, out of the sunlight—enhances our sense of Michael as a supernatural being. So do the increasingly grotesque events and dialogue: Dr. Loomis and Deputy Sheriff Brackett explore the Myers house and come across something we can't see:

> Loomis: "What's that?"
> Brackett: "A dog."
> Loomis: "He got hungry."
> Brackett: "Coulda been a skunk. A man wouldn't do that."
> Loomis: "This isn't a man."

A little later, Michael finishes off the Wallaces' German Shepherd. This stomach-churning—and *suggested* rather than depicted—motif is an elaboration of one of the classic devices of horror and science-fiction films of the Fifties: A dog was frequently the first victim of an unseen, monstrous presence that only the dog could sense. (Carpenter would put yet a different spin on the idea a few years later in his version of *The Thing*.) The dog incident sparks a dialogue between Loomis and Brackett, in which Loomis makes explicit what has so far been only suggested: "I realized that what was living behind that boy's eyes was purely and simply evil."

Visions of Michael's evanescent presence are shared by Laurie and Tommy, but never at the same time. Tommy, after a not-sure-I-saw-anything glimpse of Michael recalls the taunting of his schoolmates, asks Laurie: "What's the Bogey Man?"

Annie, meanwhile, is about to find out. Michael appears behind her as she chats on the phone, wearing a loose shirt that visually echoes the hospital gown Michael discarded after he escaped from Smith's Grove looking like one of George Romero's living dead.

As a metaphor for the intrusion of the supernatural into the quotidian world of Haddonfield, Carpenter merges the world of the horror film into the world of the characters' reality. A special Halloween night double feature is being shown by a local TV channel—*The Thing* and *Forbidden Planet* (matted-in in proper frame ratio!). We see the opening credits to *The Thing* and later hear the dialogue in the famous scene in which the soldiers and scientists discover the Object in the ice: "Spread out, everybody ... we're going to try to figure out the shape of the thing." In *Halloween*'s credits, the adult Michael Myers is pointedly referred to as "The Shape."

Lindsey Wallace, whom Laurie takes on as a second charge to her evening's babysitting chores, stays glued to the movies for most of the night, while Tommy can't keep himself away from the window—a different kind of screen—through which he keeps seeing odd goings-on. He never tells Laurie what he sees, though at one point he is visibly, and inarticulately, upset by it. Laurie, upon going to investigate, of course sees nothing.

Laurie tells Tommy, "The Bogey Man can only come out on Halloween night"—a point that's not especially reassuring on Halloween night. What she thinks of as an entertaining scary tale is to Tommy confirmation of his worst fears. Informing Carpenter's atmosphere of terror in *Halloween* are a number of the elements of fairy tales—which is to say, of the human personality's deepest native fears and desires. The primitive fear of darkness is evoked throughout the film by underexposure. Parents are relatively absent, serving only to give an instruction or two (the Strodes to Laurie, Brackett to Annie) and vanish into the realm of ineffectuality, leaving their offspring to face monumental horrors alone. A supernatural presence—witch or Bogey Man—roams abroad. There is at least one haunted house (the Myers place), though by the end of the film two others are possessed by the monster's presence.

It is not only dialogue and innuendo that suggest Michael's superhuman attributes. There is much in the events depicted on the film's own terms that is explainable only in supernatural terms: The escape from Smith's Grove (how did Michael know? How did he get out?); Michael drives a car well, without ever having had the opportunity to learn; he gets into the Myers house (his *own* house) despite the locked door; he gets into Annie's locked car; he repeatedly returns from the dead; he manifests a strange power over space, being able to inhabit any part of the frame, emerge from any dark area at any time. After *Halloween*, in the hands of inferior imitators, such carefully composed shots became clichés of the horror film, and we are now conditioned to distrust any portion of the frame that's slightly darkened. But in *Halloween* the innovation and visual mastery of John Carpenter is still present in every frame.

Carpenter's cross-tracking of Laurie's approach to the Wallace house cues us to the coming of disaster, much as did Hitchcock's cross-tracking of Melanie Daniels's approach to the Brenner house in *The Birds*. The inside is no longer a haven: Being inside can be as frightening as being outside. Laurie, in the gardening shed, tries to break through a locked door to get away, while Michael tries to break through a locked door to get at her. Moments later, she finds herself trapped *outside*, the opposite of claustrophobia being invoked at the very crescendo of the film: "Let me *in*!"

The final battle takes place inside the Doyle house. Laurie struggles to conceal the children—who, from what we know of Michael's choice of victims, aren't really in any danger—while she delays protecting herself against the monster. After the first encounter, Laurie tells Tommy (mistakenly, it turns out), "I killed him." Tommy knows better: "You can't kill the Bogey Man." Twice Laurie commits the blunder of dropping her weapon beside the killer, assuming he's dead.

As Laurie sits panting in the hallway, and with the children safely dispatched down the street to a neighbor's house, the presumed-dead Michael returns to life in the just-out-of-focus bedroom beyond, sitting up stiffly, corpselike, and swiveling his head robotically our way, an almost mechanical move that visually reverses the stiff keel-over of the psychotic gang killer shot by Lawson in *Assault on Precinct 13*—and in so doing associates Michael with the conscienceless "pure evil" of the Street Thunder psychopath who shot Kathy Lawson.

In the last battle, Laurie rips Michael's mask off to briefly glimpse an unimpressive face that Michael again immediately covers. He must be masked—as if the mask is a persona he hides behind, as if the mask gives him strength—and, masked, he faces Dr. Loomis's pistol. Michael is, in fact, always in costume, imparting to him a kinky suggestion of sadistic fantasy: boy in clown suit, man in hospital gown, masked murderer in garage mechanic's overalls, in a sheet as a bespectacled ghost. Danny Peary sees Michael as a mischievous boy trapped in a man's body, playing tricks and games with his victims, never losing his profound sense of the pain of his own childhood—and, pointedly, never harming a child[6] (though this characteristic of Michael changes in *Halloween 4: The Return of Michael Myers*).

Finally, climactically, a man (if it is a man) is shot six times, falls from a second story window, and yet vanishes into the night. Nothing can ever be the same again. "[I]n my opinion," says John Carpenter, "evil never dies."[7]

Halloween in Its Time

The classic horror films were morally ambiguous. Mr. Hyde and Dr. Jekyll were two sides of a normal, even likeable, human personality. Although Dr. Frankenstein suffered from hubris, he probably didn't deserve the downfall he got, and our response to his monster wavers between horror and sympathy. Larry Talbot, the Wolf Man, commits unspeakable murders, but is ultimately a victim of fate, not an instrument of evil. The great Val Lewton horror films of the Forties used images of horror as metaphors for the psychological state of troubled characters: Does *Cat People*'s Irena *really* metamorphose into a cat, or does she merely *think* she does?

Even in the Fifties, dominated by science fiction invaders from space who were mostly crypto-Communists, monsters tended to arise as correlates to the upsurge of a dark side of the personality of one of the lead characters, or as a symbol of some aspect of modern sociopolitical life. The late Fifties and the Sixties saw the return of Dracula and Frankenstein, courtesy of Hammer Films, and *Psycho* spawned a rash of imitations, all about two-sided personalities—good-bad characters rather than all-bad ones.

But in the Seventies, horror films abandoned the tradition of moral ambiguity and unleashed monsters that were purely evil. No amount of deference to "mental illness," "inbreeding," or "the dark side" can make morally ambiguous the out-and-out evil of the hillbilly killers in *The Texas Chainsaw Massacre* and *The Hills Have Eyes*. The Devil himself set the tone for the decade in *The Exorcist*, a film that, on its worst level, dared to explain troublesome children as a simple epitome of evil. *Jaws* is perhaps the least morally ambiguous horror thriller of all. Its villain is nothing more than a killing machine, and there is no shame or hesitation in wanting it not simply stopped but utterly destroyed.

Halloween falls squarely into that tradition. Even Carpenter's atmospheric music for *Halloween* seems derivative of Mike Oldfield's "Tubular Bells," which contributed so evocatively to the atmosphere of *The Exorcist*. Combined with the teacher's lecture on fate, Dr. Loomis's explanation of Michael as pure evil completes a thematic thread of supernatural possibility, tying in Tommy Doyle's (and *all* children's) fear of the Bogey Man. At the climax, after Michael's clearly superhu-

Monsters and victims
Above: Battling the Id-Monster in *Forbidden Planet*, a scene from
which is glimpsed on a TV screen in *Halloween*. Foreground, left to
right: Jack Kelly, Leslie Nielsen, Warren Stevens.
Below: The Shape (Nick Castle) drops in on Annie (Nancy Loomis)
in *Halloween*.

man effort to keep on coming despite repeated lethal injuries, Laurie breathes with recognition: "It *was* the Bogey Man!" Loomis agrees: "As a matter of fact, it was." Laurie begins to cry anew—though from where she sits she can't possibly know what Loomis, at the window, has just discovered: Michael's thrice-stabbed, six-times-shot, pushed-out-the-window corpse (?) has, impossibly, disappeared. There ensues a brief montage of places—the Doyle house, the Wallace house, places Michael has been, places he might be now, places that will never again be the same because he has been there and left his mark on them— ending at the Myers house, where it all began, reprising from the opening shot the sound of heavy breathing behind the mask. Michael Myers has come home to die ... or to live forever.

The Moral Dimension

Halloween has been accused of being a sick film, primarily for the often-cited reason that the film's (and the subjective camera's) most visible victims are women who indulge their sexuality. But to talk of the film as being about the sadistic victimization of women is to over-simplify. Michael Myers kills men, too, and animals. He fixes on vulnerability, on weakness, not simply on femininity or sexuality. And when he fixes on Laurie, he makes his first mistake.

Loomis, describing Michael in the sanitarium, says "15 years ... waiting"—as if to suggest a real motive in Michael's atrocities. Jealousy? Revenge? Punishment of the wicked? Moments after Michael has carried Annie's dead body into the house, Bob carries Lynda into the house in an evocation of the traditional prelude to intercourse between both the married and the unmarried. Not just sexuality but domesticity is associated with impending violence. Bedrooms are the sites of the key killings. Michael arranges corpses in the bedroom where Lynda and Bob have recently enjoyed sex. Michael's sister Judith, then Annie, then Lynda are all glimpsed partly nude before they are murdered, and their sexual liberty seems to be a motivating force for Michael's murderous wrath. This is a tempting argument, and one that has attracted many critics. But if there is anything to it, why does Michael fix on Laurie, who is the exact opposite of these other girls?

In his major killings—Judith, Annie, Lynda—Michael seems to associate sexuality with the need for punishment. But those who mess around—men *or* women—are insufficiently vigilant to protect themselves against death (an idea that acquires greater potency from the retrospective vantage point of the era of AIDS). Laurie, by contrast, *is* able to protect herself, albeit at great risk.

The nakedness of the female victims seems to suggest punishable sexuality. But with the exception of the nurse in the van, *all* of Michael's victims are at some time or other naked, including the male victims: the garage man, whose clothing Michael takes, and Lynda's boyfriend Bob. Nakedness is not here a simple suggestion of sexuality, but the most extreme image of vulnerability. All of Carpenter's early films evince an interest in people who are trapped, and—in the Hawksian tradition—consistently contrast characters who are "good" in such situations, and thus save themselves, with characters who are distracted by self-interest and thus fail to protect themselves adequately. Broncho Billy is rewarded for his vigilance against the entrapment of contemporary urban stress; Laura Mars's understanding of the camera eye enables her to solve the murders and to protect herself from the killer; the astronauts of *Dark Star* are self-absorbed in their claustrophobic plight and thus unable to prevent the final conflagration; the defenders of Precinct 13 break down into the Hawksian "good" and "bad."

To the suggestion that Judith, Annie, and Lynda are "punished for their sexuality," Carpenter responded in a 1980 interview,[8] "No, they're unaware because they're doing something else. They're interested in their boyfriends, so they're ignoring the signs." And of Laurie: "*She's* aware of it because she's more like the killer, she has problems. She and the killer have a certain link: sexual repression. She's lonely, she doesn't have a boyfriend, so she's looking around. And she finds someone—him." Laurie and The Shape connect in a darker version of the passing spontaneous attraction between Leigh and Napoleon Wilson in *Assault on Precinct 13*—itself based on the coming together of Howard Hawks's couples in *Red River*, *Rio Bravo*, and the Bogey-and-Bacall films.

Richard Jameson noticed it, too: "*Halloween* establishes an unverbalizable but completely compelling connection between its teenage female protagonist and the murderous male interloper from the hometown past, simply by photographing a virginal Jamie Lee Curtis walking away from us singing a song about a secret love, with the dark-jacketed shoulder of 'The Shape' sidestepping into foreground right."[9] The image Jameson describes is all the more potent considered alongside Annie's joking "He wants to take you out tonight" to Laurie. Jameson has been virtually alone in noticing that the movie is more about the *killer*'s sexuality than the victims'.

In this sense, *Halloween*—as Robin Wood has noted—has much in common with the films of David Cronenberg (and for that matter David Lynch's later *Blue Velvet*), in which sexuality is treated as an infectious, corrupting disease. This, in turn, is little more than a development of the traditional horror theme of vampirism, consistently treated on film as a combination of eros and pestilence.

The madman, always a force of disorder in the world, is himself a very ordered figure: He sees the world too clearly, too simply. That is the danger of true madness. It is a comfort for the Loomises and the Lauries of the world to describe him as "the Bogey Man." It is somehow simpler—more *ordered*—to see the evil as a supernatural intervention rather than the darkly possible human aberration on whose fringes we all must live.

Halloween, with its roots in *Psycho* and *The Texas Chainsaw Massacre*, follows *Assault on Precinct 13* in recognizing psychosis as the real horror of contemporary life. However, from this point, Carpenter begins a gradual return to more fantastic, more conventional supernatural horror, signaled by the identification of Michael Myers as the Bogey Man, and pointing toward the ghost and possession stories recounted in *The Fog, Christine, Big Trouble in Little China, Prince of Darkness*, and *In the Mouth of Madness*.

Finally, it really *was* the Bogey Man: Laurie wants to believe these things can't happen; Loomis knows all too well that they can and do. Much as he may want to be able to explain the workings of psychopathy in terms of his own commitment to psychiatric science, he is forced to confront the reality of Michael not as a measurable and understandable phenomenon of mental illness, but as a manifestation of evil abroad in the world. Seeking a scientific order, he instead must confront a larger metaphysical one—just as Professor Birack and his students will do in *Prince of Darkness*.

Knocking Wood

Robin Wood's analysis and criticism of the contemporary American horror film in *American Nightmare* damns *Halloween* with faint praise: "[T]he pleasures of *Halloween* are not of the kind that (in D. H. Lawrence's words) 'lead the sympathetic consciousness into new places, and away in recoil from things gone dead.' *Halloween* in fact, does nothing new, but does it with extreme cinematic sophistication and finesse."[10] It is particularly disturbing that a critic of Wood's experience should so cavalierly separate style from content, praising Carpenter's technical skill while dismissing the very viewpoint that informs that skill. However jarringly conservative it may seem to Wood, the insistence upon a classical cinematic order mirrors an insistence upon a certain social and psychological order. "Style *is* content," as Raymond Durgnat pointed out.[11]

As we saw in his comments on *Assault on Precinct 13*, Wood has a tendency to use his own radicalism not as a vantage point but as a criterion: "*Sisters, Demon, Night of the Living Dead, The Texas Chainsaw Massacre*, in their various ways reflect ideological disintegration and lay bare the possibility of social revolution; *Halloween* and *Alien*, while deliberately evoking maximum terror and panic, variously seal it over again."[12] It never seems to bother Wood that "the possibility of social revolution" invoked in the American horror films he most admires is depicted in wholly negative terms—murder, dismemberment, cannibalism—with no suggestion of a positive result for society *after* the metaphoric "revolution." The aim, in Wood's view, seems to be entirely vindictive, purgative at best.

But the viewpoint of *Halloween*—"reactionary" as it may look to Wood—is yet entirely legitimate. Carpenter's work in *Halloween* is not invalidated by the fact that his monster doesn't comfortably fit the revolutionary, anti-family pattern that Wood perceptively finds in the threatening forces of the films of Wes Craven, Tobe Hooper, and Larry Cohen.

Trying to track the meaning of Michael the monster, Wood notes that the characterization of Dr. Loomis—and his conviction that Michael is the embodiment of pure evil— represents "the most extreme instance of Hollywood's perversion of psychoanalysis into an instrument of repression."[13] Worrying over how Michael learned to drive, Wood suggests that either Michael has *not* spent the intervening years between the murder and the present staring blankly at an asylum wall, or he really *is* possessed of the supernatural powers Dr. Loomis attributes to him. "The possibility that this opens up," reasons Wood, "is that ... Michael's 'evil' is what his analyst has been projecting onto him."[14] This possible subtext, though not pursued by Carpenter in *Halloween*, has honorable cinematic roots going back to *The Cabinet of Dr. Caligari*, and *is* pursued in the treatment of Loomis's increasingly obsessive behavior in *Halloween II, Halloween 4: The Return of Michael Myers*, and *Halloween 5: The Revenge of Michael Myers*. In his analysis of *Halloween*, Danny Peary says Loomis "seems a bit batty ... but it probably takes an insane type to want to track down the destructive Michael. So we're glad he's on our side."[15]

Wood sets the doctor's obsession off against another possibility, that of "psychoanalytical explanation" for Michael's actions: that Laurie is his real quarry because she reincarnates the sister he murdered as a child. (Interestingly, the metaphor is needlessly extended into literalism in *Halloween II* with the revelation that Laurie *is*, in fact, Michael's sister—a "lost" sister, given up for adoption by her parents without Michael's knowledge.) Michael's fixation on Laurie in *Halloween* is further supported by the fact that Laurie is seen in relation to the little boy she's babysitting—a little boy reminiscent of the young Michael of the film's prologue. Here again the possibility of Michael's representing the Return of the Repressed comes into play, for—unlike the other victims—Laurie is visually associated with images of domesticity: She stays home, she cooks, she washes dishes, she takes care of children. She wears an apron and enters the room wiping her hands with a dishtowel (after carving a pumpkin in the kitchen). In her final combat with Michael, her weapons are a knitting needle, a coat hanger and a kitchen knife.

The small-town order that Michael Myers destroys is a social order in which people don't kill one another, and a sexual order in which young women find young men, mess around a little, and eventually settle down to a quiet life of raising children. It is, in other words, the very kind of world that is threatened by the Return of the Repressed in Robin Wood's interpretation of the American horror film.

The tension between Michael's assault on the rebellious sexuality of Judith, Annie, and Lynda and his assault on the conventional domesticity of Laurie, between the hint of a "psychoanalytical explanation" and Loomis's (Carpenter's?) insistence on treating Michael as the personification of pure evil, finally confounds Wood, in much the same way that the sex-as-pathology conservatism of David Cronenberg has always confounded him. What bothers Wood most is that Michael Myers refuses to fit Wood's formula: "[T]he monster becomes ... simply the instrument of Puritan vengeance and repression rather than the embodiment of what Puritanism repressed."[16] But if this is so, then *Halloween* speaks for itself: The image of the repressor is as scary as the Return of the Repressed.

Notes

1. McCarthy, Todd, "Trick and Treat" [John Carpenter interviewed by Todd McCarthy], *Film Comment* 16:1, Jan/Feb 1980, p. 21.
2. The "edited for television" version of *Halloween* damages this opening sequence by narrowing the eyeholes of the "mask" through which much of opening scene's action is seen. The purpose of making the eyeholes smaller is, of course, to obscure Judith's nudity and the graphic shots of her stabbing. But its effect is to compromise the compositional virtuosity of that stunning opening shot.
3. The "edited for television" version of *Halloween*—though *not* the video version—contains a transitional sequence that was not in the theatrical release version. Labeled "Smith's Grove, Illinois, May, 1964," this sequence takes place at the hospital and has Dr. Loomis arguing with hospital administrators. He claims that Michael's catatonia is feigned and that the boy is too dangerous for a minimum

security environment. He loses the argument, then walks down the hall and drops in on Michael, who sits in his room staring out the window. He tells Michael words to the effect that "You fooled them, but you don't fool me." Besides doing little to elucidate or color the characterization of Michael, the scene distorts the original film in several ways. It doesn't mesh well with the preceding "Halloween, 1963" opening, because it shows us all too clearly a Michael who doesn't look like the Michael we just saw unmasked, and whose daylight-visible presence takes away much of the menace and mystery of the Michael Myers character. The sequence also becomes, after the fact, the first in which Dr. Loomis appears, and has the effect of introducing him to us with the Michael-obsession that haunts his character later on already in place. For this reason, the inserted sequence also doesn't mesh well with the ensuing, redated "second introduction" sequence, "Smith's Grove, Illinois, October 30, 1979," whose original force and economy are diminished by dialogue that now seems redundant.

4. Jameson, Richard T., "Style vs. 'Style'," *Film Comment* 16:2, Mar/Apr 1980, p. 12.

5. Fox, Jordan R., Interview, "Riding High on Horror," *Cinefantastique* 10:1, Summer 1980, p. 40.

6. Peary, Danny, *Cult Movies*, New York: Dell, 1981, pp. 125-6.

7. Fox, "Riding High on Horror," p. 40.

8. McCarthy, *op. cit.*, p. 24.

9. Jameson, "Style vs. 'Style'," p. 12.

10. Wood, "World of Gods and Monsters," *American Nightmare*, pp. 85-6.

11. Durgnat, Raymond, "The Mongrel Muse," *Films and Feelings*, Cambridge, Mass.: M.I.T. Press, 1971, pp. 19-30.

12. Wood, "Introduction," *American Nightmare*, p. 28.

13. Wood, "Introduction," p. 26.

14. Wood, "Introduction," p. 26.

15. Peary, *Cult Movies*, p. 125.

16. Wood, "Introduction," p. 26.

Intermission:

Halloween—The Sequels

The success of *Halloween* combined with the sequel-hungry market of the early Eighties to make *Halloween II* inevitable. The *Halloween* series was controlled by a five-party partnership involving Carpenter, Moustapha Akkad, Debra Hill, Joseph Wolf, and Irwin Yablans. *Halloween* had been John Carpenter's first association with Akkad, the Syrian producer who helped finance the film. Akkad went on to act as uncredited coproducer (under Dino de Laurentiis) on *Halloween II* and *Halloween III: Season of the Witch*, and eventually came to manage the *Halloween* property with his own company, Trancas Films International.

Halloween II

"Basically, sequels mean the same film," says John Carpenter. "That's what people want to see. They want to see the same movie again. [*Halloween II*] was just the same film."

Halloween II takes up exactly where *Halloween* left off. The opening is particularly rhythmic: Expecting the eerie, tinkling *Halloween* theme, the viewer is instead bombarded with a playful, upbeat song, "Mr. Sandman," by the Chordettes, ironically played over a track-in on the place where the old Sandman himself, Michael Myers, has just wrought holy havoc. The song fades, and we see played out once again the events of the closing moments of *Halloween*. But this time, after finding the blood in the grass and the expected corpse of Michael Myers long gone, Dr. Loomis begins to rouse the neighborhood, calling for help. The man next door comes out: "Is this some sort of prank? I've been trick-or-treated to death tonight." Dr. Loomis looks scornfully at the man: "You don't know what death *is*." And *now* the soundtrack slams into Carpenter's familiar *Halloween* theme, with a new, heavy edge of doom in the bass line.

It's all downhill from there. *Halloween II* comes up with nothing new or inventive, and the film that follows can't match the compelling energy of that opening. The director, Rick Rosenthal, strives to deliver the same atmosphere and look of *Halloween*. He makes a noble effort at recapturing the Carpenter feel in some places, but an attempt at another virtuoso long-take tracking shot is wrecked by intercutting it with objective-point-of-view shots, suggesting that the long takes couldn't be sustained or that Rosenthal didn't trust them. Quick shots of *Night of the Living Dead* on television don't serve mood and atmosphere the way *The Thing* and *Forbidden Planet* did in *Halloween*. Instead of amplifying the thematic and stylistic impact of the film, the Romero quote here amounts to little more than a throwaway.

Halloween II is emphatically more gruesome than its progenitor, possibly because the enormously popular killfests *Friday the 13th* and *Friday the 13th, Part 2* had intervened between the success of *Halloween* and the release of *Halloween II*. More attention is paid in the sequel to the *ways* in which Michael Myers dispatches his victims, and less to the psychosexual menace he represents to the characters threatened by him. Among the distractions: slashed throats, burned bodies, hypodermic needles to the brain, and a woman scalded in a therapeutic tub until the flesh peels off her face. Henceforth, the *Halloween* progeny films mark themselves more as "splatter" movies than as the psychological thriller that *Halloween* was.

It's essentially a chase movie: Michael chases Laurie; Loomis chases Michael. In fact, despite Laurie's continued presence (mostly as a bandaged patient in a hospital bed), this film is really about Dr. Loomis and his growing obsession with Michael. Owing to Loomis's zeal in wanting to rid the world of Michael, an innocent—albeit drunken—teenager is burned to death in an accident. The *real* Michael is burned, too, but he emerges from the flames still walking and he continues to haunt Laurie's memories and dreams as the film ends.

Dr. Loomis's self-sacrifice in blowing up himself and Michael is thus ineffectual as regards disposing of Michael, and from the hindsight of *Halloween 4* it wasn't even a self-sacrifice, because Loomis survived, too. But the motif of self-sacrifice suggests other Carpenter films, past and to come: Father Malone's welcoming of his deserved death in *The Fog*; Maggie's combined revenge and self-sacrifice when she kills the Duke in the climax of *Escape from New York*; MacReady's destruction by fire of the outpost's life-sustaining systems, and his willingness to face freezing death if it means defeating The Thing; Catherine's self-sacrifice at the climactic confrontation with primordial evil in *Prince of Darkness*; Nada's sacrificial destruction of the aliens' transmitter-receiver at the end of *They Live*; and the sacrificial gestures of Alan Chaffee in *Village of the Damned* and Crow, Montoya, and Father Guiteau in *Vampires*.

Finally, the seemingly important message that Laurie is really Michael's sister—a second sister given up for adoption years ago after Michael murdered his older sister and was committed—is sheer nonsense. In the first place Michael couldn't know this. In the second place, even if he did, Laurie's being Michael's sister adds nothing to the plot and tension of the film or its character relationships. Michael's psychological fixation on Laurie was already established in *Halloween* without the benefit of any such explanation.

Halloween III: Season of the Witch

For John Carpenter, *Halloween III* represented a long-dreamed-of opportunity to collaborate with Nigel Kneale, whose writings Carpenter had admired from youth.

Kneale created Professor Bernard Quatermass, head physicist for the British Rocket Group, and sustained the character through several television shows and four feature films. The first two Quatermass films—*The Quatermass Experiment* (*The Creeping Unknown*) and *Quatermass II* (*Enemy from Space*)—were directed by Val Guest in 1956 and '57 respectively, and starred Brian Donlevy as the scientist-hero. The best known and most celebrated of the series, *Five Million Years to Earth* (*Quatermass and the Pit*), starring Andrew Keir, is one of the most revered science fiction films. A latter-day Quatermass film, *The Quatermass Conclusion*, was directed in 1980 by Piers Haggard and starred John Mills. Carpenter still credits *Enemy from Space* as the best of the Quatermass series, and the film that first attracted him to Kneale's work.

Here's how he tells the story of his long-hoped-for, ill-fated collaboration with Kneale:

Nigel Kneale was one of my heroes growing up. The first movie I saw of his remains my favorite, and that is *Enemy From Space* (*Quatermass II*). I think it is the best of his work. It is the movie that really inspired me a lot to get into movies, and his writing, and so forth. I then saw *Quatermass Experiment*, and then I saw *Five Million Years to Earth*.

I went to London in 1977 to the London Film Festival with *Assault on Precinct 13*, and I was able to buy over there copies of all the Quatermass serials as done on the BBC. And also, some of his other work, which has not been seen in this country—*The Stone Tapes, Year of the Sex Olympics*—these are all stories and plays done for television. And it's sensational stuff. He's a great writer; and the best written of them—not the

Above: *Halloween III: Season of the Witch*
The evil genius Conal Cochran (Dan O'Herlihy)
Below: *Five Million Years to Earth*
Roney (James Donald) and Quatermass (Andrew Keir) remove a
Martian from the London underground in the film based on Nigel
Kneale's *Quatermass and the Pit.*

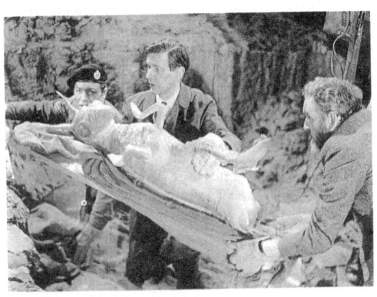

scariest, but the best written—is *Five Million Years to Earth* or *Quatermass and the Pit*. It has a lot of great ideas—it's basically science fiction and the mythological beginnings of evil. And it's something that has always stayed with me—but I must say that in terms of simply pure enjoyment, I still can't get over *Quatermass II*. I think it's the best, and it's still riveting.

When you compare the films in terms of movies, *Five Million Years to Earth* was done by Roy Ward Baker, whose work I have enjoyed but I feel is much more of a journeyman. He uses a lot of close-ups and a lot of kind of arbitrary moves, a little hand held. He seems to be well in control of what he's doing, but I felt that there was really a mind behind Val Guest ... he really had a style that I admired. It was also black-and-white. There's something about that plant that I always loved, and I always loved Brian Donlevy.

But anyway, I met up with Nigel Kneale in ... '81 ... we were working on *The Thing*. ... Kneale was working on *Creature from the Black Lagoon*, scripted it, never got done. ... As a matter of fact, I have the script. I may do *Creature from the Black Lagoon* here in a couple years. It would be fun to do. Anyway, he had an idea for *Halloween III*. Joe Dante got together with us, and all of us went to dinner with him. He had a great idea, and it is *Halloween III*—exactly that story—and we hired Nigel to write it, and he wrote it, and it was great, but it was odd, and there was this ... anti-Irish bitterness throughout this story.

I felt, "Well, what this needs is a real quick polish," and I worked with Nigel, but he didn't care to change anything. There came a point where I had to say to him, "Yeah, but the audience comes to these movies to have fun and to be scared." And he said, "I don't *care* about the audience." ... So Nigel departed, and I never could quite figure it out, because it was like three-fourths of a great script, but there was this kind of disillusioned old man behind it. I don't mean to be too harsh, but I could never figure it out until I read his novelization of *The Quatermass Conclusion*. I think if anybody has any doubts about the changes that have gone on in his life since his early work, you should read that. He's an angry man who doesn't understand what the world has become, and he really doesn't like people very much.

So, it was disappointing. I think sometimes when we have heroes, if we make them into too much of a god, we can get really disappointed by them. He's just a man, in fact. I still have the utmost admiration for his ability, and I love his early work. You probably could say that about *me*, you know. We're just humans, and we change and grow, and I think that, unfortunately, *Halloween III,* whether we shot his script or the one that was eventually written—was basically the same exact story, the same exact structure. I would say that the version you see now has a little bit more heart to it. It's a little bit more human.

In *Halloween III: Season of the Witch,* the sacrificial Celtic harvest ritual of Sahwain—referred to in *Halloween II* to further the suggestion that Michael Myers is really an embodiment of a long-dormant supernatural force of evil—occasions contemporary Irishman Conal Cochran's demonic plot to kill children and unleash hideous evils. Heads melt and disgorge spiders and snakes under the influence of an ancient curse coaxed forth by an electromagnetically activated microchip made from rock stolen from Stonehenge.

Cochran's nefarious Silver Shamrock toy factory is like the dark side of Willie Wonka's Chocolate Factory (which was itself none too benign). Moreover, it's located in the mythical town of Santa Mira, California—scene of the beginning of a world takeover in Donald Siegel's classic *Invasion of the Body Snatchers.* But *Halloween III* shares neither vision nor metaphor with the Siegel film and there seems to be no compelling reason for the cross-reference. The mixing of the primitive with the futuristic is a Nigel Kneale trademark, but here it serves little more than a cruel sort of chase thriller, far from the intellectual and cultural detective-story structure of Kneale's best work.

A more assured and productive fruition of Carpenter's admiration for Kneale was yet to come: *Prince of Darkness,* produced in 1987.

Halloween 4: The Return of Michael Myers

John Carpenter's account of the changing of the guard on the Halloween series:

> How did I finally relinquish control of *Halloween*? It was something that became as much a curse as a joy. After the first one, you know, when the sequel came up, I just couldn't imagine doing it again. ... And I figured it was a chance to let new directors try their hand at it, and Rick Rosenthal and Tommy Wallace both were new directors, and they each directed one of the sequels. And after awhile, my involvement became just

a little too painful. ... I just didn't want to be involved anymore, so the partnership threatened to sue me unless I let them
make a sequel because I'm holding up them making money on
a property. ...

There was an original bunch of partners: Moustapha Akkad, Joe Wolf, Irwin Yablans, Debra Hill, and me. And I
would always get threatened with, "Listen, you get involved
with this because you'll make it good. You know, your executive producing will make sure it's ..." And after a while, it
wasn't true anymore, you know. I mean, other people can do it
just as well as I can because my inclination would be to go
away from the original story and do something different.

I think it's in much better hands now. Moustapha Akkad
bought the rights to the sequel, and he's doing them. And, he's
going right back to the first one and remaking it again and
again, which is fine. And they may still be able to go off that
into some other area.

John Carpenter sold his rights in the *Halloween* series to producer
Moustapha Akkad and the other three partners and had only one creative connection with *Halloween 4*: the film's reuse of his familiar—and
essential—theme music.

Halloween 4—its title's switch to Arabic numbering reflecting a
conviction that the audience can count tick marks but can't read Roman
numerals—appeared in 1988, with the startling information that neither
Dr. Loomis nor Michael Myers perished in the monumental explosion
that climaxed *Halloween II*. Loomis continues his obsessive pursuit of
Michael after the killer escapes while being transferred from one sanitarium to another. There are some subjective tracking shots and in one
hallucination the eerie swivel-headed movement of Michael is reprised
from *Halloween*. There is a clever and uncompromising plot twist at
the finale. But none of the stylistic invention and audience-involving
moral depth of *Halloween* survives.

Halloween 5: The Revenge of Michael Myers

Halloween 5: The Revenge of Michael Myers appeared in the fall
of 1989, with Donald Pleasence again reprising his Dr. Loomis role.
Michael's curse continues to menace his little niece, Jamie, Laurie's
daughter—and the structure of the film, with its increasing emphasis on
a series of brutal and imaginative killings rather than on the tension of
an unpredictably recurring presence, makes the *Halloween* films increasingly indistinguishable from those of the *Friday the 13th* ilk.

Michael Myers, having already been awarded the vampire's immortality, now gains also the vampire's power to possess others by telepathy. Dr. Loomis recognizes the link between Michael and his niece Jamie, which enables the little girl to know where Michael is about to strike. Based on this prescience, Loomis keeps the entire Haddonfield police department shuttling from one end of town to another—and, of course, they're never in the right place at the right time. There is also a link between Michael and Loomis, in that each man is willing to victimize the little girl in order to satisfy his thirst for revenge.

Halloween 5 contains nods to several previous (and better) horror films. The psychokinetic link between Michael and Jamie recalls a similar link in John Boorman's *Exorcist II: The Heretic*, and Loomis's claim that "the little girl can stop the rage—she knows how" looks unashamedly stolen from the Boorman film's transformation of *The Exorcist*'s demonically possessed little girl into a Princess of Peace. Michael's chamber of horrors, in which he has arranged the remains of his victims, invokes *The Texas Chainsaw Massacre*. Even *Alien* seems to have influenced *Halloween 5*: Tina chases a kitten in a darkened barn, with Michael Myers lurking in the shadows. But these are not the playful in-jokes of the Carpenter touch so much as kitchen-sink borrowings from everywhere in the genre. The characters rarely act as they should—or realistically *would*—in the situations in which they find themselves.

The vaunted unmasking of Michael takes place in darkness, and all we see of his face is a single tear-streaked eye. Loomis almost talks Michael out of his knife and Jamie almost shames him into gentleness, but these moments are not character exploration—they are red herrings. Michael remains a killing machine, and *Halloween 5* delivers an even bigger body count than its predecessor, under increasingly preposterous circumstances. Only Alan Howarth's variations on Carpenter's original theme music impart any of the compelling atmosphere that informed the film that inspired the series.

Halloween: The Curse of Michael Myers

Halloween sequels continued to appear, with the numbering of sequels altogether dropped. The 1996 film *Halloween: The Curse of Michael Myers* was technically "*Halloween 6*" and took place six years after its predecessor. In it, Jamie Lloyd and Michael Myers are revealed to be both under the Curse of Thorn, a Celtic evil kept alive by a Druidic cult that has kept both Jamie and Michael in their power for the intervening six years. After Jamie escapes and Michael comes after her, targeting the old Myers (now Strode) house once again, Tommy Doyle and Dr. Loomis return to do battle with the ancient evil.

Halloween H20: Twenty Years Later

Halloween H20, released for the original film's 20th anniversary in 1998, is the seventh movie in the *Halloween* series and the first since *Halloween II* to star Jamie Lee Curtis as Laurie Strode. But while its resurrection of the Michael Myers myth is the closest in spirit to the original film, no *Halloween* film after *Halloween III: Season of the Witch* can be considered, in any measure, a John Carpenter film.

6

He's Controlling All of Us

Someone's Watching Me!

On November 22, 1978, about a month after the premiere of *Halloween*, NBC-TV broadcast a "Movie of the Week" entitled *Someone's Watching Me!*, written and directed by John Carpenter. It confirmed, even to those viewers unfamiliar with *Dark Star* and *Assault on Precinct 13*, that the sure-handed, visionary direction of *Halloween* was no fluke. John Carpenter was the real thing.

Someone's Watching Me! began life as an original story idea entitled "High Rise" and based loosely on an actual event that had occurred in Chicago. To people who wanted to typify John Carpenter too quickly, it looked like another—albeit skillfully directed—woman in jeopardy story à la *Halloween*. But *Someone's Watching Me!* is not only an inventively directed thriller—it is a film *about* film direction.

Someone's Watching Me! opens with a brief prologue: shots of a high-rise apartment by night, a ringing phone, a tape recorder, a telescope's eye scaling the wall, and a brief dialogue between a threatening voice and a frightened woman named Elizabeth. Then the film's main title enters, evoking the opening of Hitchcock's *North by Northwest*: Lines cross each other, shape themselves into a grid, and dissolve finally into the criss-cross, egg-crate image of a modern glass tower. Harry Sukman's music even deliberately mimics Bernard Herrmann's opening title music to the Hitchcock film.

To the ominously named Arkham Tower Apartments (Arkham, Massachusetts, is the site of Miskatonic University, where scores of H. P. Lovecraft characters suffered devastating encounters with things from beyond) comes Leigh Michaels, looking for a place. Her first name recalls Janet Leigh of *Psycho*, Hawks screenwriter Leigh Brackett, and the heroine of Carpenter's own *Assault on Precinct 13*. Her last name can't but have a certain ring after *Halloween*, especially suggesting as it does the possibility of *belonging* to a man ("Michael's"?). We soon learn that getting over a man is the central struggle at this point in Leigh's life.

She likes the apartment. "I'll take it. It'll be like living in the top drawer of a glass box." And a glass box it is: She has already fallen under the telescopic eye of the faceless tormentor. After watching Leigh with our own eyes, we now watch her with his, and things change.

As with Laurie Strode and Michael Myers, however, there is a strange sort of affinity between Leigh and her anonymous nemesis. In her job as a director at KJHC-TV, she looks at TV screens the way he looks at apartment windows, scanning his telescopic gaze from one to the next, picking, choosing, deciding, controlling. And it is only when Leigh finally turns the manipulator's techniques back on the manipulator that she is able to confront him.

Much of her ability to do so depends upon her confidence, which in turn is a function of her sense of herself as a woman. Sexual identity plays an important part in all this. Sophie, the assistant director with whom Leigh works, picks up on the fact that Leigh is on the rebound from a relationship with a man. She's had a similar loss herself, she tells Leigh, but reveals that her lost love was a woman. "Don't worry," she quickly assures Leigh: "You're not my type." Leigh allows as how she's not worried. She has, in fact, more to fear from men, who keep hitting on her. Just after Sophie's moment of self-revelation to Leigh, their coworker Steve, a typical predatory male, tries to pick up Leigh. He's persistent, but so is Leigh. The answer is no, and after Steve leaves Sophie refers to him as a "Mountie." Leigh replies, "Well, this time he's not going to get his ... whatever." The word "man" is inappropriate, but her opting for "whatever" suggests a sexual identity crisis that is counterpointed by Sophie's lesbianism.

But a little later, after rejecting the advances not only of Steve but also of a slick stranger in a singles bar, Leigh proceeds to reverse roles, aggressively (but charmingly) hitting on and picking up a man herself. Her insistence upon hitting on a man herself after rejecting a man who hit on her emphasizes the degree to which Leigh wants to—and *can*—take control of her life. She *chooses*.

Her instinct is good: He's a right kind of guy, a USC philosophy professor who takes her interests in hand and stays patient with her, but whose efforts in her behalf ultimately prove ineffectual. (David Birney says the full name of his character only once in the film, but it sure sounds as if Carpenter has christened him with the name of fellow television and B-film director Paul Wendkos.)

Leigh's approach to Paul is filmed subjectively, the camera tracking quickly in on Paul from Leigh's point of view, receding, then returning for another run. It's a threatening move, a hawklike swoop, and all the more menacing after *Halloween*, in which the use of subjective camera became a kind of shorthand for incipient assault. In this way, the shot suggests an affinity between Leigh and her predatory nemesis, and implies that, in fixing on Leigh, the killer may this time have met his match.

Leigh is not easily scared. Even when she comes home and finds her door ajar, she confidently wisecracks: "Hello, burglar ... I feel it only fair to warn you that I studied with Bruce Lee before he died." With the eye of a camera, she tracks and pans her apartment and finally fixes on the newly installed telephone in the foreground. She uses it to call the apartment manager and complain that the phone man left her door open; the man on the other end of the phone claims he locked it himself. As she half-jokingly quarrels with him, a figure darts through her apartment in the background and slams the door on the way out. This kind of jump-out-of-your-seat shock isn't supposed to work on TV, but Carpenter, through constant reversal of tone and expectation in the scene, and through a frame composition that reassures the viewer even as it sets him up for the jab, brings it home in spades.

He pulls it off again a little later. After her first evening with Paul, Leigh realizes he's walked away without her phone number. She jumps out of her car and follows him, but he's disappeared. Returning to her car, muttering to herself for fumbling her keys, she's suddenly set upon by the looming, ghostly lit, rake-angled figure of a burly, scruffy looking man. "It's a hell of a life, isn't it?" he opines, and shuffles off into the darkness. This pop-out-and-go-boo device broadens itself from what might seem a gratuitous effect to a thoroughly integral image of the urban paranoia that Carpenter assayed in *Assault on Precinct 13* and that pervades not only *Someone's Watching Me!* but virtually all of his work, looking forward particularly to similar street people images in *Prince of Darkness*, *They Live*, and *In the Mouth of Madness*.

The device the killer uses to invade his victims' lives is a bogus operation called "Excursions Unlimited." The target gets a letter inviting her to deduce her destination from a series of gifts to be mailed to her. If she guesses correctly, she gets a free trip to the place. By the end of the film, Leigh Michaels has managed to guess her intended destination all too well.

Present Number One is, significantly, a telescope. Leigh assembles it and toys with it insouciantly; it's only much later that, on an explicit suggestion from the tormentor, she uses it to make visual contact with her menace. The killer wants to be found; he wants her to see him and know what he is doing to her. (Of course he also wants to mislead her and to frame another man for his acts.) Twice during the film Leigh's gift telescope scans the opposite building—apartment windows like so many TV screens in the wall, an image already chillingly hit upon by Hitchcock for *Rear Window*—and comes to rest on another telescope looking back at her. The image of a telescope watching a telescope recalls the moment in *For a Few Dollars More* when, from hotel windows facing each other across a dusty El Paso street, the bounty killers played by Clint Eastwood and Lee Van Cleef set eyes on each other, aided by binoculars and a telescope. The connection between an Italian western and a high-tech suspense thriller is not so far-fetched in light of the spaghetti western roots of *Assault on Precinct 13*, and especially not in a film in which the apartment manager is named Mr. Leone.

The telescope, a surrogate camera, reiterates in *Someone's Watching Me!* the shared killer's-eye view of *Eyes of Laura Mars* and the opening of *Halloween*. But here a vision, a way of seeing, is not so much shared as *imposed*—imposed upon Leigh as surely as she, a TV director, imposes her way of seeing on the audience at home. Carpenter draws a chilling equation between framing the visual image and controlling the viewer's response—and then, by extension, the viewer's life. He doesn't stop there: Throughout *Someone's Watching Me!* violation and violent, emotional control are described precisely in terms of the filmmaker's art: The killer frames Leigh's image in his telescope, adjusts the lighting in her apartment, manages the sound by means of telephone and tape recorder, and even gives her costume and blocking directions by phone ("Look through the telescope," "I like you better without the robe; take it off"). The scary subtext of this not-so-superficial thriller is Carpenter's ambivalent vision of the power of the film director.

It's no accident that the bad guy of the film is named Stiles.

Of course, of all the writers and directors whose influences can be found in Carpenter's work, Hitchcock's is the one most profoundly present in *Someone's Watching Me!* Witness the *North by Northwest* style of the opening credits; the many references to the *Rear Window* moral/visual motif; the pairing of a light and a dark woman à la *The Birds*; the combination of a telephone and a knife as in *Dial M for Murder*; evanescent hand lettering on a steam clouded mirror like the writing on a fogged train window in *The Lady Vanishes*; and the outstretched fingers straining for a knife dropped down a grating à la *Strangers on a Train*. The Hitchcock influence is as carefully worked out here as are the Hawks influence in *Assault on Precinct 13*, the Kneale influence in *Prince of Darkness*, and the Lovecraft influence in *In the Mouth of Madness*. Each of these voices, and others, may be heard throughout Carpenter's work, but to each of these three prior artists he has also devoted one film in particular. This one is Hitchcock's.

Just after Leigh hears "I like you better without the robe" on the phone and realizes she is being watched *at that moment*, Carpenter quotes Hitchcock's famous *Vertigo* shot—a combination track-out/zoom-in that "stretches" the space around the central image. Hitchcock invented the shot to express the dizzying tension between fear and desire that informed Scotty Ferguson's (and our) attitude to the possibility of falling from a high place. Claude Chabrol used it in the finale of *La Femme Infidèle* to express the pain of separation by combining emotional movement *toward* with physical movement *away*. Steven Spielberg used it in *Jaws* to express simple disorientation—the rending of space suggesting a severance between the individual at the center of the shot and the world around him, but from an objective, not a subjective viewpoint. Since *Jaws*, that has become the stock "meaning" of the *Vertigo* shot, and that is how Carpenter uses it here. Immediately afterward, when Leigh runs into the bathroom and cowers there, Carpenter uses an overhead shot that not only emphasizes her smallness and vulnerability but also, inevitably, evokes *Psycho*.

As in Hitchcock's most important films, the stakes in *Someone's Watching Me!* are nothing short of life and death: Early in the film a news report is heard on a radio playing in the background. The item concerns the apparent suicide of a single woman, Elizabeth Solley, who jumped from the window of her high-rise. This is the Elizabeth of the film's opening scene; but only we are privy, at this point, to the knowledge that she was murdered and it is her killer who is now menacing Leigh. The notion of a heritage of suicide—the killer's m.o. is to make the killing look like suicide, possibly even to hound his victims *into* suicide—suggests Roman Polanski's *The Tenant*, and the escalating emotional stakes of the Carpenter film suggest Polanski's classic study of psychosexual collapse, *Repulsion*. But Leigh is tough enough that the killer's use of nuisance and suggestion doesn't break her down—in fact, it only makes her angry.

"He's controlling all of us," she exclaims in frustration, when she sees how cleverly the killer has manipulated things so Leigh's friends can no longer help or even believe her. Paul's analysis: "He's trying to hurt you without touching you, working from as far away as he can get and still get to you." But when Paul suggests that Leigh move, she refuses: "He's not going to chase me out. ... How dare he invade my

Someone's Watching Me!
Leigh Michaels (Lauren Hutton) can't get the lights on.

life?" It is here, as her terror turns to rage, that she gains the strength and determination to see the ordeal through to its end. She has been violated, dirtied. This is the way victims of crime feel—the way it feels to come home and know someone has been there and taken something.

What is most threatened by the killer's intrusion is the very thing Leigh has changed jobs and homes in order to try to find and preserve: her independence—and, in particular, her independence from *men*. She comes to L.A. unable to shake off the vestiges of a relationship gone bad, and she tries to avoid defining herself in terms of men. Her ability to initiate a relationship herself, aggressively, rather than being a passive recipient of men's attentions, is a strong first step. But now virtually stripped of friends and of help from the law, she rediscovers her purpose: She *has* to do it all herself. She must exorcise the power of predatory men altogether from her life by confronting and defeating—unassisted—her nemesis.

Her campaign—like her spunky pickup of Paul in the singles bar—is an aggressive and determined one. The killer has invaded her space; now she invades *his* space. First Leigh ventures into the apartment from which the killer has menaced her, only to look back and helplessly watch a murder committed in her own apartment—another evocation of *Rear Window* as well as of Brian De Palma's *Sisters*. Undaunted, Leigh even invades the killer's own home. Returning to her apartment, she senses his presence, and finds the suicide note he has already written for her. This is too much. He has manipulated her life; now he is manipulating her words, her motivations, her death. And even in this he is keeping his distance, as Paul suggested he would. It dawns on Leigh that Paul was right about the killer: "You're afraid of me—afraid to get too close."

Trapped in her apartment, the lights out, the switches back-wired to give a shock if touched, the phone dead, Leigh shatters a window to scream for help. As she raises her chair to smash a second window, *he* appears, almost imperceptibly; one instant Leigh is heaving a chair toward the window, the next she is struggling with the killer. He comes out of the darkness, we're not sure from where. He is suddenly and simply *there*, having that strange power over space that Michael Myers possessed.

The climactic struggle recalls the final moments of *Halloween*: a faceless tormentor; a desperate grab for the nearest sharp weapon; the way the killer staggers backward, befuddled, and pulls the shard of glass from his neck; a fall from a window.

It's over. Leigh looks downward after him, in an evocation of the final shot of *Vertigo*, but with altogether different impact: For the first time in the film Leigh is her own woman, completely and triumphantly alone, haunted by nothing and no one. She sums up the killer's mistake: "Got too close." Leigh Michaels can, at last, take care of herself—and rather better than Laurie Strode could. She is, in fact, Carpenter's archetypal tough woman. Don't mess with her.

7

There's a Reason for Everything

Elvis

Elvis is about a guy who wants to be an entertainer. He's a hillbilly, and he's unprepared for what happens to him. He did a lot of great music and a lot of bad music, but I've always loved Elvis and even loved his bad stuff and have been mesmerized by him since I was a little kid. I wanted to get my licks in and do something that I felt had some quality to it, because most of what's involved with Elvis—all the movies and the shows— they're really kind of shuck-and-jive stuff. There never was anything with any heart to it, and I felt that after *Loving You*, Elvis was never really portrayed as a *savage* anymore. He was never dangerous. He was always kind of whitewashed. So we wanted to do something that dealt with it all, including him being kind of a wild man.

—John Carpenter

Two cars speed along a Nevada desert highway to a string band blues instrumental. A title tells us it's July 26, 1969. They arrive at a Las Vegas hotel and disgorge an aging Elvis Presley and his retinue of advisers and bodyguards. Moving backward, the camera tracks them as they push through the aisles, past the slot machines, toward the sanctity of a room where Elvis sits down to watch a movie on TV while others decide his fate. In moments a temper tantrum erupts and Elvis shoots the television set. It's a moment of inexplicable emotional intensity that is echoed throughout this film about the stresses of success and the desperation of a simple man in a complex world.

The film is framed in flashback, Elvis's life passing before him *and us* as he prepares for the comeback performance on which hangs the fate of his career. You can't "explain" a life, but this is Carpenter's effort, as a film biographer, to bring to Elvis's life something of the order and meaning the singer himself failed to find. *Elvis* is in some ways a remake of Elvis Presley's most unabashedly autobiographical film, *Loving You*. In that sense, John Carpenter's *Elvis* is a return to the source. The real life to which it returns begins in Tupelo, Mississippi, in 1945, as young Elvis gets a guitar for Christmas. Music is proposed as The Way, something to bring meaning to this troubled young life.

Why troubled? The film's early images suggest the elements at war in the film's interpretation of Elvis Presley's psychological makeup. We see him at the grave of his prematurely dead brother—arguably the key disruptive force in the life of young Elvis. Throughout the film, when Elvis needs counsel, he "talks to" his dead brother. In the later scenes, after Elvis's mother, too, has died, the brother becomes visually associated with a shadow on the wall—Elvis's *own* shadow—an intimation of his own mortality and a suggestion that talking to his brother is a way of addressing a hidden part of himself. The death of his brother seems to have overwhelmed him with a sense of his own alone-ness, and to have cemented his dependence on his mother.

That aloneness, imposed partly by circumstance, partly by him-self, separates Elvis from those who might have been his friends. He is abused by his peers, unaccepted, an odd kid out (a Carpenter theme we have already seen in the teasing of Tommy Doyle in *Halloween*, and sensed in Ethan Bishop's cryptic reminiscence of his ghetto childhood in *Assault on Precinct 13*). We see Elvis struck by a neighbor kid who calls him a mama's boy and later, in high school, he is teased and roughed up over his pomped hair and "different" clothes. The sense of alienation will haunt his entire life, as the youthful aloneness is re-placed in the mature man by the loneliness of fame. He feels himself missing out on the experience of being an ordinary person. "Sometimes I'd just like to be one of them," he tells his wife Priscilla, who replies, "You can't ever be. You're very special." The sense of self is both a handicap and a gift.

When Bonnie, his high school girlfriend, encourages young Elvis to perform at an assembly, he is terrified ("You know I'm chicken"), but he needs acceptance so desperately (and seems to sense that he is good enough to get it), that he takes the chance. He sings "Ole Shep," a sentimental country tune, and gets a wild ovation. "They really like me," he says. He is clearly not used to being liked, but he enjoys the new feeling. Eventually it becomes addictive and it's a shock, though not a surprise, that already early in his career he collapses from exhaus-tion. An increasingly obsessed Elvis sacrifices personal relationships to fame: "I *have* to work." The pivotal event of the film, the framing event to which *Elvis* inevitably returns, is Elvis's need to risk his marriage, his career, and his reputation to go on in Las Vegas. He even ignores threats on his life (though, in the end, the comeback did cost him his life).

It's no wonder that an outcast kid would get used to the feeling of being accepted, but the film's Elvis is not only interested in fame as compensation for social rejection. He's also interested in his music and in the art of performance because they give him a sense of himself that he is otherwise unable to achieve, unable to separate from his brother and his mother. At a studio to make an audition recording Elvis is asked, "Who do you sound like?" He replies, "I don't sound like no-body." He instinctively knows he is a true original.

A later sequence, one of the film's most invigorating, shows Elvis and his backup musicians building "Heartbreak Hotel." After several abortive beginnings, Elvis says to cut the musical intro. They try it that way—the way the song was finally recorded—and we see Elvis as a singer who makes his own style by asserting himself, influencing the process of production in ways most singers can never do.

As the film creeps back toward the Las Vegas present, Elvis's musical performance style becomes identified with his sense of him-self. One of his increasingly frequent and violent tantrums is occa-sioned by his producers' decision to amplify his voice. Then, troubled by his own outburst, he wonders, "What's happenin' to me?" Moments later, as if recognizing and articulating a part of what's happenin', he says, "That's my music. It ain't theirs, it's mine." One whose work is so intimately associated with him*self* finds it increasingly difficult to cope with the stress of becoming an institution, a public property.

Indeed, the film's Elvis often seems a person manipulated by stronger circumstances and personalities than himself: Sam Phillips, the record producer who gives him his first chance; Colonel Tom Parker, who becomes his manager; Hal Wallis, who produces his movie *Love Me Tender*; Ed Sullivan, who brings him into the nation's living rooms; the U.S. Army, which writes a new chapter in his career ("You got nothin' to worry about," Col. Parker tells him) and alters his life for-ever.

But without question the dominant force in his life is his mother. As played by Shelley Winters, Mama is a powerful and loving woman, not a pushy and domineering one. We never see a real illustration of Mama's unique strength and the love with which she has bound her men. The control she exerts over Elvis's psyche is quiet, not demand-ing. She doesn't drive him; he drives himself. It almost seems as if her dominion over him is willed by Elvis himself.

In any case, the film abounds with images and evidence of the centrality of Mama to Elvis's life. Young Elvis is considered a mama's boy. He makes his first record for Mama; Graceland is built first and foremost as a home for Mama; and one of the film's best images of the inherent contradiction of Elvis Presley is the shot of Mama feeding chickens on the lawn of the palatial estate, and her furtive look (of jealousy?) as Elvis brings home a date.

Elvis's conversation relates virtually everything to Mama. "You like my hair?" Priscilla asks him, and Elvis answers, "It's almost the exact same color as my Mama's." Mama is, of course, dead by this time: Elvis meets Priscilla, significantly, at a party soon after Mama's death. His father introduces Elvis to his own new love interest, so that the party scene becomes an intriguing depiction of two men "on the rebound" from Mama. When Elvis and Priscilla get the nursery ready for the coming of their child, Elvis's comment is, "I wish Mama could be here to see it."

Inside the fabulously successful, fabulously wealthy performer lurks a lonely, empty man (or boy?) who reaches out for guidance and finds only a dead brother, a dead mother. His ability to respond to the enormity of his situation extends no farther than his ability to understand himself and reach some point of contentment, and so he lashes out at those closest to him. Early on he rejects his old friend Red. Unable to manage the growing tension between his "friends" and his music on the one hand, and his wife and child on the other, he alienates both with his mood swings and tantrums. In one powerful scene he fires every one of his associates in a rage, then quietly asks his father to go hire them back again.

"I wish I didn't have to be all confused," he tells Priscilla in a moment of self-honesty. He tells his shadow-brother, "I still feel like there's something missing." At one point, in a sudden burst of enthusiasm, he shares with Priscilla something he has discovered in the Bible: "Life and death are one." The dead are still here, he concludes. He doesn't *have* to carry on without his brother and Mama. It may be that the order, the "something missing" he has been seeking, is a justification of his having survived while his brother and mother died. "Why did everything in my life happen the way it did?" he wonders aloud. "Ain't no such thing as coincidence. There's a reason for everything." From this scene Carpenter cuts, ironically, to a road shot to the music of "Suspicious Minds": "We're caught in a trap ..."

The film exists in two versions. The original 150-minute cut was designed as a special event, to fill an evening of prime time television. At 119 minutes, the more often seen truncated version plays like "Scenes from the Life of Elvis," rather than like a continuous, unified portrait of the man and his career. Carpenter has said, "I did not get to edit and score the film. So it's not my film in the end. It was taken away because I didn't contract to do it. I was a director for hire."[1] But in either version, the film is alive with the Carpenter style.

Elvis
The universal appeal of Elvis Presley (Kurt Russell)

Not the least of his touches is the inspired performance he evokes from Kurt Russell, in the first of several collaborations between director and actor. Essential to the film is The Voice, and Russell's mastery of it quickly makes us forget we are not watching the "real" Elvis. Russell had had an opportunity to study the original up close: As a child, he made his film debut with Elvis Presley in *It Happened at the World's Fair*. When he outgrew child roles, Russell moved away from film, even playing minor league baseball for a while. *Elvis* was the film that brought him back and established him as a screen presence to be reckoned with—though until Mike Nichols's *Silkwood* Russell remained pretty much Carpenter's discovery. Talking about the *Elvis* performance, Russell said later, "Elvis Presley is the second most recognizable unit to Coca-Cola. The only thing tougher to do is play the Coca-Cola logo."[2]

The visual style Carpenter establishes for the film evinces an affinity for what might be called the corridor composition: numerous hallways, rows of slot machines in the Las Vegas casino, hotel corridors, high school halls, hallways and doorways of Graceland, rows of suits in a clothing store, rows of fans pressing in on him, mobbing him. All are suggestive of life as a series of passages, and the dominant image that emerges from the film is one of Elvis trying to steer the strait and narrow among obstacles—and people—that crowd in on him. The use of constraining images also suggests a self-discipline Carpenter may have employed to accustom himself to the television frame: His compositions in *Elvis* tend of necessity toward the vertical, as opposed to the horizontalism of his Panavision theatrical films.

That emphasis on the vertical is seen, too, in the cliché-parodying shot that introduces Col. Tom Parker, who will loom large in Elvis's life: a slow tilt up from the feet to the glowering eyes of Pat Hingle.

Another characteristic Carpenter touch is the use of the film quote. There are worlds of connections to be drawn between Elvis and the James Dean movie he watches on TV in one scene: Presley and Dean were contemporaries and rebels who, through the performance medium, became spokesmen for a generation. The visual comparison underscores Carpenter's avowed intent to get the sense of Elvis as "kind of a wild man." We are reminded, too, that Dean was long dead by the time of Elvis's comeback, and there may be an element of nostalgia and loss in Elvis's watching Dean's frozen Fifties image on a television screen.

One seminal stylistic idea in *Elvis*—the use of rock 'n' roll songs to counterpoint the moods and the stages of Elvis's life—serves as a reminder that this film about a musician is directed *by* a musician. Though of course virtually dictated by the film's subject matter, the period music in *Elvis* is not just source music; it is also used repeatedly to "comment" on the action, the song lyrics often giving the lie to Elvis Presley's appearance-heavy public life. Thematic and stylistic integration of period music with the film's action resurfaces in a later "for hire" job that is more emphatically a John Carpenter film: *Christine*. But one sees it in *Elvis* in such touches as the establishing shots of Graceland frequently accompanied by ironic lyrics—"so lonely they could die ..." and "Are you lonesome tonight?"—conveying a profound sense of a house that's not a home.

Carpenter also relies on the music to sustain an underlying religious theme in *Elvis* that reminds us of the gospel roots of his Presley's sound. The joyful "Rock My Soul," for example, amplifies the birth of Elvis's and Priscilla's baby. Elsewhere we hear "Rock of Ages" and "Crying in the Chapel."

This quasi-religious tone, which underscores Elvis's own inner search for meaning, is sustained in the film's finale: As Elvis's comeback performance begins, the orchestra mimics the majestic opening to Richard Strauss's *Also Sprach Zarathustra* to open his show. He walks—*hurries*—onto the stage and into history. The last thing we hear Elvis singing is the "Glory, Hallelujah" of the "Battle Hymn of the Republic"—a culmination of the film's religious subtext and a resolution, it seems, of Elvis's struggle to find meaning in his life and justification in his work.

Notes

1. McCarthy, Todd, "Trick and Treat" [John Carpenter interviewed by Todd McCarthy], *Film Comment* 16:1, Jan/Feb 1980, p. 19.
2. Interviewed in Associated Press wire story, January 6, 1989.

8

We're All Cursed

The Fog

I don't want to make a film where the story is subordinated to technique. We're all storytellers here.

—John Carpenter[1]

In some circles, *Halloween* was accused of being all style and no substance—thrills for the sake of thrills. As if in reaction to that attitude, Carpenter's films from this point on evince a fierce insistence on the primacy of narrative. *The Fog* is, in many ways, a film about narrative—about storytelling and its impact on our lives.

The Fog opens with an epigraph from Edgar Allan Poe:

Is all that we see or seem
But a dream within a dream?

Underscoring this suggestion that the film that follows is a framed narrative, the first scene of the film features John Houseman, playing Mr. Machen (an *hommage* to Arthur Machen, great writer of ghost stories), spinning a scary tale for a shivering clutch of boys gathered around a campfire. This evocation of the power of storytelling—and hence of film—serves to set the mood for what follows, and also to provide the historical narrative background for the resurrection of the vengeful dead.

With the fireside story of a shipwrecked crew who return to haunt the town whose citizens engineered the wreck, Houseman's voice does the whole job: No flashback, no fanciful depiction of the events described. "What you *don't* show is often stronger," says Carpenter.[2] The sequence is a paean to the lost art of storytelling—especially the telling of *scary* stories, which has now become the domain of movies. The sequence announces *The Fog* as a good old-fashioned ghost story—and it *is*, its unsteady hokiness more than offset by its many moments of chillingly competent manipulative filmmaking.

"When the fog returns to Antonio Bay," Machen intones at the climax of his tale, "the men of the *Elizabeth Dane* will rise up." Now it is nearly midnight, coming up on April 21—as Machen can tell from his swinging pocketwatch—the 100th anniversary of the founding of the town, and a strange fog bank bodes ill to the contemporary inhabitants of Antonio Bay. That fog causes machines and other objects to animate, or to fail to operate properly, much in the manner of *The Day the Earth Stood Still*—but the film treats this phenomenon as a selective process: Some things work, others don't. It seems random, but there may be some power *selecting* the interference.

One of the disruptions is a brick that falls out of the wall of the church office of Father Malone, revealing the hiding place of his grandfather's 1880 journal. This book recounts the facts on which Machen's fireside story was based: The people of Antonio Bay, California, are descended from a small band of settlers who deliberately devised the wreck of a ship called the *Elizabeth Dane* in order to prevent the ship from landing with its cargo of lepers bound for a tiny colony to the north. Adding insult to injury, the six conspirators stole the gold that Blake, the wealthy leader of the lepers, had offered to pay for the right to found the colony.

Moments before discovering the book, Father Malone dismisses his helper, Bennett, who, observing that Father Malone is in his cups, offers to stay. Upon his dismissal, Bennett disappears from the film, along with any help he might have offered. The role of Bennett is played by John Carpenter, in a joke much like the one John Huston played in *The Treasure of Sierra Madre*: After being hit up by Humphrey Bogart's Fred C. Dobbs for two handouts in the space of a few minutes, Huston's man in a white suit tells Dobbs, "From now on, you're going to have to make your way through life without my assistance." The man in white disappears from the film, and the director abandons his characters to their fate.

The first ten or twelve minutes of *The Fog* match real time, from Machen's reading of his pocketwatch at five minutes to twelve to disc jockey Stevie Wayne's announcements of the time over KAB-FM. As the fog rolls in, the town begins to come apart, a character named Nick Castle (Tom Atkins) picks up a hitchhiker named Elizabeth (Jamie Lee Curtis), and a terrible fate befalls the crew of the trawler *Sea Grass*.

Elizabeth tells Nick he is her 13th ride, and suggests that she might be bringing "bad luck." Shortly after he picks her up, his windshield is shattered by the force loosed on Antonio Bay by the fog. Later, when Nick puzzles over the knocking at his door, the smashing of his clock, and the disappearance of the *Sea Grass*, Elizabeth says, "Ever since you picked me up things have been going wrong ... I'm bad luck"—an echo of the suggestion made about the visiting Melanie Daniels in Hitchcock's *The Birds*, another film about a California bay town beset by avenging horrors—all the more significant in light of Elizabeth's shared name with that of the ill-fated ship of lepers.

But it might also be that the eerie old salt Machen "caused" the whole thing by the spell woven with his campfire ghost story at the beginning of the film. Indeed, the film *is* the tale he tells (neither the first nor the last instance of self-referential filmmaking in Carpenter's work), and there is a sense in which all that follows that simple prologue is mere embellishment, the fleshing out in movie language of a ghost story that, once told orally, becomes a part of the collective imagination of the story's listeners, its characters, and *us*. The little boys who hear the tale go on to live it.

Stevie Wayne's little boy Andy sees a doubloon among the rocks on the beach, but the doubloon disappears, leaving instead a piece of driftwood from the hull of the *Elizabeth Dane*, which he gives to his mother. In her studio, the wood drips water onto her equipment, causing a short. In the shower of sparks, the word "*Dane*" on the driftwood becomes a legend, "6 must die."

Storytelling occurs again, as Nick and Elizabeth search for a clue to what happened aboard the *Sea Grass*. Their search of the trawler is intercut with Father Malone's telling of the story from his grandfather's journal to realtor Kathy Williams (whose husband, Al, is the skipper of the *Sea Grass*). On board, Nick tells Elizabeth a story of how his father found an old gold doubloon that later disappeared. As Nick reaches the climax of his story, working himself and Elizabeth into a tension that infects us as well, an upright locker flies open: We start; a heap of rolled-up charts tumbles out. Elizabeth is relieved and makes a joke as she regains her composure: "I think I'll go to Vancouver now." As she does so, the locker *behind her* pops open and she finds herself in the chilling embrace of an eyeless corpse. Drawing a connection between the techniques of oral narrative and of film art, Carpenter tops the obvious set-up with a *real* scare utterly unexpected.

At the medical examiner's office, as Elizabeth sits in the foreground, the corpse under the sheet moves in the background, echoing a composition from *Halloween*. The living dead thing shuffles toward Elizabeth, then collapses, scrawling the number "3" on the floor.

Elizabeth's increasingly credible suggestion that her "bad luck" might have something to do with the strange goings-on is now abandoned from the tale, in favor of the growing sense of guilt that centers on Father Malone. He *knows* who "caused" the visitation, and he, almost Christlike, takes onto his shoulders the burden of guilt shared by

The face of horror in *The Fog*
Above: Stevie Wayne (Adrienne Barbeau)
Below: Father Malone (Hal Holbrook)

the six original conspirators. "We're honoring murderers," he says of the upcoming centennial celebration, and adds, in either a drunken stupor or an obsessive daze, "Antonio Bay has a curse on it ... we're all cursed"—an evocation of the supernatural that seems to disclaim his own assumption of responsibility and that echoes the recourse to "fate" and "the Bogey Man" in *Halloween*. But *The Fog* reverses the theodicy of *Halloween* and *Assault on Precinct 13*, in which essentially good protagonists face off against avatars of pure evil; here, the avenging supernatural beings are fundamentally righteous, and the human victims are targeted because they assume the responsibility for a heritage of guilt.

Malone's realization that "we're all cursed"—that the people of Antonio Bay all bear the guilt for their ancestors' atrocity because their city and their lifestyle was built on the ill-gotten riches of the founders' wrongdoing—is an acknowledgement that the fog and the avenging spirits it spews forth are a form of Robin Wood's Return of the Repressed. In fact, though it is not finally as good, as troubling, or as deep-cutting a film as *Halloween*, John Carpenter's *The Fog* comes closer to Wood's model of the American horror film—for here the monsters represent precisely the return of the unnatural, not to say evil, beginnings on which Antonio Bay's settled domesticity is based, the self-denying lie that the town's citizens have suppressed for generations.

Malone finally seeks his own death as the only expiation available to him and equal to the enormity of the communal guilt he takes onto himself. He babbles the impossible truth to anyone who will listen (and few do): "Blake and his men have come for us!" (This comes shortly after a rich moment of Carpenter wordplay in which Kathy Williams has praised the founding fathers to the listening crowd at the centennial celebration, saying, "It's up to us to keep their kind of spirit alive.") Malone finds the cross into which his ancestor had melted Blake's gold, shoulders it Christlike, bears it to the ghostly Blake, and returns it to the drowned lepers. "Take me," Malone tells the ghosts, and wonders why he is not killed—wonders so that it may be his own will that finally brings the lepers back, in the film's final shot, to put an amen to it all, the hooded, red-eyed swordsman visually replacing the crucified Christ in the background as he strikes the final blow.

Just before that happens, the narrative frame in which Machen's campfire story fixed the film at the beginning is closed with Stevie Wayne's remark to her listeners, "If this has been anything but a nightmare, and if we don't wake up and find ourselves safe in our beds, it could come again." We're forced to recall the "dream within a dream" of the film's epigraph, and wonder whether this *has* been only a narrative nightmare, or if the storytelling has intentionally been bled into reality.

The frame is broken now, for Carpenter doesn't close his film here. Stevie goes on, in an evocation of the "watch the skies" ending to the 1950 Howard Hawks-Christian Nyby film *The Thing* (which Carpenter would remake two years after *The Fog*): "To the ships at sea who can hear my voice, look across the water into the darkness. Look for the fog!"

Even that isn't enough. Now Carpenter returns to the church and Father Malone, as Blake and his crew, almost as an afterthought, return to claim their sixth victim with a single stroke. Cut to black.

Both *The Fog* and *Halloween* are traditional subgenres of children's fright tales: the Bogey Man and the ghost story. Stevie's little son Andy is analogous to the little boy in *Halloween* who first mentions the term "Bogey Man." As in *Halloween*, children are portrayed ambivalently here: both victims and creators of grim mischief. (Interestingly, *The Fog* is the last Carpenter film in which a child is specifically placed in jeopardy. From here on out, it's an adult's world. Indeed, in his later films, children become specifically menacing, particularly *In the Mouth of Madness* and his remake of *Village of the Damned*.)

Both *Halloween* and *The Fog* tell tales wrought from factual occurrences whose anniversaries are commemorated by a haunting return of fatal figures from the past. In each event, once-human beings are transmogrified into supernatural creatures of abnormal power. In both films, Carpenter's evocative use of music for dramatic effect has the added advantage of giving the occasional moment of silence a heightened aura of terror. The "real" characters in each film are taken from "real" life into the world of impossible horror, and no one can tell where the line has been crossed. When in *Halloween* did the story of a "real" psychopathic kid become the story of a malevolent "Bogey Man"? When in *The Fog* does the story of a "real" atrocity become the story of a bunch of ghosts—or, perhaps, the story of *the story* of a bunch of ghosts?

In *The Fog*, Carpenter extends his concern for the behavior of human beings in traps. "It's a lot like *Assault on Precinct 13*," he told Todd McCarthy, "in the sense that it's structured night-day-night. It's a group of people who are trapped in a room at the inn."[3] The cute-meeting, wisecracking Elizabeth and Nick are a typical Hawksian couple, perhaps even Bogart and Bacall through a distant mirror. They're good. They survive (another reversal of the moral universe of *Halloween*, in which their spontaneous, free-spirited sexual coupling would

likely have marked them for death). Father Malone, the town's reposi-
tory of intellectuality as well as of communal guilt, breaks down, and it
may be precisely *because* he breaks down that Blake returns to dispatch
him in the film's final shot.

If we *are* all cursed, then *The Fog* may be something of a curse in
the Carpenter canon. *Halloween* was, first of all, a tough act to follow.
After *The Fog*'s spellbinding opening and its real-time first sequences,
it is hampered by trying to do both too little and too much. For a film
that insists upon narrative, story logic is not this California *Flying
Dutchman*'s strong suit. For one thing, the film can't make up its mind
whether the leprous crew of the *Elizabeth Dane* have come back for
revenge, or merely to recover their stolen gold. The ghostly avengers
write numbers to suggest the number of villagers they intend to kill.
But how could the shipwrecked lepers have known how many people in
the village conspired against them and who those people were? And if
their intent is to kill six people, why do they go after so many more in
the course of the film?

Once the gold is returned to the ghosts, they leave—the job seemingly unfinished, Father Malone amazed that he has been spared. But
the ghosts return abruptly to claim him as the final victim, apparently
for no better reason than to provide a downbeat ending for the film—a
horror film device inspired by Carpenter's own *Halloween* that quickly
became obligatory with such pop-out-and-go-boo endings as those in
Brian De Palma's *Carrie* and *Dressed to Kill*, John Frankenheimer's
The Prophecy, Sean Cunningham's *Friday the 13th* series, and many
others. (A better ending might have been to have Malone live, only to
discover that he has contracted the living death of leprosy.)

The portion of the plot dealing with night-time KAB-FM radio
jock Stevie Wayne—Adrienne Barbeau in a performance that comes
off as a female version of Clint Eastwood's mellowed-out-and-riding-
for-a-fall disc jockey in *Play Misty for Me*—is only skimpily integrated
with the rest of the film. When the power and phone lines go out, she
fires up the generator and uses the airwaves to call from the studio for
listeners to help her son Andy as the fog engulfs their beach house. But
how does she know Andy is trapped in the house? How does she know
"there's something in the fog"? We're not told—nor does the emergence of the ghosts to menace her at the climax serve either the narrative logic or the style of the film.

It is possible, of course, to labor *The Fog* and many another B-
horror film at great length with such quibbles of plot consistency and
integration. But to do so is to miss the point of the genre, and the role
that atmosphere and convention play in it. Further, it is to miss the

point of the delirious *fun* John Carpenter is having with it. "*The Fog* is an EC horror comic," Carpenter said, shortly after the film was released.[4] *The Fog*'s compelling first reel may be an opening that deserves a better movie, but it, and many incidental moments throughout the film, bear up the promise of *Halloween* and the suggestion of greater things to come.

Film on Film

Carpenter laced *The Fog* with more cinematic cross-references and in-jokes than any other film he had done up to that time. The film's idea and atmosphere are rooted in *The Beast from 20,000 Fathoms*, Eugene Lourié's 1953 programmer in which a resurrected sea monster attacks a tugboat and a fogbound coastal village before moving on New York. In *The Fog*, Carpenter acknowledged the contemporary horror film's debt to many precursors both within and outside of the genre, but he also continued to acknowledge a debt to Hitchcock. *Psycho* references, which already abounded in *Halloween* (the pursuer of the murderous Michael was named Sam Loomis, as was the pursuer of the disappeared Marion Crane in *Psycho*; Nancy Loomis acted in the film, as did Jamie Leigh Curtis, daughter of Janet Leigh, the original Marion Crane), proliferate in *The Fog*: Nancy Loomis reappears, along with both Curtis *and* Leigh, and Carpenter himself appears in a Hitchcockian signature cameo. *The Fog*'s Hitchcock references multiply with the layering on of ideas from *The Birds*: the suggestion that the natural phenomenon (birds, fog) is actually the agent of some supernatural, avenging force caused by the presence of a "bad luck" character in the film (Melanie Daniels, Elizabeth Solley); a California bay town under siege; a corpse with its eyes poked out; visual emphasis on phone booths and a gas pump spilling gasoline in the early sequences; a deliberate reference to a boat "coming back from Bodega Bay" in the dialogue.

But *The Fog* has roots that run deeper than Hitchcock's Sixties films: Its depiction of a small town besieged by evil owes a debt to several monochrome British science fiction–horror films of Carpenter's youth, including Leslie Norman's *X–The Unknown*, Val Guest's *Quatermass II* (*Enemy from Space*), and Wolf Rilla's *Village of the Damned* (which Carpenter would later remake), in each of which a lonely village on the British countryside is further isolated by an invasion of forces from beyond. Of course, all of these films are arguably variations on Jack Arnold's *It Came from Outer Space*, the archetypal aliens-take-over-the-community movie.

Besides the joking references to other films, Carpenter also peoples his films with characters named after his real-life associates. In the cast list to *The Fog*, we find characters named for Carpenter collaborators Nick Castle and Dan O'Bannon, for effects man Tommy Wallace, and for producer Richard Kobritz. Jamie Lee Curtis's character, Elizabeth Solley, has the same name as a woman whose apparent suicide, reported in a background radio broadcast in *Someone's Watching Me!*, marks her as an early victim of the killer who stalks that film's heroine.

The Fog, though not exactly a "big studio" film, may be justly seen as Carpenter's first "Hollywood movie," and the degree to which jokes and cross-references abound is a measure of the energy and enthusiasm of a young director enjoying the toys of his success. Soon he would put the toys and budget of a major studio to work to a more serious purpose in *The Thing*. But first, he had one more "fun" film to make for Avco-Embassy.

Notes

1. Fox, Jordan R., Interview, "Riding High on Horror," *Cinefantastique* 10:1, Summer 1980, p. 10.
2. Fox, *op. cit.*, p. 43.
3. McCarthy, Todd, "Trick and Treat" [John Carpenter interviewed by Todd McCarthy], *Film Comment* 16:1, Jan/Feb 1980, p. 24.
4. Fox, *op. cit.*, p. 43.

9

I Heard You Were Dead

Escape from New York

All the criminals in the world are confined there for life. They have their own society. It's hell on earth.

—John Carpenter, 1980
(on his then unproduced script for *Escape from New York*)

Escape from New York is a comic book of an action movie, whose tongue-in-cheek tone—unexpected from the newly acclaimed auteur of *Halloween*—left its viewers a little disoriented. Only *Dark Star* could have prepared audiences for whimsy of this kind, and in 1981 *Dark Star* hadn't been widely seen, despite Carpenter's growing reputation. Certainly the studied terror of *Halloween* and *The Fog* suggested a writer-director concerned with the serious exploration of the dark side of human experience. So when *Escape from New York* burst onto the screen, many thought the comedy had been unintentional, the film merely inept.

Though far from inept, the film *may* have been a miscalculation. Not until *Big Trouble in Little China*, five years later, would the Carpenter wit again drive a film so boldly—and by that time, it would do so with much more assurance. The balance between science fiction adventure thriller and action comedy is less easily maintained in *Escape from New York*.

The film is not without its glories, however, and among these are the music, the production design, Dean Cundey's masterful cinematography, Carpenter's compelling synthesizer score, and the wildly original idea itself.

The film's premise is that New York was turned into a penal colony in 1988. The action, described in the titles as taking place "Now," is set in 1997. The problem of dating one's prognostications is, of course, that when the chosen date actually arrives, the predicted disasters are seen not to have occurred, and the prognosticator's vision is discounted—witness the widespread, point-missing commentary about how "wrong" George Orwell was when the year 1984 actually arrived without evidence of enslavement by mass mind control. The year 1988 has come and gone since the release of *Escape from New York*, and Manhattan is still alive, if not entirely well. But the preposterousness of Manhattan's actually being abandoned to a penal institution is ample evidence that both the date and the premise are not prognostications but metaphors for the quality of life that already infects New York—and much of urban America—"Now," today. The concern for the dehumanizing impact of urban crowding is echoed in such later Carpenter films as *Prince of Darkness* and *They Live*. *Escape from New York* takes the street gang atmosphere of *Assault on Precinct 13* and turns it into the social norm.

Liberty Island has become the vestibule of a prison, but ironically retains its original name even though it now functions as antechamber of a Dantesque hell. Changes have occurred in the governmental structure of the United States. It's become more authoritarian, more militaristic—perhaps a police state. There is a U.S. Police Force and the country is currently at war, though negotiating for peace. A key tool in those negotiations is the MacGuffin of the film: a tape cassette that contains some kind of vital information the President must present at a summit conference within 22 hours. That the fate of the world would hinge on the playing of a tape cassette is as unlikely as the President's having the only copy of that cassette in his pocket—but there's more spoof in *Escape from New York* than there is narrative credibility.

The President's plane has been hijacked by terrorists and deliberately brought down over New York. The President has ejected in a capsule, and subsequently been kidnapped by persons unknown. Enter Snake Plissken, a new candidate for admission to New York Prison. Snake has a reputation as a war hero, but also as a criminal, which has ultimately earned him a sentence in New York unless he is willing to help the government by rescuing the President. He has the skills to do it—but he has an attitude problem.

Snake is an authority-resisting maverick, a rebel with no discernible cause. Like Bogart's Rick in *Casablanca*, he sticks his neck out for nobody; like Brando's Johnny in *The Wild One*, he's anti-everything, rebelling against whatever you've got.

And it's hard to blame him. The authoritarian order outside the walls of New York is no better nor less brutal than the one inside. The world of *Escape from New York* is, like that of *Assault on Precinct 13*, a world in which institutions have failed, and there is little to choose between the good guys and the bad guys. Moral meaning, if it is to be redeemed at all, must be on the level of individual heroism and humane treatment of one's fellows.

But Snake Plissken is no Ethan Bishop, and if the relationship he cements on the "inside" with Cabbie, Maggie, and Brain is stronger than any loyalty he has for the President or the system he represents, it is still nothing like the bond between Ethan Bishop and Napoleon Wilson. It is an uneasy truce, marked by double crosses and distrust—an alliance more of convenience than of commitment.

With his eye patch—and later his wounded leg—Snake is a Byronic hero in spite of himself. He commands some respect ("You're a special case, Snake"), and his reputation precedes him: Despite the reportedly huge criminal population of this future New York, everyone Snake meets seems to know him already or at least have heard of him, but we never find out why his reputation precedes him so emphatically—especially among criminals—and why even those who have never met him recognize his face.

The unifying factor among all those who recognize him, though, is that they thought he was dead. "I know who you are ... I heard you were dead" becomes a kind of ritual incantation uttered when anyone meets Snake. Most of the time Snake makes no reply. But the first time the phrase is uttered, by the young woman Snake encounters in an abandoned Chock Full o' Nuts diner besieged by Crazies, he *does* have an answer. "I thought you were dead," she says, and he replies: "I am." The sardonic rejoinder expresses Snake's opinion of himself (he has sold out, working for the government) and of his situation (virtually hopeless, and the "bomb" in his head sealing his doom). It further suggests that he is a kind of avenging angel, returned from the dead, like the Clint Eastwood characters in *A Fistful of Dollars*, *High Plains Drifter*, and *Pale Rider*. And it underscores the film's vision of urban chaos as an image of hell. (Brain, the old partner-in-crime Snake meets inside, is really named Harold Hellman.)

Kurt Russell's parody of Clint Eastwood—not an idle notion, but an integral part of the character of Snake—is brought off with delightful deadpan, especially in light of his playing opposite Lee Van Cleef, the nemesis of the "Man with No Name" in two of the Sergio Leone spaghetti westerns that made Eastwood's name and style so familiar. When Russell's Snake Plissken (a character as firmly Leone-based as *Assault on Precinct 13*'s Napoleon Wilson) faces Van Cleef's Bob Hauck at the climax, it's Carpenter's variation on Eastwood facing Van Cleef at various points in *For a Few Dollars More*, a film characterized by an uneasy partnership, double crosses, offers made and refused, and, at last, a grudging mutual respect: Hauck: "You gonna kill me now, Snake?" Snake: "Not now—I'm too tired."

Hauck and Snake are, like their namesakes, predator and prey, equally dangerous, equally adept, mortal enemies. Van Cleef's Hauck is a sharp-eyed watcher (Van Cleef's film roles have made ample use of the penetrating, powerful eyes that in *The Good, the Bad and the Ugly* earned him the epithet "Angeleyes"); Russell's Snake is a devious (and one-eyed!) adversary with a poisonous bite.

The characters insist on being called by their chosen names. Brain (Harry Dean Stanton walking through his role) tells Snake, "Don't call me Harold." The Duke of New York demands to be addressed as "A–Number One"—an oblique reference, perhaps, to the lyrics of the Kander-Ebb tune "New York, New York" (which Carpenter would reference again later in *Starman*, when Jeff Bridges imitates an alien imitating a Planet Earth Person imitating Frank Sinatra)—and teaches the President to call him that by standing him against a wall and firing a machine pistol at him until he says it right. Snake himself stresses his seemingly honorific nickname: When Hauck calls him Plissken, he insistently replies, "Call me Snake." This is a setup for the conclusion of the film, in which Hauck offers Snake a permanent job. "We'd make a good team, Snake," he says, to which Snake replies, "The name's Plissken." Does his switch to the surname suggest that he's coming around to Hauck's way of seeing things and is thinking about the offer? Or that he is throwing off the criminal association with his nickname, becoming his own man by emphasizing the dignity of his surname? The cryptic Leonean word play suggests a character change, but leaves us to surmise what it might be—as does the dialogue in the final scene of *For a Few Dollars More*, arguably the source of this scene: Clint Eastwood's Man With No Name asks Lee Van Cleef's Colonel Mortimer, "What about our partnership?" and Mortimer replies, "Maybe next time."

Escape from New York owes much to Leone: not only the insistence on character nicknames, but also the elemental, violent confrontation, the simplified universe, the strong motivation of revenge, the cryptic dialogue, the episodic structure, the quest-narrative and, of course, the presence of Lee Van Cleef. One passage could almost have been conceived by Leone himself: Finding the President's wristband life monitor in the possession of a freak, Snake concludes that the President must be dead and tells Hauck. Hauck, assuming Snake is proclaiming the mission a failure, tells him he'll kill him if he tries to come back out of New York. "No human compassion," mutters Snake, in one of Russell's best Clint Eastwood impressions.

Escape from New York
Above: Snake bound for New York. Below: Snake drives home.
Cabbie (Ernest Borgnine), Brain (Harry Dean Stanton), Maggie
(Adrienne Barbeau), Snake Plissken (Kurt Russell), the President
(Donald Pleasence, hidden).

People in the film's time of 1997 talk not much differently from the way they do now, or did at the time the film was released. This vision of a future world, like most film images of the future, is grounded firmly in the present. The pastiche of costume and personal manner may be intended to suggest the era in which each of the film's characters was imprisoned: There are punks, rockers, a few aging hippies and even some classic winos. The decor is the junkyard futurism of such previous science fiction films as *Soylent Green* and *A Boy and His Dog* (a design concept that would have profound impact later on *The Road Warrior*). The characters suggest a cross section of society's dregs and misfits: the Duke's punk-styled adjutant, like an attendant fool; Cabbie, a New York hack for so many years he apparently opted to stay when the city became a prison and somehow survived the transition; Brain, always above his situation, always thinking fast enough to keep himself alive, but never more than a small-time hood; Maggie, with a heart of gold (one man's throwaway is another man's angel); and the Duke himself, a small-minded, two-bit punk who commands physical power almost by accident, and whose *inside* hierarchy mocks the authoritarian structure *outside*.

The night drive down Broadway is urban blight gone mad: In the firelit darkness we glimpse deteriorating walls and buildings, discarded junk, furtive characters darting here and there (like the nocturnal attackers of *Assault on Precinct 13*)—a visual environment that would be echoed in Walter Hill's *Streets of Fire*. The atmosphere is so nightmarish that the coming of the dawn is less a relief than an anomaly.

Carpenter's music for the film is as relentless and unforgiving as his visual concept. The main and end title theme is a pulsing slow march to which Carpenter appends a slight medieval spin not inconsistent with the film's almost feudalistic vision of character relationships. During Snake and Cabbie's journey to Brain's stronghold, Carpenter repeats a tinkling vamp like that used in his *Halloween* theme, over which he lays repeated pulsing chords in pairs—a device reused in *The Thing*, in which Carpenter's and Alan Howarth's music shares the soundtrack with Ennio Morricone's.

In his narrative style, Carpenter enjoys himself by lovingly lampooning B-film conventions. One of these is the creatively bankrupt expository device in which people tell each other things they both already know, just so the audience will understand the situation. The classic example of this is the tired old scene in which one person reads another's dossier out loud to him—as Hauck does with Plissken near the beginning.

The gratuitous fight scene is another B-film convention, common especially in programmers and serials. Carpenter mocks it in the wrestling match between Snake and an enormous opponent in Madison Square Garden as an imperious Duke looks on. The improbability of the Duke's risking Snake when he needs him, or of a gladiatorial diversion being indulged in just when time is of the essence to everyone, is exactly the kind of inconsistency that never seemed to bother the makers of the cliff-hangers. (This scene, by the way, is just one of many debts that *Mad Max Beyond Thunderdome* owes to *Escape from New York*.)

Another point scored off old programmers is the use of technological MacGuffins—made-up machines and devices—to explain plot points. In dime-store science fiction, if you need to achieve a certain result, just make up a machine that does it. That happens several times in *Escape from New York*, and Carpenter's tone in these parodistic scenes is often so deadpan that the comedy *seems* unintentional even when it isn't.

But comedy it is—and much of it runs to self-referential in-jokes about the world of film. The Crazies, for example, may be a reference to the little-seen George Romero film of the same title, even as they invoke the "Screamers" in L. Q. Jones's screen version of Harlan Ellison's *A Boy and His Dog*, and the subterranean mutants of *Beneath the Planet of the Apes*. In-jokes also pepper Carpenter's cast-list: The Liberty Island security controller played by Tom Atkins bears the name of Robert Rehme, the president of Avco-Embassy at the time *Escape from New York* was produced. There are also characters named Romero and Cronenberg; and Carpenter himself, with his band, the Coup de Villes, reportedly performed the music for the drag rendition of "Everyone's Coming to New York" in the shabby movie-house-turned-music-hall that is the only thing left of the theatre capital of the world.

But the film references that most pervade the film are, predictably, to Howard Hawks: The maverick hero, unwilling to compromise; the portrayal of institutional authority as the tool of effete windbags or dangerous sadists; the formation of a ragtag team of professionals to fulfill a mission that the authorities cannot even undertake—all are hallmarks of the Hawksian vision. So is the characterization of Brain's "squeeze," Maggie, a creation firmly in the Hawksian tough woman tradition. Maggie's last stand against the Duke after Brain is killed, her devotion, and her death are portrayed with the right combination of guts and sentiment. She is the first—though not the last—Carpenter woman to specifically give her life combating evil, and she just might be the quintessential Woman of Carpenter's film vision.

She's not the woman for Snake, of course. She's bound herself to Brain, and Snake respects that. Carpenter resists what must have been an obvious temptation to start something between Maggie and Snake.

Even at the film's climax, when Brain is killed and Maggie has the option of escaping from New York with Snake across the mined 69th Street Bridge, she chooses to stay behind and face the Duke's oncoming car. Snake doesn't baby her or patronize her; he gives her his gun ... and his admiration.

There *is* no woman for Snake, and that only enhances the loneliness with which he walks the world. He does meet a woman in the Chock Full o' Nuts diner, of course. She's played by Season Hubley, who also played opposite Russell as Priscilla in *Elvis*. "Got a smoke?" she asks him, recalling the Bogey-Bacall banter of Napoleon Wilson and Leigh in *Assault on Precinct 13*. Snake gives her a cigarette, but immediately scolds her for lighting it openly, allowing their position to be seen. Their relationship never gets off the ground: After a terse exchange of dialogue she is set upon by Crazies and literally dragged through the floor into the earth. Goodbye to all that. Though the influence of Howard Hawks remains profoundly discernible in Carpenter's work, this is the last time a film of his will so directly invoke the smoky, competitive aura of Hawksian sexual attraction.

It's interesting to note that *all* of the women in *Assault on Precinct 13*, *Halloween*, and *Escape from New York* are either wounded or killed—a phenomenon that suggests not a sadistic attitude toward women but a willingness to place them, as Hawks did, alongside men in the center of the arena of physical action.

Though Carpenter frequently references Hawks through dialogue and visual style, the most profound Hawksian trait he evinces is his sense of an underlying code of behavior—one sharp enough to distinguish bad guys from good, yet broad enough to redefine the very notion of goodness in terms of skill and responsibility, not social or political alliance. Thus we have seen in *Assault on Precinct 13* that both a criminal and a cop emerged as paragons of goodness, while the institution of the Police in general, and most of its exemplars in particular, came off as no better than the amoral street criminals whose revenge they precipitated by their oppressive tactics.

In *Escape from New York* as well, the notion of moral right as defined by alliance quickly collapses. The constituted government is no more moral than the Duke's reign of terror, and in fact the Duke comes off a little better for being at least honest about his tyranny. The Duke is nothing if not direct: He hits Snake bang on the head with a tire iron; then, while our hero slips into unconsciousness, climaxes a running gag by commenting ironically, "I heard you were dead."

The authorities, by contrast, plant "microscopic explosives" in Snake's arteries and tell him about it afterward. In fact, if the doctor hadn't insisted, there's every indication that Hauck wouldn't have told

Snake at all. (The device of the killer charge implanted in the hero's body was also used in J. Lee-Thompson's *The Chairman*.) Why put it there when they could achieve the same effect by merely *telling* him it's there? The only conclusion is that they really *want* the option of letting him die—a recognition that goes far toward explaining Snake's bitter attitude. But it raises a further question: Why go to the trouble of neutralizing the charge after the job is done? Why should Hauck keep his word to Snake?

The killer charge operates as a built-in time limit on Snake's activity, and the film's implicit code of conduct is thematically tied to a sense of timing. When Snake runs into Brain for the first time and recalls that his old partner in crime had run out on him two years before in Kansas City, Brain replies: "You were late." What Snake sees as desertion, Brain sees as a justified reaction to a behavioral failure in the other. The exchange between Snake and Brain gives new weight to the time limit at work on Snake, and to his cryptic query after the charges have been implanted: "What if I'm a little late?" This time the stakes are higher, and throughout the film little reminders of the crucial importance of being on time not only help build suspense, but also play a larger role in the framework of narrative and character.

In the event, Snake's interpretation of the Kansas City incident seems more likely than Brain's, for, given the opportunity, Brain once again deserts Snake, attempting to flee New York with Maggie in Snake's glider. Snake catches up with them, and once again the quick-thinking Brain redeems himself by being the only one who knows where the all-important tape cassette is. He knows because Duke's punk, who had picked up the tape when it fell out of the President's briefcase, is now seen wearing Cabbie's hat, and Cabbie has the only cassette player around. (The cleverness, though, saves Brain's skin only temporarily. He belongs to the Duke, body and soul, and it isn't long before A–Number One claims his own.)

The tape becomes the means by which Snake gets his revenge in the end: He nonchalantly unfurls and snaps the vital tape, after substituting a cassette from Cabbie's car that absurdly spews forth the "American Bandstand" theme instead of the expected solemn message about nuclear physics and world peace. (A similar device informed the end of the James Bond film *Diamonds Are Forever,* in which a tape of a program sequence leading to nuclear destruction is replaced with an innocuous recording of British military marches.)

Why does Snake trash the tape? Maybe it's just to embarrass the President who, moments before, has shown himself to be a treacherous and ungrateful windbag, insensitive to the deaths of those who helped him escape. Maybe it's to the darker purpose of deliberately sabotaging the government's efforts toward peace—either because he doesn't trust those efforts, or because he stands for anarchy and wants to hasten the old order's destruction of itself.

When the prisoners of New York state their terms—amnesty for all of them in exchange for the return of the President—the President becomes identified with their chance for freedom; and freedom can only be a key theme in a film set in a penal colony and on Liberty Island. But what is freedom to such as these? Not escape from hell but a chance to bring hell with them to the world outside. Like Street Thunder in *Assault on Precinct 13*, or Michael in *Halloween*, the Duke and his cronies are portrayed not as suitable subjects for rehabilitation, but as pure evil—evil that must be *contained* at all costs.

Snake and the President get out. No one else does. The walls stay up, but they might as well not have. It is the President himself who kills the Duke, and he does so savagely, ironically reciting the Duke's nickname, "A–Number One," as he riddles him with bullets. Whether it is an image of the corruption of even the highest levels of constituted authority by the forces of evil, or whether it means that the President has been a treacherous killer under the skin all along, doesn't much matter. Though he's left dead as a dog, the Duke wins. What *he* stands for finally holds sway. Everyone *is* coming to New York. And the only consolation is that Snake Plissken, the last, best hope, lives to fight another day.

10

Trust Is a Tough Thing to Come By

The Thing

Not so much a remake of the 1950 Howard Hawks–Christian Nyby film as a new and more faithful approach to its original source, William M. Campbell, Jr.'s *Astounding Science Fiction* short story "Who Goes There?," John Carpenter's *The Thing* is one of his least appreciated and most ambitious efforts. The ambition is not just in the intricate special effects and the challenge of making a film about a monster who can look just like the guy sitting next to you, but also in the sustained metaphor of the collapse of identity, responsibility, and trust in the modern world.

Unlike the Hawks–Nyby film, which departed dramatically from the Campbell story, Carpenter's film is less interested in its characters' response to their situation than in the growing indistinguishability of the monstrous from the human. That, actually, is the theme that has run through most horror and science fiction film since the lone hero of *Night of the Living Dead* survived a night of terror, only to be mistaken for a zombie himself, and summarily shot and burned in the film's bleak closing shots. The inability to tell the human from the horrible has its roots in *Dr. Jekyll and Mr. Hyde*. Its most relevant manifestations in contemporary cinema begin with *Psycho* and continue through *The Texas Chainsaw Massacre* and *Halloween* and the spate of horror-holiday slasher movies that followed. In the same shape-shifting vein, fresh ground was broken in the science fiction market just next door with the human-seeming androids of *Alien*, *Blade Runner*, and *Android* (directed by Aaron Lipstadt, Carpenter's associate producer on *Escape from New York*). But though the theme has been a bit overworked, it's rarely been done with such skill and immediacy as in Carpenter's *The Thing*.

Carpenter admires the Hawks–Nyby film enough to have quoted it in *Halloween*, and paraphrased its ending in *The Fog*. In his own version, Carpenter has MacReady and Garry view a videotape of the late Norwegian expedition team unearthing the alien spacecraft, and the shot (on the video!) is choreographed just like the famous shot from the Hawks–Nyby film (the same shot glimpsed on TV in *Halloween*): The men pace out along the perimeter of the icebound spacecraft and chill to the recognition of what it is they've found. Carpenter later repeats the composition in large when the men of the American crew gather around the burning Bennings replica in the snowy night. Another design echo of the Hawks film is the "bed" carved out of ice, in which the dormant alien has come to life.

But there are important differences between Carpenter's film and the Hawks model. In the Campbell story and the Carpenter film, the creature crash-landed on Earth thousands of years ago remains frozen in the ice at the South Pole. Thawed out, it proves to be an organism capable of multiplying rapidly and eluding detection by mimicking other organisms. In the Hawks–Nyby film, the invader has just landed, is at the North Pole not the South, and is a humanoid "intellectual carrot" that retains its own shape and feeds on human blood, propagating itself through planted seeds. The alien-as-plant image was one that reinforced the idea of the invader as dehumanizer in several formative science fiction films. In *The Quatermass Experiment*, *Invasion of the Body Snatchers*, and *Day of the Triffids*, the invader imposes on humankind a threat that represents absorption into a vegetative, unquestioning existence that was a widely understood metaphor for Communism: loss of freedom, individuality, mobility, and will. Carpenter's invaders, by contrast, remain distinctly animal, and (usually) humanoid, an image of what we *are* rather than of what we might become.

But the more important difference between Carpenter's and Hawks's treatment of the story is in the message underlying each film's portrayal of character interaction: In the Hawks–Nyby film, the creature is a catalyst for the confrontation of real-world conservative men of action in the service of political conviction, against ivory-tower liberal men of intellect in the service of learning for its own sake. In the Carpenter film, the creature is a metaphor for the already deteriorated condition of human interaction: deception, dishonesty, distrust. Howard Hawks's and Christian Nyby's *The Thing* is about the group and how it survives threats to its cohesion; John Carpenter's *The Thing* is about the ineluctable isolation of the individual.

Besides its debt to the Campbell story and the Hawks–Nyby film, Carpenter's *The Thing* also has roots in *They Bite*, a story developed by Dan O'Bannon and John Carpenter, in which people are menaced by an insect-like organism that biologically mimics whatever it attacks. That also influenced the creature created by O'Bannon in the screenplay for

Alien.[1] The mimicking theme is indebted, of course, to numerous science fiction invader films, including *It Came from Outer Space*, *Invaders from Mars*, *Invasion of the Body Snatchers*, and *The Quatermass Experiment* (in which the invader both absorbs *and* organically mimics its victims).

In general, the science fiction invader films of the Fifties and early Sixties begin with an emphasis on order and certainty, and an image, perhaps, of civic or domestic calmness, or of romance (a young couple walking or driving down a country road, for example). Then something arrives—usually from the sky—and disrupts that order. A hero or a team of heroes emerges, analyzes and assesses the new order, and puts things aright either by destroying the invader and reaffirming the old order (as in, for example, Hawks's and Nyby's *The Thing* or Gordon Douglas's *Them!*) or by shaping a harmonious new order that accommodates the changes represented by the invader (as suggested, for example, in the open-ended finales to *The Day the Earth Stood Still* and *It Came from Outer Space*).

Carpenter's films, by contrast, generally begin not with an order that is subsequently disrupted, but with a world in which things are already out of joint: the scratchy and disappointing "incoming communication" that begins *Dark Star*; the scuffling in the dark and the bloody shootout in the opening to *Assault on Precinct 13*; the menacing presence suggested by the disorienting camerawork in the first shot of *Halloween*; the communal guilt and terror that imbue the campfire story in *The Fog*. There is already a disorder abroad in the world, and it is up to a team of heroes to adapt to it, or to combat it and replace it with a *new* (not a restoration of the old) order.

As the simple white-on-black main titles conclude with John Carpenter's credit, stars peep into the blackness behind, recalling the background of the Universal Pictures logo. A flying saucer suddenly tumbles into view, and burns its way into Earth's atmosphere, followed by the film's title, which is visually "burned" into the frame. This is Carpenter's evocation of the visual device used for the main title of the Hawks–Nyby *The Thing*—and of the things-from-the-sky opening so common to classic science fiction horror films. Two of Carpenter's own favorite formative films, *It Came from Outer Space* and *The Quatermass Experiment*, open the same way.

In fact, if any film other than Hawks's and Nyby's *The Thing* can be viewed as a key influence on Carpenter's *The Thing*, it is Jack Arnold's *It Came from Outer Space*. Both films have at their heart the problem of trust. John Putnam, the hero of *It Came from Outer Space*, has to get other people in his town to trust him, to believe his story about space creatures inhabiting a nearby mineshaft. The crash-landed aliens have to persuade the locals to trust *them*, believe that the aliens really mean no harm and will stay only long enough to repair their damaged ship. At a crucial point in the film, John Putnam's quest for trust merges with the aliens'. He makes an act of faith: "We sit and wait and trust them to make it clear to us." He tells the others, "They want us to trust them," and his subsequent defense and protection of the aliens stresses that distrust is not something that comes naturally or easily to him.

In Carpenter's *The Thing*, by contrast, distrust is already the way of the world. Carpenter, this time out, replaces the hell of fire and darkness that characterizes *Escape from New York* with a hell of ice, the chill world of "Antarctica, Winter, 1982" (not enough that it's Antarctica—it also has to be *winter*!) providing an apt metaphor for the death of feeling and of finer human qualities. It's also a hell of boredom, like that aboard the scout ship *Dark Star*: The men at this Little America research station are already so undone by isolation and cramped quarters that they barely tolerate one another. They watch old tapes of "Let's Make a Deal." ("I know how this one ends.") MacReady plays—and loses to—a "Chess Wizard" game with an alluring female voice, a humanization of the mechanical that again evokes the world of *Dark Star*. (In both films, an electronically synthesized voice is the closest we get to a feminine presence.) MacReady doesn't like to lose; his response is to pour a glass of whisky into the computer's works, shorting it out—a premonition of the shutdown of technology at the climax of the film, and of the neo-Luddite finale to *Escape from L.A.*

The atmosphere at the research station is like *Alien* on the ground. When a pair of Norwegian scientists from a nearby station appear, shooting from a helicopter at a running sled dog (an echo of, among other things, the helicopter surveillance scene early in *It Came from Outer Space*), Doctor Copper attempts to explain the mystery: "Stir crazy ... cabin fever ... who knows?"

The claustrophobic sense of doom is reflected in the film's visual and musical rhythms. The sequences are divided by fades to black, offsetting the whiteness of ice and snow while punctuating the deliberately slow pace of the film: This world ends with a whimper, not a bang. Carpenter usually invokes the fade at an open-ended point—a sudden glance, a moment of surmise, an unanswered question.

The film's doomed pace is echoed in the music: slow, creepy, *Psycho*-like minor-key chords in the high range bleeding in over a fuzz-bass heartbeat rhythm. Most of the music for *The Thing* was scored by Ennio Morricone—another by-product of Carpenter's admiration for Sergio Leone's films:

The Thing

Howard Hawks's and Christian Nyby's *The Thing* (above) is about the group and how it survives threats to its cohesion; John Carpenter's *The Thing* (below) is about the ineluctable isolation of the individual.

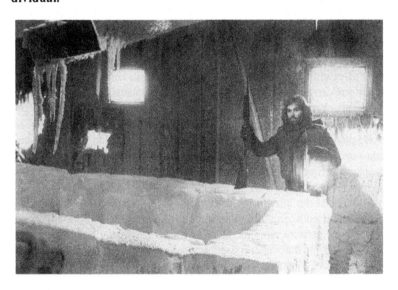

I love Ennio Morricone's work. He and Bernard Herrmann
remain my favorite composers—they're most influential. In
The Thing, that was all Ennio Morricone's work except for
some incidental music that I scored myself because there
wasn't enough quiet mood stuff that needed to be done. The
collaboration with him was fabulous. He had developed a very
musical score, but I talked him into doing one with only three
notes in it for the basic theme—that's the opening—and then
he did a kind of traditional Hollywood string score for some of
it. I thought it was beautiful, and I loved it.

The predominating quiet desperation of the film also serves to
greater amplify its climactic moments of sudden shock: Childs, Garry,
and Palmer tied up together, as Palmer starts turning into The Thing;
the Palmer-Thing absorbs Windows, head to head; Norris, dead of a
"heart attack," suddenly crumbles away when Doc puts the defibrillator
on his chest, and a huge pair of jaws munches off Doc's hands; Norris's
head sprouts legs and scuttles across the floor—these are the moments
at which the terror becomes real, and the almost resigned attitudes of
the doomed men give way to a last burst of self-preserving energy in
the face of the fury of the invader.
  The stakes are very great, indeed: There is living cell activity in
the presumed-dead Thing-replicas, and Blair's computer-assisted calcu-
lation of how long it would take the alien force to take over the entire
world once in contact with civilization comes coldly out to just over
three years. The Thing is in the best tradition of invading creatures of
the Fifties in that, apparently, nothing can stop it. But it differs from the
traditional invader in that it mimics other organisms perfectly, indistin-
guishably. You can't tell it from us—unlike the predatory aliens of *Invasion of the Body Snatchers*, *It Came from Outer Space*, or *I Married
a Monster from Outer Space*, in which the replicas don't act quite human, or of *Invaders from Mars* and *Quatermass II*, in which the Earth
hosts are left with convenient entry wounds, marking the fact that they
are possessed.
  Against the alien, MacReady and his fellows employ the weapon
of fire, as used against the giant ants of *Them!*—but to no avail, since
the cellular activity remains, as does the threat. In the end, MacReady
opts instead for the weapon used against the monster in Mary Shelley's
original novel *Frankenstein*, and later, against *The Blob*: freezing. But
this is at best the limited, temporary victory common to Carpenter
films. Freezing is more to The Thing's benefit then to humanity's, and

MacReady knows it—The Thing has already demonstrated that it can survive the cold. It waited for thousands of years. It can wait for thousands more.

The ability of the creature to mimic others makes it a natural metaphor for the same theme signified by invaders in the monster movies of the Fifties: the collapse of confidence in human beings. The subtext is no longer political; the fear is not that your neighbor has become a commie, it's that he can't be trusted and will destroy you if he has to. Blair, the first to recognize the power of The Thing, is visibly shaken. "I don't know who to trust," he tells MacReady, who answers, "Trust is a tough thing to come by these days." (And this is *before* the really awful stuff starts!) Later MacReady and Fuchs talk secretly in the cab of a skidozer, like the astronauts in *2001* going into a space pod to talk in private, only to find that there is no longer any place they can be safe.

Trust *is* a tough thing to come by these days, and the growing dehumanization of the urbanized Eighties is a theme Carpenter takes up more directly in the citified horrors of *Prince of Darkness* and *They Live*. Of course, there is no crowding psychosis in the vast wasteland of Antarctica, but the interpersonal dynamics of the crew members, under increasingly claustrophobic and terrifying circumstances, provide an apt metaphor for contemporary life. The decline of trust is symptomatic of the age, MacReady seems to recognize; the monster is only a metaphor, albeit a deadly one. What it represents, what it brings out in people, is as deadly to humankind as are its jaws.

When they can no longer trust one another, the men can also no longer trust sleep. MacReady forces himself to stay awake, like Dr. Miles Bennell in *Invasion of the Body Snatchers*—knowing that with sleep comes the silent invasion through which everything is changed utterly. The sleep of reason brings forth monsters. MacReady says into his taped log (a grim variation on Pinback's complaint tapes in *Dark Star*): "Nobody trusts anybody now."

With the loss of trust in one's fellow man comes the loss of one's own sense of identity. We rely for self-definition on the way others perceive us. Now all bets are off: "How do we know who's human? ... How would you know if it was really me?" The question, which echoes John Putnam's in *It Came from Outer Space*, and the one that Nigel Kneale and Roy Ward Baker ask on a larger scale in *Five Million Years to Earth*, points toward Carpenter's more direct approach to the theme of the merger of alien with human identity in *Prince of Darkness*.

Confronted with the question, MacReady employs a brutal, chess player's logic: I know *I'm* human, and if you other guys were Things, you wouldn't let me stick this needle in your arm, let alone carry out this electrolysis blood test I've invented, so I know *you're* human—so now we'll try the same test on the *next* guy. They proceed to draw one another's blood in a bizarre variation on the blood-oath scene in *Assault on Precinct 13*, the flesh-cutting and blood-letting emphasized in closeup as it was in the earlier film. But we already know that MacReady is not a winner at chess, and besides, the line between science and faith has begun to blur. This is no oath of loyalty; the blood is given grudgingly, apprehensively.

The pervasive atmosphere of distrust, desperation, and doom suggest another metaphor for the film, that of nuclear war and its aftermath, wrought by human intolerance, and breeding forth only more of the same. The nuclear metaphor is certainly supported by the film's finale, a fiery conflagration, followed by the shutdown of technology and the subjection of humankind to the forces of bitter nature.

Blair's ice cave and the partly built spacecraft are an escape route for The Thing—an escape route cut off when MacReady burns the ship, and then the camp's heating and life support equipment. The heat is temporary. Soon it will chill down. It's only a matter of time until the big freeze—like the final, awful preeminence of ice-nine in Kurt Vonnegut, Jr.'s *Cat's Cradle*. The stakes have changed completely. It is no longer a case of individual survival but of saving what is human.

Childs turns up. He says he thought he saw Blair, chased him, and got lost in the snow. This opens the possibility that The Thing is alive as either Blair or Childs or both—and invites the question whether the alien can escape to the civilized world or not.

> "What do we do now?"
> "Wait here awhile ... see what happens."

Self-sacrifice for the sake of the rest of us? Maybe. But something more. MacReady and Childs sit looking at each other—like Fred C. Dobbs and Curtin each daring the other to be the first one to fall asleep in *Treasure of the Sierra Madre*—waiting for the apocalyptic fires to die, waiting for the last big freeze, neither knowing for sure if the other is The Thing or not. Ennio Morricone's music continues through the final credits, bleak, eerie, until one by one the instruments drop out, leaving only the single, heartbeat-pulsing bass string—and finally not even that. It's the ultimate chilling of the soul.[2]

Danny Peary, commenting on *The Thing* in his *Dark Star* article in *Cult Movies 2*, says: "Who cares if dehumanized characters are further dehumanized? For *The Thing* to have been effective and have had an emotional impact as well as shock value, the characters needed to be more sympathetic, more *human*."³ Peary's criticism makes sense only if you assume the movie is about its characters. It isn't. It's about *us*. The decelerating heartbeat in the music is our own, throbbing in our ears. It is the last sound we will hear.

Harlan Ellison called *The Thing* "a deranged beast of a film in which special effects not only were encouraged to run amuck, but provide the *only* raison d'être for a movie we were told would be the first *accurate* transliteration to celluloid of John W. Campbell's 'Who Goes There?' when, in fact, it was a cheap ripoff of the original Hawks–Nyby version with all humanity removed."⁴ Ellison's run-on tirade overlooked the fact that the excision of humanity is precisely the point. Did he think all that ice and snow were just window dressing? *The Thing* is about the death of the heart.⁵

Notes

1. Fox, Jordan R., Interview, "Riding High on Horror," *Cinefantastique* 10:1, Summer 1980, p. 7.
2. Be warned that an unauthorized version of *The Thing* still exists on video (though not on film). Recut by Sid Sheinberg, this version inserts some overexplanatory dialogue and voice-over, and tacks on a shot-but-not-used ending that suggests that MacReady conquers The Thing, saves the world, and makes everything all right—thereby undercutting the metaphoric power of the film's downbeat, open ending.
3. Peary, Danny, *"Dark Star,"* in *Cult Movies 2* (New York: Dell, 1983), p. 55.
4. Ellison, Harlan, "Lurching Down Memory Lane with It, Them, The Thing, Godzilla, HAL 9000 ... That Whole Crowd: An Overview of the Science Fiction Cinema," in Peary, Danny, ed., *Omni's Screen Flights/Screen Fantasies* (New York: Doubleday, 1984), p.12.
5. A number of fans and critics of this film have expressed interest in a sequel in which The Thing reaches the civilized world. I have always thought that the most interesting sequel to *The Thing* would be a film in which MacReady and Childs are rescued and returned to civilization, each obsessed by the possibility that the other is The Thing—even though neither of them actually is.

11

Rock 'n' Roll Is Here to Stay

Christine

> *Christine* was about rock 'n' roll, and Stephen King wrote me a note and said, "This is really *High School Confidential* with a car in it."
>
> —John Carpenter

In the late Seventies, Stephen King emerged as the reigning emperor of horror, almost single-handedly reviving a literary genre that had lain dormant since the golden age of *Weird Tales*, and providing an incredible volume of movie fodder into the bargain. Brian De Palma's film of King's *Carrie* made the reputations—and secured the popularity—of both the novelist and the director. Tobe Hooper directed *Salem's Lot* as a television miniseries (Carpenter visited Hooper and producer Richard Kobritz on the set, sparking unfounded rumors that he had a hand in the writing of the film). Stanley Kubrick dismayed audiences and critics by making *The Shining* more Kubrick than King. David Cronenberg assayed *The Dead Zone*, and George Romero teamed with King for the anthology film *Creepshow*, a tribute to the EC Horror Comics of the Fifties that influenced both of them.

With every major practitioner of the horror film taking on a King project, it was inevitable that Carpenter do so, too. His film version of *Christine* remains one of the best to be made from a King story. Like Lewis Teague's *Cujo*, the film provides effective cinematic correlates for King's themes and devices, within a tighter, more disciplined structure. Both films actually improve on King by compressing the overwritten episodes and detail that weaken the novels.

There may be a little *too much* compression in the early section of *Christine*. People start bemoaning Arnie's "change" and his obsession with his car before we've had much of a chance to see those things develop. But this is a film about a car and about rock 'n' roll, so speed is everything. *Christine* zips along with a compelling pace that puts literary values in the backseat.

Where the novel sustains both the possibility that Christine herself is evil (and hence corrupted her former owner LeBay), and that she has *become* evil because haunted by the malevolent spirit of LeBay, Carpenter's film is unambiguously direct: Christine is the embodiment of evil from the moment she rolls off the assembly line. The film opens as an engine bursts to life and idles through the main credits. All we see is the "V" on Christine's grille—an image that will persist throughout the film, linking "Victory" with a suggestion of the female genitalia as Christine is seen as passionate lover, treacherous dominatrix and, finally, all-powerful witch.

After the credits, the first thing we see is the vortex of a ventilation fan—an image that, for some reason, became a standard symbol for menace in horror films of the Eighties (Tobe Hooper's *The Funhouse* and Alan Parker's *Angel Heart* are but two examples). "Detroit, 1957" reads a legend, and Christine rolls off the assembly line to the tune of "Bad to the Bone," along with dozens of other 1958 Plymouths. Within moments, she has severed the hand of a line inspector who carelessly leaves himself in range of her open hood. Seeming to like the taste of blood, she then dispatches by unknown means another man, who is so injudicious as to sit in her driver's seat and tip his cigar ash. Her radio blares Buddy Holly's "Not Fade Away" ("I'm a-gonna tell ya how it's gonna be ..."), and the smug tone leaves no doubt: This is a mean car, pure and simple.

Arguably, a more gradual recognition of the evil in Christine might have made for more effective horror, but the assumption is that most people going to the movie already know what it's about, and Carpenter, though a sublimely manipulative director, is not one to tease, let alone disappoint, an audience. In *Christine* he goes right for the jugular.

That's not to say that *Christine* is devoid of moral ambiguity. But like Hitchcock, Carpenter places the moral burden where it belongs: on the viewer. We *like* Christine, and cheer for her when we see how she boosts the self-esteem of nerdy, ineffectual Arnie, and how she neatly disposes of his enemies without implicating him. It's only as Arnie himself begins to change, his newfound confidence unfolding into arrogance, that we begin to feel we're in too deep. Christine has given Arnie's life a new Order—but not the one he'd bargained for.

The film proper begins in Rockbridge, California, on September 12, 1978. Christine has just turned 21 (a point is made a little later of the fact that the new cars came out in September "back then"). Arnie Cunningham is introduced as a mama's boy, with dark-rimmed glasses and a pale face, who spills the garbage in the driveway and can't make

Christine—John Carpenter's toughest woman.

a move without being reminded by his mother what to do. The first dialogue between Arnie and Dennis emphasizes Arnie's feelings of sexual inadequacy, establishing the association of car with male dominance, which was the central metaphor of King's novel. It is also a reminder of the scene between Laurie and Annie in *Halloween*—also set in a car—which first defines the protagonist's character for us in terms of inability to find a sexual companion. Laurie is looking for someone, and she finds Michael Myers. Arnie is looking for someone, and he finds Christine.

The tough kids in the school love to pick on Arnie, attracted, perhaps, by his oddness and his vulnerability. He at any rate takes his place among the hazed and abused kids who people the films of John Carpenter—a thematic interest Carpenter shares with King, whose mousy, abused Carrie fulfilled every bullied kid's fantasy by using a supernatural weapon against her enemies.

In previous Carpenter films we've seen the ruthless teasing meted out to Tommy Doyle in *Halloween* and to young Elvis Presley in *Elvis*, and we had the ghost of a suggestion of Ethan Bishop's similar childhood in *Assault on Precinct 13*. Though an incidental moment in each of those films, the bullying forms an important part of the psychological subtext of Carpenter's cinema world, where terrors are intensified when we are alienated by others and forced to realize our aloneness ... even though that aloneness may be the beginning of the individual's search for real meaning. In *Elvis*, fame and talent were the weapons Elvis used to get a kind of revenge on those who treated him less than seriously. Given *Christine*'s association of cars with music in the matrix of teenage America, one could say that Arnie, like Elvis, gets his vengeance with rock 'n' roll—and discovers that music is a harsh mistress.

John Carpenter's own view of the music has evolved:

> I love certain kinds of rock 'n' roll, but the *idea* of rock 'n' roll can often be very destructive. I mean, you've seen a lot of people who've died from it, just from the lifestyle of it. And often, rock 'n' roll's meaning has changed over the years to where now it has nothing to do with rebellion anymore, which it used to. It has to do with mainstream and selling products, so part of me says, "You know, I hate it now that it's become so acceptable." You know, you go into an elevator and you hear music that once was extremely rebellious. It has a different meaning. So, I think, I do have an ambivalence about rock 'n' roll. I mean, sometimes you have to explain to people what's great about it, and if you have to, you know they don't get it. But on the other hand, now it's become toy music—it's just so bad now.

Rock 'n' roll is a unifying metaphor of King's novel, as reflected in the use as epigraphs of lyrics from teenage love songs, car songs, and death songs. Carpenter, who had already used song lyrics to counterpoint and comment on scenes from Elvis Presley's life in *Elvis*, takes up the metaphor, and it becomes, for him, an ambivalent view of the music. He is, after all, a musician himself, and the rhythms of rock 'n' roll inform many of his films. Yet the music is here associated with a disruptive force—not simply a rebellious, liberating force, as in *Elvis*, but an *evil* force, an unleashing of much more than repressed sexual energy. It is an *order*, whether we like it or not. After all, it is emphatically "here to stay." It is not, however, the order we had in mind. At the end of the film, Leigh remarks emphatically, "I *hate* rock 'n' roll." Where rock 'n' roll music became an ordering influence in Elvis's life, it is here associated with the *dis*ordering influences in Arnie's life.

We see rock 'n' roll itself as a force throughout the film. When Dennis tries to open the car's door, the radio sings out, "Keep a-knockin' but you can't come in." Later, rock song lyrics accompany Christine's attempt to choke Leigh at the drive-in, and the car's subsequent profession of love to Arnie. Christine speaks with the voice of rock 'n' roll. Carpenter's use of the car's radio as a means of communication is a way of cinematically paralleling King's use of rock 'n' roll lyrics as epigraphs throughout the book. Rock 'n' roll, as much as cars, is the subject of both book and film, insofar as it both reflects and shapes the dreams of American teenagers. Even when crushed by a Caterpillar, Christine blares forth on her radio, "Rock 'n' Roll Is Here To Stay."

Despite the film's contemporary setting, Christine's music is period, from the era of which she is a product. The bullies, by contrast, get contemporary music—The Rolling Stones' "Beast of Burden"—to distinguish them from the classic rock associated with Arnie and Christine. The insistence on the music of the Fifties suggests that Christine is stuck in time, or that she represents the haunting of one era by another. The long reach of the Fifties in *Christine* is counterpointed by—and made emblematic of—the persistence of the scars of youth, a common Stephen King theme. Arnie is certainly a damaged kid, and it is the sense of *loss* in his life that pervades the novel (told from the viewpoint of his friend Dennis). In that sense, both book and film may be seen as a futile effort to reclaim what is already irrevocably lost. Keith Gordon takes Arnie from schlemiel to stud to shithead with splendid control, stressing the fact that the guy never gets a chance to be a normal kid. Christine becomes a symbol of that effort to reclaim loss—or perhaps a vampiric exploiter of the loss: As she cruises, her odometer rolls back-

Christine

The world of *Christine* is a world of hostility. Above: Dennis (John Stockwell, center) cannot talk his friend Arnie (Keith Gordon) out of buying Christine, even when they learn of the evil the car wrought on the life of its previous owner, the brother of crusty George LeBay (Roberts Blossom). Below: Arnie and Dennis have a run-in with foul-mouthed garage-owner Darnell (Robert Prosky).

The outrage ... and the revenge
**Above: Arnie and Leigh (Alexandra Paul) witness the spectacle of a
wronged Christine. Below: The end of Moochie (Malcolm Denare).**

ward; she's getting newer all the time, moving back to the years of her own youth.

Like the novel, the film makes a bid to be the definitive statement on the love affair between the American male ego and the automobile—the dark side of *American Graffiti*. Buddy Repperton's taunting mockery of Arnie's name as "Cuntingham" indexes the degree to which the film is about the myth of traditional American masculinity—the yearning for it, the peer pressure that informs it, the dark side of achieving it.

Christine makes Arnie a man—and becomes his lover. Both she and Leigh feel jealousy, and they do combat with each other over Arnie. Sexual competition informs the film at every level: In an early shot in the school library, the subjective camera takes Dennis's point of view, approaching Leigh to ask her for a date. As Dennis nears Leigh, another girl he sometimes dates looks up from her work and smiles at his approach, but her smile droops in the last instant as he passes her by. She slides out of frame lower right, left behind for greener pastures.

Christine's violence is, at first, the product of the passion between her and Arnie. Later, it is the wrath of a woman scorned, its key image the Plymouth's grille, a cryptic *vagina dentata*. Arnie is more of a knowing accomplice to Christine in the film than in the book. After the bullies have destroyed the car, Arnie tells Christine, "They can't hurt us any more—not if we're together." The symbiotic relationship thus established, Arnie and Christine strengthen each other: She regenerates herself before his very eyes (to the tune of "Harlem Nocturne," a favorite accompaniment to strippers' performances), and goes on to destroy his (and her) enemies while protecting him.

It is Christine's arbitrary killing of Darnell—a coarse and hostile old guy, but one we've grown to like—that finally alienates us from her. That killing alerts Arnie to the problem as well: "Why?" he wonders. But it's too late for Arnie to get out of his complicity. Passion has become possession. The changing colors of light on Arnie's flaring eyes as he talks with Dennis during their New Year's drive show that the transformation is complete ... and only Dennis can now do what has to be done.

With the front end of the car as a mock face, its monstrous, malevolent, grinning grille recalling the jack-o'-lantern logo of the *Halloween* films, *Christine* carries through Carpenter's penchant for linking primal evil with the technology of the modern world—TV, computers, and now cars. Carpenter continues to insist on simple, objective evil: Street Thunder, Michael Myers, the Fog, the Duke, The Thing ... Christine. Yet Christine may not be so simple. She provides another image of the Return of the Repressed, in Robin Wood's parlance: The evil within her is a reminder of the trade Arnie has made in order to give himself a different kind of life. The car makes that new life possible, gives Arnie confidence, enables him to affirm his sexuality and win the affection of a beautiful girl. But Christine gives and Christine takes away: The car proceeds to dismantle the very new life she has given Arnie, to besiege it on all sides, leaving it at last the unattainable illusion that it must have been from the very beginning, when Arnie Cunningham was just an outcast nerd. Arnie was lost before he ever got started.

Christine, of course, doesn't bring evil into the world. Like The Thing, she is emblematic of a world already out of order, already steeped in hostility. The camera tracks among the trees in the exterior shot of the high school, echoing similar compositions in *Halloween*, creating a sense of uneasiness, disorder. The high school bullies, eccentric old George LeBay, and even garage owner Darnell, the closest thing the film has to a benevolent character, all pepper their dialogue with threat, insult, and coarse language. Even Arnie's parents, though more decorous, are arbitrary and oppressive. Only Dennis and Leigh seem to have truly gentle spirits, and it is left to them to do final combat with Christine.

That combat, with Dennis in a Caterpillar vs. Christine alone, is a dramatic change from the novel, in which Arnie kills himself, his mother, and Christine, after Christine has killed Arnie's father. In the film, Arnie's own death, seemingly suicidal, is almost a throwaway; the crushing and regenerating of Christine gets all the stylistic emphasis. There's no question who the central character of the film is.

The junkyard compacting of Christine is filmed like a John Ford funeral, with Dennis, Leigh, and Junkins looking on. But instead of "Gather at the River," Ritchie Valens's "Let's Go" bursts out. At first we and they think it's Christine's radio again, but it turns out to be a junkman's ghetto blaster. Shaken, Leigh says, "God, I *hate* rock 'n' roll" ... and as we come in tight on the remains of Christine, the bent rods wiggle just a little. Her theme song, "Bad to the Bone," returns to accompany the end titles. Christine—like the Bogey Man, The Thing, and rock 'n' roll—is here to stay.

Starman
Two views of Jenny Hayden (Karen Allen) and the thing that is not her dead husband Scott (Jeff Bridges)

12

I Can't Get No Satisfaction

Starman

John Carpenter is emphatic about *Starman*'s having been a "for hire" job. Nevertheless, though it remains the best known and successful of his "big studio" films, it is not without a personal dimension. It is, for one thing, Carpenter's warmest, gentlest, most understanding and humane film. His vehement insistence on Dean Reisner's authorship of *Starman*, despite the Writers Guild-mandated award of screenplay credit to Bruce A. Evans and Raynold Gideon, is evidence of Carpenter's personal stake in the film.

Starman's similarity to *The Thing* is an indicator of the film's place in a continuing Carpenter vision. In fact, this film about a benevolent alien who finds that humans can't be trusted is virtually the flip side of *The Thing*, whose malevolent alien becomes a walking metaphor for the same truth.

Both films open on a starscape, through which hurtles an object bringing a visitor to Earth. *Starman* begins, after the Columbia Pictures logo, with the sound of a news report about the launch of *Voyager* and the tapes it carried, heard over a starscape. The broadcaster's voice segues into the sound of the Rolling Stones' "Satisfaction," and *Voyager* sweeps past. We *see* the tapes playing ... and then we see the Milky Way, and a new ship flashes past, hurtling into Earth's atmosphere. The commingling of space flight imagery with rock 'n' roll music echoes *Dark Star*; and like *Dark Star*, *Starman* is informed by an atmosphere of disappointment and frustration. "I Can't Get No Satisfaction" may well be Starman's theme, providing apt counterpoint to the failure of his abortive goodwill mission to Earth. The order he has found here is not the one the *Voyager* tapes led him to expect.

Identity, Science, and Politics

Starman bears another similarity to *The Thing*: The narratives of both films are built upon the alien's ability to imitate the shape and manner of a familiar creature. The character played by Jeff Bridges is not "the alien" but a clone grown from one of dead Scott Hayden's hairs, providing a temporary housing for the soul and mind of the alien. Thus the Starman, like The Thing, survives and eludes capture by mimicking a human being. But *Starman* rings changes on the "doubling" imagery of *The Thing*: Where in *The Thing* the indistinguishability of the alien from a normal human being generated distrust of others, in *Starman* the fact that the alien is able to make himself look and act like a human being is what wins for him the sympathy and empathy of Jenny Hayden, of Mark Sherman, and of us.

Because of Jeff Bridges's marvelous performance, *Starman* also comes to be about the human body as a relatively inefficient machine, and in that sense it may also be about acting: Starman tries on a body as an actor tries on a role; Bridges portrays a truly believable alien who's unfamiliar with the body in which he finds himself.

The idea of an alien able to mimic humans springs, once again, from Jack Arnold's *It Came from Outer Space*. That film's hero, John Putnam, tries to stretch the minds of the townspeople and persuade the bellicose Matt to tolerate the brief visit of the crash-landed space visitors ensconced in a nearby mine. He says only half rhetorically, "Wouldn't it be interesting if I weren't John Putnam at all, but something from another world?" In a later scene, Putnam actually meets his own "double" in the mineshaft. At the end of the film, he says, "They'll be back," and for him it is a hopeful thought, whose childlike wonder would ultimately be fulfilled in Steven Spielberg's *Close Encounters of the Third Kind* and *E.T.*—and in John Carpenter's *Starman*. Generally, though, Carpenter's vision of alien invasion has been distinctly darker, as evidenced in *The Thing* and *They Live*.

John Putnam's welcoming approach to the aliens of *It Came from Outer Space* is set off against the belligerence of Matt, who wants to attack and destroy where Putnam wants to trust and learn. *Starman*'s characters map interestingly onto those of *It Came from Outer Space*, Fox playing Matt to Sherman's Putnam. Through this contrast of characters *Starman* reiterates the tension between scientist and militarist that informed Hawks–Nyby's *The Thing*, but with a difference. Hawks and Nyby were interested in their characters' *reaction* to an extraordinary situation, while Carpenter saw the extraordinary situation as a metaphor for the condition in which his characters already found themselves.

In the Hawks production, the scientists are effete, idealistic crypto-commies who would let us fall victim to a malevolent enemy by preferring study to action, however swift and terrible. The militarists' propensity for vigilance and immediate action makes them the better equipped to deal with the invasion. *Starman*, by contrast, actually has more in common with Jack Arnold's *It Came from Outer Space* and *Creature from the Black Lagoon*, both of which feature colliding viewpoints about the proper response to alien invasion, with the filmmaker's sympathies reversing those of Howard Hawks. In *It Came from Outer Space*, John Putnam asks his buddy Pete, "What would you say if I *had* found a Martian down there?" Pete replies, "I'd say hold it for a circus." John disagrees: "I'd say wait. Find out why they're here first." Similarly, in *Creature from the Black Lagoon*, the confrontation is between two scientists, one who favors killing the creature first and studying it later, the other who advocates the more humane approach of studying the creature in its habitat and learning from it without doing it violence.

Starman's Sherman and Fox are *both* proponents of a military establishment (National Security), but only Fox prefers to shoot first and talk later. He stands in the tradition of the conscienceless politician, typified by the character of the President in *Escape from New York*. Sherman, on the other hand, is the good-guy scientist, and at least one thing the movie is about is how he redeems himself and our species by his humane attitude toward the alien.

Starman does, however, retain a touch of the mean-spirited and simplistic anti-intellectualism seen in Hawks's and Nyby's *The Thing*: Fox is introduced to us dressed in a tux, emerging from a concert hall; we first glimpse Sherman sitting down with an array of junk food to enjoy a basketball game on TV. The course their characters take for the remainder of the film charts for us a subtext in Carpenter's films that becomes explicit in *They Live*: The truly human and humane are usually salt of the earth, lowbrow, blue-collar types; those who embrace a higher aesthetic and a higher learning are suspect. The Hawksian stereotyping is further confounded by the fact that, for all his folksiness, Sherman the scientist comes much closer to being an intellectual than does Fox the politician. But the theme of the lowbrow good guy persists in Carpenter's work, particularly evidenced in the unbroken chain of working-class heroes played for Carpenter by Kurt Russell in *Elvis*, *Escape from New York*, *The Thing*, and *Big Trouble in Little China*.

In *Starman*, the whole situation of the film arises from the tension between the humane scientist and the reactionary militarist: Sherman, we are reminded, was part of the process that put *Voyager* into space in the first place, and he believes in the gesture of peace that it stands for. The difference between the *apparent* intent of Earth, as evidenced by *Voyager*, and the *actual* intent, as represented by Fox, is what creates Starman's dilemma.

Fox is the hard-headed reactionary who resists the new order; Sherman the open-minded liberal with a sense of wonder, who opens his arms to it. The two stalemate. Fox's opposition to Sherman—his refusal even to listen to Sherman's views—is an immovable assertion of raw power. It may seem unlikely that he wouldn't listen even for a moment, but he knows Sherman well enough to know what he is going to say. He also knows himself and the political pressures of his own job. Fox is the heavy, but Richard Jaeckel plays him with understanding and respect for the man that Fox has to be. Fox has every right to expect Sherman to be a "member of the team." But when he gratuitously attacks Sherman's personal tastes and image—"Get rid of that damn cigar!"—the attack makes the cigar an easy emblem of Sherman's rebellion, and of his dignity and humanity. So when Sherman, exulting in a temporary victory, blows smoke in Fox's face, he says, almost as if Carpenter is apologizing for not resisting the cheap shot, "As much as I hate to stoop to symbolism ..."

Sherman enjoys a limited victory in the sense that he blocks Fox long enough for the alien to escape, but Sherman loses Starman and the biggest opportunity of his life. Still, the tenor of the ending, in both Mark Sherman's and Jenny Hayden's reactions, is something closely akin to the quiet confidence of *It Came from Outer Space*'s ending: "They'll be back."

Songs and Movies

Starman seems to inherit from *Elvis* and *Christine* the device of songs commenting on the action. Shortly after Starman enters Earth's atmosphere on echoes of *Voyager*'s recording of "I Can't Get No Satisfaction," Jenny Hayden is introduced to us looking at an old home movie of her and her husband Scott singing "All I Have to Do Is Dream." This device effectively limns both characters for us—they are searchers whose object is out of reach. Starman's goal eludes him because Earth turns out to be rather more hostile than *Voyager* had given him reason to expect; Jenny's dream—the return of her dead husband—is beyond any reasonable reach. Yet both Starman's dissatisfaction and Jenny's dream will be resolved in each other.

Despite the fact that it's the mid-Eighties, Jenny is watching a home *movie*, emphatically *not* a videotape. That gesture is typical of the Carpenter who put *Forbidden Planet* on a TV screen in *Halloween* in its proper widescreen frame ratio, and who continues to insist on his debt to a tradition of film. *Starman*, among the many things it is about, is yet another paean to that tradition, and it doesn't take Jenny and Starman driving among the familiar mesas of John Ford's Monument

Valley to make us aware of it. In a way, *Starman* gives us life imitating art, in its purest form: Starman learns appropriate gestures and expressions from watching film, just as he learned speech from the *Voyager* tapes. He learns about love partly from Jenny and partly from movies he sees on the motel room TV, most visibly the beach scene of *From Here to Eternity*.

Of course, *Voyager*, with its sound tapes and visual images, has prepared the alien Starman for this kind of media-based learning experience. *Voyager* has done its job as a media-educator of visitors from other worlds: "I send greetings," says Starman, trying out his newfound human voice. In reply to Jenny's many questions, he responds in a halting tone that she misinterprets as madness: "I can't get no satisfaction."

Interestingly, *Starman* is not the only science fiction film built on a *Voyager* premise. *Star Trek—The Motion Picture* was also based on *Voyager*. In that film, the exploratory satellite comes back as a potential destroyer of Earth; but in both films, *Voyager* is emblematic of the double standard of Earth (and specifically American) society: superficially welcoming ("Please come and visit our planet"), but actually profoundly xenophobic. In both films, the resolution and redemption is achieved by uniting a human being with the alien life form.

Starman taps another standard invader-movie theme as well: Starman describes his planet: "We are very civilized, but we have lost something." In *This Island Earth* and *The Man Who Fell to Earth*, to name only two of many examples, a dying civilization sends an emissary to Earth to try to gain something from the contact. It is typical of this subgenre that the visitor ends up giving more than he gets, and Starman will be no exception. But his visit is not without its little benefits for him, too, largely the result of his extraordinary adaptability.

Hitching a ride, trying a cigarette, coughing violently, and not understanding why a species would do such a thing to itself—it's all a learning experience. "You're not from around here, are you?" It's the experience of physical pleasure—Dutch apple pie, love, sex—that really renews him (suggesting that his species has forgotten how to enjoy itself, or perhaps has lost its physicality altogether): "I think I am becoming a Planet Earth Person."

But as open as he is to the terrestrial experience, Earth is, in general, no friend to strangers. This planet isn't big enough for Fox and Starman. Even Jenny, destined to love the alien, is at first no more immune to xenophobia than the rest of us. In the home movie she watches in her first scene, she says to a raccoon, "Don't be afraid ... we mean you no harm." But in moments, she's ready to shoot the Starman: She screams; he screams: The sight gag goes *E.T.* one better: In the Spielberg film, both creatures were frightened; here, Starman is responding to what he perceives to be a form of communication. And it is his response in kind—not so much the scream as the threat of violence—that finally gives him the upper hand. "We go," he says, and starts her car with a touch, demonstrating his power over terrestrial machines, and Starman and Jenny start out to drive across the country, as the Invader movie meets the Young Lovers on the Run movie.

The lover part comes slowly, of course. For all that he looks like her dead husband, he is, after all, an alien life form, and one capable of tremendous power. But his touch, the touch that influences electronic instruments, is also the touch that heals. When she gets shot in their attempt to escape from police (another tough, wounded Carpenter woman), Starman emerges from the flames carrying her in his arms in an audacious inversion of the classic Beauty and the Beast image of the invading monster carrying away the beautiful woman (*The Cabinet of Dr. Caligari*, *King Kong*, *Creature from the Black Lagoon*). Only this time he's not monstrous, and she's dead. Jack Nitzsche's majestic music—for all its uncomfortable similarity to "Five Circles" from Vangelis Papathanassiou's *Chariots of Fire* score—calls attention to the sheer *movie*-ness of the scene.

We've seen him bring a slain deer back to life. We know he can restore her, give life with a touch. This time he chooses a kiss, an evocation of the fairy tale magic of Sleeping Beauty or Snow White—and an acknowledgement of the narrative and cinematic tradition in which Carpenter's vision is rooted. He is Prince Charming as miracle-worker, and he brings Jenny back to life literally, as well as metaphorically, even as, in a sense, he brings her dead husband back to life by recreating himself in the image of Scott Hayden.

Starman stands in the honored film tradition of the ill-treated benevolent visitor from beyond. His manner, his mission, his powers, and the treatment he receives all recall Klaatu, the peace emissary, from *The Day the Earth Stood Still*; the cute little healer of *E.T.*; and another film that premiered the same week as *Starman*: John Sayles's *The Brother from Another Planet*.

Bigger than Jesus

Every benevolent, super-powered alien from the skies is to some degree a Christ figure, and that includes Superman and Santa Claus. "Environment hostile," Starman reports to his home-planet controllers, "Rendezvous third day." That "third day" business may seem a bit heavy-handed, but *Starman* is, to no small extent, a parable of the Second Coming. The "third day" is just a part of the trimming.

More to the point, the Starman is beaten by those who don't understand, or who fear, or feel threatened, and pursued by authorities who must do away with him for reasons predominantly political. (Pontius Pilate, however, gets a second chance in Mark Sherman, who doesn't fail the test.) The Starman is seen as the power of life, opposing the forces of death. The hunters, with a slain deer tied to the hood of their car, are bringers of death, to whom Starman stands in opposition, representing a race that reveres life in all its forms. This opposition exactly mirrors the tension between Sherman and Fox.

He gives life in other ways. He restores Jenny Hayden, trapped in the living death of her grief and loss, and he engenders in her a child. "I have given you a baby. ... It is a boy baby. He will be human, the baby of your husband; but he will also be my baby. He will know everything I know, and when he grows to manhood he will be a teacher." This powerful gesture points not only toward the then-unanticipated TV series spun off the movie, but also toward nothing short of the *Third* Coming. He tries to find his star in the night sky and at first makes a mistake about it, so long has he been away already, so far has he come: "No ... *there.*" Jenny beams at this new Star of Bethlehem. She wants to be able to show the baby "where his father came from." All of which, if the imagery is consistent at all, suggests that Starman is not a new Jesus after all, but something bigger. The new Jesus is only the missionary he leaves behind.

Sherman catches on. When Starman makes a reference to having to get to the Crater (the inverse of Devil's Tower in *Close Encounters of the Third Kind*) for his escape-rendezvous, Sherman asks, with a wild surmise, "Why the Crater? Have people from your world been here before?"

Starman: "Before ... yes. We are ... interested ... in your species. You are not like any other ... and you would be surprised to know how many others there are ... intelligent but savage. ... Shall I tell you what I find beautiful about you?" Sherman nods. "You are at your best when things are worst." Sherman (sure-man, as opposed to his boss, the fox) is the blessed recipient of the closest thing Starman has to a Message. Cigar and all, he epitomizes what is best about human beings.

Love Conquers All

But more than the anti-xenophobia statement that Spielberg delivered in *E.T.*, and more than the messianic myth typical of benevolent-extraterrestrial films, *Starman* is also a love story, and that's the gimmick that made it so successful and popular. It is a particularly audacious tale about the experience of falling in love with a stranger—

though this motif, too, is not without time-honored precedent in the science fiction film tradition. In a sense, *Starman* reverses the process, though not the premise, of *I Married a Monster from Outer Space*: In that remarkable film, a woman's experience of her husband taken over by an alien invader became a metaphor for the psychosexual awakening of the new bride upon the discovery of the stranger—the *monster*—inside the man she's married. In *Starman*—much as in Cocteau's haunting and erotic *La Belle et la bête*—the man is a monstrous stranger first, *then* a lover.

Jenny answers his question about love: "Love is when you care more for someone else than you do for yourself ... but it's more than that ... it's when someone is a part of you." Though Carpenter has been consistently sensitive to the value of human relationships, *Starman* is the first film in which he demonstrates conclusively that there is room, even in a vision rooted in horror and science fiction, for a belief in the saving power of love.

Nowhere is that conviction more illuminated than in the wondrous face of Karen Allen—just one more thing that *Starman* is about. Jenny Hayden's theme, "All I Have to Do Is Dream," tells us of wanting her dead husband back ("whenever I want you ..."), but it's that *face* that tells us he's dead, long before the fact is confirmed to us in words.

With *Voyager*'s orbit and Starman's entry into the atmosphere as prologue, it is really the face that opens the film and sets the situation for us, and appropriately it is the face that ends it. "Tell the baby about me," the alien says, leaving her one of the power-spheres that help him control matter and energy. He walks into a mist of particulate matter suspended in a field of reddish light. We never see his ascension into the spacecraft, or the departure of the vessel. Instead, the end of his visit is reflected wholly in the watching face of Jenny Hayden. The colored lights bathe her features, then fade to bring her back to normal color as the music swells. We end on her face, watching, and in the uncorniest way possible *glowing*—a final shot that would be the less if it were any face but *that* face; a final shot I wouldn't trade for a hundred eyes-uplifted, jaws-agape onlookers from any half dozen Steven Spielberg movies. The luminous magic of this movie is untouchable.

Intermission:

The Philadelphia Experiment and *Black Moon Rising*

In 1984 and 1985, two films appeared that were based on screenplays Carpenter had written earlier. *The Philadelphia Experiment* is a time travel film with an intriguing premise: When a Navy experiment in the Forties goes awry, two sailors are hurtled into 1984. Given the opportunity to bear witness to what the future has in store, they must find their way back, and also come to terms with their altered sense of their own identity. Carpenter's screenplay was rewritten by at least four other credited writers, and little remains of it, by his account. He is dissatisfied with what the filmmakers did with the premise:

> *The Philadelphia Experiment* was going to be a film of mine right after *The Fog*, and I became fascinated with it, but I realized that it was a story without a third act, and so I abandoned it to do *Escape from New York*. Later, the company came back and said, "We want to do *Philadelphia Experiment*, but we want to base it on your screenplay," so they bought it from me and asked me if I wanted to executive produce, and I was seduced into doing that. Awful movie.

On *Black Moon Rising*, director Harley Cokliss has a possessory credit, though the film has no perceptible authorial style. A taut action tale based on a Carpenter screenplay, the film involves a freelance trafficker in information who steals a cassette for agents of the government, then hides the cassette in a futuristic car to keep it from being co-opted by rival agents. When the car itself is stolen, the hero has to crack the stronghold of a corrupt company in order to recover his tape—and save his life. The film evinces elements of the Carpenter vision: a loner with a mission forms a loose team to tackle a big job (cf. *Escape from New York*); the mission is crossed by treacherous government agents (cf. *Starman*); the antagonism is based on a simplistic depiction of corporate evil that Carpenter would assay more broadly in *They Live*.

In a sense, *Black Moon Rising* is a revision of *Escape from New York*: the lone antihero in unwilling service to government agents who are even less principled than he is; the daring rescue mission; the tape cassette as MacGuffin; the blend of contemporary and futuristic milieus.

The involvement of at least two other screenwriters may have effectively diluted the original Carpenter contribution. *Black Moon Rising* is a good high-action film, but one that never realizes—nor even very seriously explores—the full potential of its premise.

13

It's All in the Reflexes

Big Trouble in Little China

Trying to change my image? No. I'm just trying to do good stories. You should service your story. If your story is about fear, then, certainly, you should draw from real fears. If your story is about myth, you connect the myth to the human condition.

—John Carpenter
on the set of *Big Trouble in Little China*.[1]

The attorney seems mildly threatening as he asks Egg Shen if he knows the whereabouts of one Jack Burton. Egg is unflappable. He wants to protect Jack, whom he describes in reverent tones as something like a savior. None of this makes much sense to the attorney—nor to us at this point. Egg's talk of magic and supernatural goings-on isn't alarming so much as amusing to the attorney. He's smug and condescending to this quaint Oriental, as he tells Egg he'd have to have some proof that sorcery exists. Egg obliges by whipping up a little electrical storm between his fingertips—just a little one, a few blue arcs, nothing to write home about. The attorney's jaw drops. "That was nothing," says Egg. "But that's how it always begins—very small."

Egg Shen's opening monologue tells us of a Jack Burton who has already become a legend, and now we slam into the main title sequence, Jack himself driving his semi through a driving rain and holding forth his philosophy on the CB: "A man'd hafta be some kinda fool ta think we're all alone in *this* universe." It frames the film cleverly, so that it's both the beginning of the film and the beginning of a flashback from which we never escape. In this sense, the action of *Big Trouble in Little China* seems to arise from a told story, as it did in *The Fog*, underscoring Carpenter's insistence on film as a narrative form, and suggesting once again that it is the storyteller's art that gives life to the tale.

It was inevitable that such a staunch believer in classical narrative as John Carpenter should be drawn to the fertile ground of the cliff-hanger, already ably exploited by George Lucas and Steven Spielberg in the Indiana Jones films. *Big Trouble in Little China* is a fast-paced, one-thing-after-another action thriller with roots in westerns, martial arts, and sword-and-sorcery fantasy. But the film's enormous, infectious sense of fun masks an inner seriousness; its narrative order reflects a thematic concern with Order in the Universe. For all its apparent eclecticism, its spoofery, and its lack of artistic pretension, this was the purest and most mature Carpenter film to date.

Egg's opening performance for the attorney sets the stage for the film's vision of the *order* of magic. Jack Burton, when we first see him, lives in an orderly, somewhat amusing world, until events turn surreal on him. A routine trip to the airport turns into a double kidnapping and a furious car chase. A turn down a quiet blind alley in Chinatown makes him witness to a Chinese standoff, the spectacle of ancient warriors falling from the sky, and the emergence into daylight of the long-hidden, cursed sorcerer Lo Pan. The impossible becomes the norm, and the only way Jack can adapt to the new order is by becoming *himself* a proponent of magic. He does this at the climax by allying himself with the good warriors (ragtag lot though they are) who strengthen themselves with Egg Shen's potion before going forth to do battle with the powers of darkness.

He's an odd image of primordial evil, this Lo Pan, a sort of Chinese Howard Hughes, a reclusive tycoon running both a commercial and a supernatural empire from subterranean headquarters stretching out beneath a dozen or more warehouses and restaurants of Chinatown. Now a flamboyant wizard parading mystical powers, now a doddering old fool wasting away in a wheelchair, this 2,000-year-old man has spent centuries seeking a green-eyed blonde to be his bride and victim. Now he suddenly finds himself in possession of *two* of them. He logically decides to marry both, sacrifice one, and keep the other for himself. He eagerly prepares for the ceremony that will make him young again. He's a walking anachronism, part ancient god, part contemporary iconoclast. Seeing the upstairs arrival of Gracie Law and her friends on the video security monitor, he snaps to Burton and Wang: "Now who is this? Friends of yours? This really pisses me off to no end!" Lo Pan is "a dream," in Egg's parlance, a deathless demon; but he wants only to be young and human again. Yet sympathetic as his plight is, he is never *treated* sympathetically.

Wang's Uncle Chu and Egg Shen describe Lo Pan's powers as the product of the tension between positive and negative (a good order and a bad one). They read the signs. "Finally," says Egg, "we shall bring order out of chaos"—and Carpenter characteristically punctuates the important line by cutting abruptly to the next scene.

Egg is both sage and tour guide: literally, a tour bus driver; figuratively, the Virgilian guide who takes Jack and his friends into the subterranean hell of Little China (a more classical and magical hell than that of *Escape from New York*). Egg's ways die hard: He can't resist giving Jack and the others a guided tour of the underworld. As they cross a bridge beneath which oozes a dark fluid, Egg says, "Black blood of the earth." Jack responds, "You mean oil?" Egg replies, "I mean black blood of the earth! A thousand years ago ... huge earthquakes turned the world upside down. Many normal people were killed. Many unnatural people roamed free to commit great offenses against the gods." It's an evocation once again of the world view of Nigel Kneale: the contemporary battle against an evil that gained primordial entry into the world and is only now revealing its fullest power.

Warriors who defy gravity, a monstrous centipede that eats human beings, a floating wad of flesh covered with eyes, a hairy beast skilled in abduction—these are the minions of this power, the stuff that nightmares are made of—and Lo Pan is their prophet. "Only a dream can kill a dream," pronounces Egg, and he offers the good guys a drink. The power in the flask is nothing so simple as a drug. It's the antidote to evil, the magic potion that imparts secret powers. "I took something" is Jack's only explanation for his feeling of power.

This realm of magic recalls the world of fantasy literature: Margo, the vapid reporter, says, "It's like a radical *Alice in Wonderland*." But *Big Trouble in Little China* is more like a raid on Oz. In fact, Carpenter says his own view of the film was "as a sort of Chinese *Wizard of Oz*."[2]

But it's not mainly the world of literature that the film invokes; it is, of course, the world of film. *Big Trouble in Little China* abounds in movie parody. It's like a surreal, comic, back-lot nightmare, and the targets come from both high and low. The battle of the Lords of Death against the Tong in that foggy Chinatown alleyway combines martial arts parody with a lampoon on Akira Kurosawa's color-coded warriors in *Kagemusha* and *Ran*. The hairy monster's abduction of Gracie is another off-the-wall version of the Beauty and the Beast image already parodied in *Starman*. Egg's stand against Lo Pan is a battle of the sorcerers like the one between Boris Karloff and Vincent Price at the climax of Roger Corman's *The Raven*.

As Snake Plissken in *Escape from New York*, Kurt Russell did Clint Eastwood. Here he does John Wayne—and, of course, he is doing Howard Hawks's John Wayne: the fast, overlapping dialogue, the swaggering bravado, and the combination of titanic strength and self-mocking buffoonery. In combat against the Lords of Death, Burton

Big Trouble in Little China
**The Team in Little China: Gracie Law (Kim Cattrall), Jack Burton
(Kurt Russell), Wang Chi (Dennis Dun), Miao Yin (Suzee Pai).**

finds himself bested by Wang, who doesn't need his help. Burton fires a machine gun at the ceiling ... and is knocked cold by falling plaster. Burton walks through the climactic combat with lipstick on his face, at once heroic and ridiculous.

Jack is *good* in the Hawksian sense. He gets confused, but he's never at a loss. He catches things that come hurtling his way (a bottle, a knife): "It's all in the reflexes." (And that's *Carpenter*'s timing, too, in this sure-handed, rhythmically paced film.) So it's okay if Jack is often the butt of his own joke, or the object-lesson of his own criticism, as John Wayne was darkly in *Red River* and more lightly in *Rio Bravo*. And when, in the last shot, the hairy monster reappears on Jack's truck, a last vestige of Lo Pan's world, and a suggestion that the forces of disorder are still abroad in the world, it doesn't really scare us. It's just one more bit of movie parody—Carpenter sending up the contemporaneous vogue for the socko, pop-out-and-go-boo ending that Brian De Palma virtually created in *Carrie*. That monster could hardly be a problem to our Jack. We know he can handle it. Besides, he's already paid his dues. The check's in the mail.

He's leaving without the woman, of course, like a classic Hollywood cowboy, or one of Sergio Leone's revisionist titans, or one of Akira Kurosawa's *ronin*, who must ritualistically decline the offer of a more permanent arrangement and ride away alone. Gracie virtually proposes to Jack, but like Snake Plissken, unwilling to commit to a partnership with Bob Hauck at the end of *Escape from New York*, Russell's Jack Burton says, "Lemme think about it."

There won't be much thinking. Jack Burton is moving on—*has* moved on, as we know from the beginning of the film. "We really shook the pillars of heaven, didn't we, pal?" he says to Wang, then rides into legend—in the cab of a semi. This is one cowboy who can afford his own horse.

Notes

1. Interviewed in Fourzon, Pamela, "*Big Trouble in Little China*," *Cinefantastique* 16:2, May 1986, p. 53.
2. In Taub, Eric, *Gaffers, Grips, and Best Boys*, New York: St. Martin's Press, 1987, p. 74.

14

Not What We Had in Mind

Prince of Darkness

A clear white full moon beams from a dark night sky. An old man dies in his bed, holding a tiny trunk on his lap. The camera tracks uneasily among trees. In an old handwritten diary, the words: "The Sleeper wakens. I have witnessed his stirrings." A swarm of ants covers the ground. The sun is eclipsed.

John Carpenter's vision culminates in *Prince of Darkness*. Not particularly strong with American critics, it nevertheless was enormously popular with audiences, and scored a big success in Europe, receiving the Critics' Award at the Avoriaz science fiction film festival. *Prince of Darkness* is as ambitious and inventive a reminder as any since *Psycho* that the well-crafted horror film is not a thing of the past.

Psycho, of course, was the key influence on *Halloween*. Ironically, *Halloween* and Tobe Hooper's *The Texas Chainsaw Massacre*, both films of uncommon integrity and visceral power, unintentionally introduced a decade of decline in the horror film when they spawned a host of "stalk and slash" imitations by far less skilled and visionary filmmakers.

A whole generation of young filmgoers—and film*makers*—came of age thinking of the horror film as nothing more than a gore-laden psycho-killer thriller. The spate of imitators of *The Exorcist* during the Seventies were only a variation on the psychopathic murderer theme, their demonically possessed characters doing little more than contriving the graphic, brutal deaths of those around them. Few and far between were the films that actually tapped the mythic richness of the horror genre in all its multidimensional resonance with the dark side of human hope, human fancy, human fear.

The rediscovery of the vampire myth in the early Eighties began to rehabilitate the genre—a rehabilitation in which *Prince of Darkness* takes a proud place. But through nearly two decades of work in film, John Carpenter had already been building a vision that developed and unified the broad range of traditional horror film themes and conventions.

In this deceptively simple film, tricked out as a run-of-the-mill low-budget horror movie (and mistaken for nothing more than that in many critical circles), we find an integration of all of the basic motifs that recur throughout Carpenter's films:

- the underground world of *Big Trouble in Little China*

- the Hawksian team of professionals at work against a threatening force: *Assault on Precinct 13, Dark Star, Escape from New York, The Thing, Big Trouble in Little China*—and the limited victory of the team: "We stopped it here," the priest says proudly, recalling the end of *Big Trouble in Little China* and Jack Burton's boast, "We really shook the pillars of heaven ..." (But it *is* a limited victory. "We *stopped* it here" doesn't mean we destroyed it. Evil never dies.)

- the reality of the supernatural: *Halloween, The Fog, Christine, Big Trouble in Little China*

- the extraterrestrial as a metaphor for the demonic (*The Thing*) or the messianic (*Starman*)

- the restlessly tracking subjective camera, sneaking around trees, suggesting an unseen presence: *Halloween, The Fog, The Thing, Christine*

- the resurgence of an age-old evil, waiting for its time: Michael Myers' 15 years in the hospital ("waiting ...") in *Halloween*; the avenging zombie seamen in *The Fog*; the combat against a thawed out, centuries-old alien in *The Thing*; the long-lived curse of the car in *Christine*; the eternal quest of Lo Pan in *Big Trouble in Little China*

- the reach across time: old timers with pocket watches in *The Resurrection of Broncho Billy* and *The Fog*, in which the contemporary world is haunted by images from another time; the deadline and the our world/future world comparison in *Escape from New York*; *The Thing* lain frozen all these years; the resurgence of Sahwain in *Halloween II* and *Halloween III*; *Christine* bridging the Fifties into the Eighties; *Starman* has "been here before"; Lo Pan's eternal struggle for youth in *Big Trouble in Little China*; and races against time in *Escape from New York* and *Black Moon Rising*

- an old diary provides the key to a mystery of dormant evil rising to life: *The Fog*

- the claustrophobia of being locked in and under siege: *Assault on Precinct 13*, *Halloween*, *The Fog*, *The Thing*

- a heritage of evil dating from colonial Spanish California: *The Fog*

- a powerful evil being that seemingly cannot be destroyed: Michael Myers in the *Halloween* films; the crew of the *Elizabeth Dane* in *The Fog*; *The Thing*; *Christine*; David Lo Pan in *Big Trouble in Little China*

- shape shifting and the theft of a human image as an alien being's means of establishing itself: *The Thing*, *Starman*, *Big Trouble in Little China*

- love as a saving force against evil: *Halloween*, *The Fog*, *Christine*, *Starman*, *Big Trouble in Little China* (This Christ-theme becomes explicit just after the climax, when Birack comforts Brian after Catherine has gone through the mirror and it has been shattered behind her: "She died for us.")

So Carpenter's definitive film operates to bring unity and order to his own body of work as a filmmaker. But besides integrating all of Carpenter's basic themes, *Prince of Darkness* is remarkable in its ability to encompass and sensibly interrelate most of the elemental ideas and images of horror and science fiction. In fact, you'd be hard put to find a theme or image of the horror genre that *isn't* woven into its texture. A partial catalogue would include:

- the dream, or nightmare, as gateway to another world, a world of evil that stands as a metaphor for the realm of the unconscious, which surges up while the rational mind sleeps

- the devil, and possession by the devil, as an explanation for evil, and an assertion that evil is an objective, absolute reality abroad in the world

- the evil-in-a-bottle, whose eventual escape signifies the return of the long-repressed primitive human consciousness, on whose denial is based the shaky fiction of civilized life

• psychokinesis, the power of mind over matter and, particularly, the power of the evil or possessed mind over the forces that good marshals against it

• the possessed bodies of the walking dead attacking and infecting the living, an evocation of the vampire myth that reflects humankind's simultaneous fear of and fascination with death, and gives that fascination an erotic significance (Wyndham, after being killed by the possessed mob, is reanimated to give the team members the grisly message, "Pray for death.")

• the association of the spread of evil with the spread of a communicable disease (a common theme also in the films of David Cronenberg), represented here in the passage of demonic possession by means of fluid transmitted from one body to another (The alien creature in *The Thing* also infects by liquefying—a not unlikely metaphor during the era of AIDS; and apropos the religious basis of *Prince of Darkness*, cf. *Revelation* 12:15: "And the serpent vomited water from his mouth, like a river, after the woman.")

• the association of darkness and night with evil, playing on fear of the dark, one of our most primitive impulses, and one of the most explainable: Darkness abridges eyesight, arguably human beings' most crucial sense, resulting in a feeling of weakness, even helplessness

• the fear of certain types of animals (here, maggots, worms, ants, and roaches)—another primitive impulse, relating to the threat that small, creeping things pose to large, erect human beings (This fear alone accounted for the success of dozens of giant insect and giant reptile movies during the Fifties.)

• the mark of evil: Kelly's bruise develops into hideous facial disfiguration: the mark of Cain, or of The Beast

• demonic possession as a metaphor for psychopathic violence, the loss of control over the unconscious, the upsurge of the dark side of the personality

• the mirror as an image of the distorted self, with an unknown presence lurking "behind the mirror," within the human unconscious: looking—and reaching—into the mirror as the confrontation with the dark side of the self

• the climactic battle of a few good people allied against the forces of evil, with the fate of the world hanging in the balance: nothing short of Armageddon

• the Antichrist theme: the Bride of Satan and the Terrible Child as images of the tangible challenge of evil against good for dominion over the world (The transformed Kelly's call to the dark side of the mirror—"Father ... Father ..."—echoes not only the cry of another Terrible Child, the spawn of Yog-Sothoth, in the climax of H. P. Lovecraft's great story "The Dunwich Horror," but also the bubbly cry of another lost son, seeking his father underwater, in Walt Disney's *Pinocchio*. If Kelly has become the Son, the One, the literal Prince of Darkness, whose "purpose is to bring the Father back from the dark side," if Kelly has become, in short, Antichrist, then Catherine is the opposing Christ image in the film, the one whose sacrifice saves the world, the one who "died for us." Catherine is the noblest of Carpenter's tough women, and the closest to the standard he set with Leigh in *Assault on Precinct 13*: Instead of being brought down by the forces of evil, as most of Carpenter's women eventually are, she sacrifices herself. In this sense, she wins, though her victory is a Pyrrhic one.)

Singly or in combination, these themes have characterized the horror genre from the very beginnings of imaginative art. But rarely have they occurred together, and almost never in a work that unites them into a sensible whole, rather than shambling pastiche.

The Quatermass Connection

There is, however, one memorable and crucial precedent: the 1968 film directed by Roy Ward Baker for Hammer, *Five Million Years to Earth*. Also known as *Quatermass and the Pit*, this film remains the most celebrated of the four films featuring the British scientist Bernard Quatermass, created by novelist and screenwriter Nigel Kneale, much admired by John Carpenter.

In its story, Quatermass, investigating a strange object found during construction of a London underground station, makes a chilling discovery: Five million years ago, as man-apes walked the earth, they were captured by invaders from a dying world, taken to Mars, altered to become host to the Martian consciousness, and returned to earth to become the dominant species. (Aliens-among-us is the theme of all of the Quatermass films, as it is with the television programs of Quatermass's goofy successor, Dr. Who. Kneale's Quatermass stories predate Stanley Kubrick's *2001: A Space Odyssey*, which deals more metaphysically

with a premise similar to the primordial Martian takeover of *Five Million Years to Earth*.) The Martians, who could not survive physically
on their own planet or on ours, survive in our collective consciousness.

Of course not *all* the man-apes were so altered. So, as all of them
evolved into modern man, some retained the Martian consciousness—
the collective memory of ritual killings, destruction, the death of a
planet—while others did not. These are the more susceptible, imaginative humans—and the ones who experience emotional imbalance and
destructive impulses. They were endowed with "higher intelligence—
perhaps something else," says Quatermass—a suggestion of what we
call the soul, blotted by what we might think of as Original Sin. In
short, a science fiction theodicy.

The religious theme is sustained throughout *Five Million Years to
Earth*, with the collective Martian memory seen as the source of human
myths about demons, devils, ghosts, poltergeists, ESP—the diabolical
occult in general, attributable in large part to the Martian power of energy over matter. "Myths, magic—it all came from *there*," Quatermass
recognizes. The young woman whose psychic sensitivity has been instrumental in the revelation concludes, "*We're* the Martians now."

It is daring enough to suggest that evil entered the world through
the specific, material intervention of an extraterrestrial intelligence, and
that human "superstition" is based on actual prehistoric occurrence. But
to go farther, to suggest that the product of that primordial intervention
has evolved parallel to ourselves, and that today the distinction between
good and evil, within and among individual humans, is positive and
objective, measurable by scientific technology—it is perhaps the most
audacious and relevant moral fantasy science fiction film has given us.

Human beings have always been comfortable seeing good and
evil in absolute, objective terms. The proposition of *Five Million Years
to Earth*—that the human instinct for violence and war is specifically
rooted in man's extraterrestrial origins—is enough to shake not only
20th-century relativism but also the very roots of human religious and
ethical awareness.

The truth about the Martian consciousness of man is revealed
only gradually in the film, by means of a machine that can record random mental images and play them back on a video screen ("People
don't believe anything these days unless they've seen it on the telly,"
one character comments). As the mounting evidence becomes irrefuta-
ble, the military—true to the archetypal science fiction pattern established by Hawks's and Nyby's *The Thing*—squares off against science,
though Kneale and Baker are more sympathetic to the scientists. The
tension is between men of wonder and inquiry (anthropologist Dr.
Roney and rocket scientist Professor Quatermass) on the one hand, and

Influences on John Carpenter
Above: Marion Crane (Janet Leigh) battles her dark side in Alfred
Hitchcock's *Psycho*. Below: Quatermass (Andrew Keir) and Roney
(James Donald) get more than they bargained for when they tap
the pre-human consciousness of Barbara (Barbara Shelley) in *Five
Million Years to Earth*.

men of aggression and intractability (Colonel Breen and the government minister) on the other. "Your imagination is running wild," says Breen to Professor Quatermass; whereupon Quatermass replies, "Isn't yours?"

The opening of the ancient object—a Martian vessel—coincides with the awakening of a long dormant force we could call pure evil. (A workman overcome by the horror of the vision visited upon him when he comes in contact with the vessel later calls out, "Them! Them!"— echoing the terror of the little girl who first sees the giant ants in the classic *Them!*) On the streets outside the underground station, susceptible people stand and stare, using their communal consciousness to channel the unleashed force against non-Martian-influenced fellow humans. It remains for a few strong people to marshal the powers of good against the force; and in the film's climax (which involves a church, television transmission, and an electric power line, much as the finale to *The Quatermass Experiment* did), Dr. Roney gives his life to destroy a giant demon who is a quite traditional image of the devil. In the "limited victory" image typical of the endings of the Quatermass films, Quatermass recognizes that this hard-won battle will not be the last.

John Carpenter's *Prince of Darkness* is virtually an American palimpsest on *Five Million Years to Earth*. An ancient vessel is found beneath a California mission church where it has lain for centuries, guarded by a mystic subsect of a Catholic monastic order (the "Brotherhood of Sleep," bound together by a literally shared dream), whose last guardian is the priest whose death opens the film. But has the object been confined or *protected* by the priests? A cosmic event signals the revitalization of the seven-million-year-old Force contained in the vessel, and it sends out emanations that *possess* those who come near— beginning with the highly suggestible "street schizos." Dreams—and later video screens—transmit a message sent from the distant future, warning the people of the present about the danger and the need to do something.

The radical professor of physics (and practitioner of *meta-physics*), Dr. Howard Birack, of the Doppler Institute, is enlisted by a troubled priest to put a team of scientific experts to work to find a way to analyze the Force and, with luck, to *stop* it. Birack is a kind of Chinatown Quatermass, and a breath of fresh air in the often anti-intellectual atmosphere of Carpenter's films. Birack puts together a crack squad of his best colleagues and grad students who, with their technological weaponry, ensconce themselves in the increasingly claustrophobic church to do battle with something bigger than they have ever imagined. Even the evil-in-a-bottle is small potatoes compared with the being behind the mirror, the anti-God for whom the ancient vessel is just one of many means of gaining a foothold in the world of human beings. In the end, dedication, self-sacrifice, and love are the values that defeat—or at least defer—the forces of evil.

Besides offering an objective explanation for evil, *Prince of Darkness* has a number of other features in common with *Five Million Years to Earth*. Communication of a cautionary message across time (ordinarily a science fiction, not a horror, theme) is in both films the mechanism whereby the good are prompted to take action against evil. The evil has lain dormant (in a container impervious to human interference, made of an unknown substance and of extraordinary age, "predating anything of human origin") but steadily growing in strength for millions of years, awaiting a specific moment to make itself known and take power. Brian describes it haltingly: "A life form ... self-organizing ... it's *becoming* something ... what?" Passive crowds of street people are possessed by the force and become killing mobs. And the shared dreams in *Prince of Darkness* parallel the shared brain waves in *Five Million Years to Earth*; both barely glimpsed images transmitted across time, seen dimly on a television screen like a video transmission of the mind: "This is not a dream."

Churches, abundant crucifixes, graveyards, and echoes of the occult form a matrix of the Gothic alongside high technology in *Five Million Years to Earth*. In the same way, Carpenter's film mingles the ancient and the modern, the primordial with the futuristic, interlacing traditional mythic images with its contemporary story. At one point we glimpse the traditional red-skinned, horned, pointy-tailed, pitchfork image of the devil in a Tom 'n' Jerry cartoon on one of the film's many video screens. At another, Walter casually munches an apple as he approaches a woman who has already been claimed by Satan. A crucified dove warns the good guys that the day of Antichrist is at hand. Maggots in a beggar's cup give a new dimension to a traditional image of death and corruption.

And then there's Wyndham, whose name evokes John Wyndham, the British novelist whose *The Midwich Cuckoos* and *Day of the Triffids* were both filmed during the Sixties, the former as the classic *Village of the Damned*, which Carpenter would remake in the mid-Nineties. Just before his death, as he attempts to escape from the church, Wyndham condemns the "superstitious" fears of his colleagues by calling them "caca." As his conviction fades, he emphatically repeats the word. "Caca," comes from the Greek "kako-," the prefix for evil, root word of "cacophony," conjuring the screeching of many demons, the sound of hell. Whereupon Wyndham is killed by the street schizos, only to reappear later, reanimated, warning the team to "Pray

Prince of Darkness
Above: Catherine (Lisa Blount) and Brian (Jameson Parker) are
drawn to each other. Below: Susan (Anne Howard) and Lisa (Ann
Yen) are fatally attracted to the force in the crystal cylinder.

for death," then collapsing into a bug-riddled shell of a corpse, in an image not unlike the one Nigel Kneale envisioned for the victims of Conal Cochran's mad genius in *Halloween III: Season of the Witch*.

Kneale and *Five Million Years to Earth* loom large in Carpenter's cinematic consciousness. The way the autopsy of an alien creature in the Kneale-Baker film resonates in Carpenter's *The Thing* is just one example of the influence of the film on his work. Despite the breakdown of the collaboration with Nigel Kneale on *Halloween III: Season of the Witch*, Carpenter's admiration for Kneale has remained unabated. In the early classroom lecture sequence in *Prince of Darkness*, Brian Marsh (Jameson Parker) wears a sweatshirt containing the word "Kneale."

And then there's that screenplay credit for *Prince of Darkness*: Martin Quatermass. The promotional material for the film contains the following "biographical information":

> Martin Quatermass, born in London, England, is a former physicist and brother of Bernard Quatermass, the rocket scientist who headed the British Rocket Group during the 1950s. Quatermass graduated from Kneale University with a degree in theoretical physics. *Prince of Darkness* is his first screenplay, and he assures that all the physical principles used in the story, including the ability of subatomic particles to travel backward in time, are true. Author of two novels, *Schrödinger's Revenge* and *Schwarzchild Radius*, he currently lives in Frazier Park, Calif., with his wife, Janet.

John Carpenter has acknowledged that Martin Quatermass is a pseudonym for John Carpenter.

The intellectual component of the film and its basis in particle physics evoke Kneale's vision as much as they reflect Carpenter's own recent interest in quantum mechanics. Walter and Catherine discuss the theoretical problem of Schrödinger's Cat; Professor Birack is accused of trying to mold philosophers instead of physicists. Birack references Heisenberg's Uncertainty Principle: "Our logic collapses on the subatomic level into ghosts and shadows," he remarks in the opening montage, whereupon Carpenter cuts to Brian's vision of the moon, then racks focus to the haloed leaf in front of it. The clear vision of science meets the mythic, the demonic, the unordered, unorderable reality of nature. (The collision is enhanced by the fact that Birack is played by Victor Wong, whose character Egg Shen opens *Big Trouble in Little China* with a haunting challenge to his interrogator—and, spoken straight into the camera, to *us*—that he should believe in magic and sorcery "because they're *real*," something he calmly proceeds to demonstrate.)

Early in *Prince of Darkness*, Birack lectures: "While order *does* exist in the universe, it is not at all what we had in mind." Subatomic particles behave in defiance of our concept of reality, our sense of logic, our expectation of causality. Reality is upset—as later, the fluid containing the life force of the son of anti-God flows visibly upward. "He lives," says the priest, "in the atom. He lives in all things. ... No prison can hold him now." The appearance of a new supernova (echoing *Dark Star*'s finale and *Assault on Precinct 13*'s "sunspots" parody of *The Texas Chainsaw Massacre*) accompanies the awakening of the long-dormant spirit of the evil one: Particles on the macrocosmic level behave as unpredictably as those on the microcosmic.

Mythic conjecture becomes one with scientific inquiry: Lisa, the expert in ancient languages, translates an old manuscript, learning that "the Father of Satan, a god who walked the earth before man, but has somehow passed to the dark side," sealed his own son, the Prince of Darkness, into a vessel. (Just as the Starman proved to be something bigger than the Jesus he seemed, so does the enemy in *Prince of Darkness* prove to be something bigger than the Devil himself.) The physicists become reluctantly persuaded of the real consciousness of the evil-in-a-bottle. "Faith is a hard thing to come by these days," says Brian, echoing a line from *The Thing*. As the force exerts a mighty squirt and possesses Susan with an image of impregnation, Catherine asks Brian, monitoring a video readout of the force's activities, "What's it doing?" He replies, "Reaching out ... influencing ... changing things ... moving objects by thought."

In another room, across a wide desk, Birack and the priest share a wild surmise. Birack, whose answers always take the form of suppositions, says, "Suppose there is a universal mind controlling everything ... a God willing the behavior of every subatomic particle. Now every particle has an anti-particle, its mirror image, its negative side. Maybe this universal mind resides in the mirror image instead of in our universe, as we have wanted to believe. Maybe he is anti-God, bringing darkness instead of light."

This is no mere lip service to a scientific explanation, as are the cosmic events in such films as George Romero's *Night of the Living Dead* and Tobe Hooper's *The Texas Chainsaw Massacre* and *Lifeforce* (which itself mimics *Five Million Years to Earth* to the point of borrowing whole shot compositions, but to never so meaningful a purpose as *Prince of Darkness*). It is rather the suggestion that no explanation is possible: If the ordered view of the world that we base on scientific

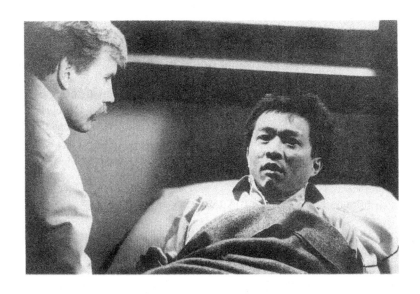

Warriors against Darkness
Above: Brian and Walter (Dennis Dun). Below: Professor Birack
(Victor Wong) and The Priest (Donald Pleasence).

observation can be *collapsed* by that same observation, then what is *not* possible? Even ideas traditionally held to be superstitious may be grounded in *reality*—as was proposed by *Five Million Years to Earth.*

The extraterrestrial origin of evil is, of course, not an excuse but another metaphor. There *is* order in the universe—but it is not at all what we had in mind: a statement of human awareness on the brink of a discovery as devastating as it is illuminating. It would be as appropriate on the lips of medieval monastics, who never dreamt that the pains they took to demonstrate the rationality of the universe would lay the foundation of a new order of thought—science—that would move human consciousness away from, not closer to, God.

Film on Film

Even if that were all, *Prince of Darkness* would be a rare horror film. But it is elevated to the rank of a minor masterpiece in that, like so many definitive films by visionary filmmakers, it transcends its genre and becomes meta-film: a movie that, in addition to its immediate material and metaphysical subject matter, is also about movies. It is filled with allusions to a plethora of film genres, conventions, and specific films. Carpenter indulges in in-jokes and cross-references throughout his films, but the deliberate references to other films in *Prince of Darkness* form a subtext of film-on-film that becomes part and parcel of Carpenter's vision, taking it beyond the world of Nigel Kneale and Bernard Quatermass by employing imagery that symbolically addresses the epistemology of film itself.

Walter (Dennis Dun, another magic-oriented icon from *Big Trouble in Little China*), gets trapped in a confessional-like closet between the room where the possessed Lisa and Susan wait for Kelly to become the host of the son of anti-God, and the room where Birack, Brian, and Catherine have barricaded themselves against the evil and try to dig through to him (recalling the dilemma of Laurie Strode in the laundry room in *Halloween,* trying to break out one way before Michael Myers breaks in another). Walter keeps his spirits up by wisecracking to the possessed women: "You seen any movies you like?"

The window through which he watches them is like a confessional screen, and that's just one of many film-related visual puns with which *Prince of Darkness* is laced. The church in which the scientist-philosophers face the evil force is called St. Godard's. Worms squirming against a window are watched as yet another crypto-filmic image. Such things don't happen by accident in a film made by a writer-director with a profound sense of cinematic tradition. Neither do the abundant references and similarities to other films:

• the stairsteps outside the church, shot from a low angle in a composition that recalls the most famous shot from *The Exorcist*—a film also echoed when the maggot-bearing female street schizo speaks with the throaty voice of a (male?) demon

• the street schizos, a threatening, mindless crowd lurching along in groups like George Romero's Living Dead

• a Tom 'n' Jerry cartoon glimpsed on a TV screen

• St. Godard's as a carefully guarded doorway to another world, as in *The Sentinel*

• transmitting a message mentally across time in an effort to save the people of present Earth through a saving act of love, recalling not only *Five Million Years to Earth*, but also Chris Marker's powerful short film *La Jetée*

• insects and vermin as emblems of the upsurge of a corrosive force, as in David Lynch's *Blue Velvet* and David Cronenberg's *The Fly*, as well as in the horrific ancient-modern curse Kneale envisioned for *Halloween III*

• the commingling of scientific technology and terminology, and science fiction themes, with demons out of Gothic horror, as in *Alien*, *Poltergeist* and *Lifeforce*—and, of course, the Quatermass films

• Lisa repeatedly keying the message "I LIVE!" on a computer terminal—an image of possession employing the same technique as the pages and pages of "All work and no play" meticulously typed by Jack Torrance as his mind crumbles in Stanley Kubrick's *The Shining*

• Kelly's disfiguring marks as signs of possession by an alien force, as in *Invaders from Mars* and *Quatermass II* (*Enemy from Space*)

• Calder, possessed, singing "Amazing Grace" (laughing ironically as he reaches the lines "I once was lost, but now I'm ..." and stopping there to cut his own throat with a broken stick of wood)—the spiritual associated with the downbeat finale to Philip Kaufman's remake of *Invasion of the Body Snatchers*, in which the alien possessors of the world finally get *everybody*

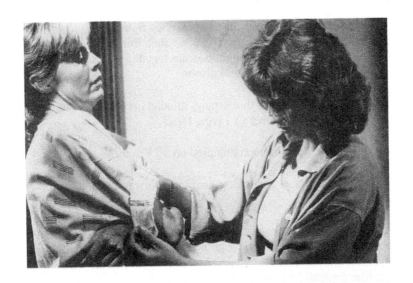

Prince of Darkness

The world of *Prince of Darkness* is filled with traditional symbols of the battle between good and evil. Facing page: Above: Catherine (Lisa Blount, right) examines the bruise that Kelly (Susan Blanchard) bears like a mark of Cain. Below: Brian (Jameson Parker) among the icons and crucifixes adorning the old church.

This page: Above, left: The Priest (Donald Pleasence) with the ancient box and key. Above, right: Mystic tools, ancient and modern: Brian (Jameson Parker) with cards and computer.

• pinning the conventional horror story to a scientific and philosophical vision that is forced to become theological, as in William
Peter Blatty's intriguing, little-seen *The Ninth Configuration* (also
known as *Twinkle, Twinkle, "Killer" Kane*)

The message from the future is "seen" in dreams as a wavy video
transmission, a kind of filmed image that links the world of the screen
with the world of dreams—the oldest and still the most valid observation about the way film works on the human unconscious. The cautionary dream-message suggests that film may be our salvation ("*Saint
Godard*"). But it is also the thinnest of protective layers between our
comfortable, complacent sense of reality, and the dark side: In the climax of the film, the world beyond is seen in the traditional image of the
other side of the mirror.

Though not without its underpinnings in the world of literature
and art, the mirror image in film is frequently a metaphor for the movie
screen itself, a layer of illusion through which a greater reality breaks, a
layer both protective and expressive, which shows us images that
stimulate our fancies even as they reflect our realities. Beyond it lies a
darkness that we recognize as the darkness of the movie theatre, but
also of something more.

Everyone knows that a broken mirror means bad luck. In *Prince
of Darkness*, while the shattering of that mirror (an echo of the shattering of the lens-like windows of Leigh Michaels's apartment in *Someone's Watching Me!*) closes the door through which evil enters our
world, it also traps human consciousness in one world or the other,
breaking the uneasy but vital link between the conscious and the unconscious.

By the end of the film, communication between the worlds is
once more confined to dimly glimpsed dream images. Brian receives a
new dream-message showing Catherine in the world beyond, coming
through the portals previously transgressed by the dark Father, then
wakes to a hallucination of a demon Catherine in bed beside him. He
reaches out to the mirror, wondering about that link, his mind alive
with possibilities. But Carpenter shoots him straight on, so he's reaching out to *us*, as if to penetrate the literal screen on which we are watching *Prince of Darkness*.

Then, just as we get it, just as the point is driven home, cut to profile: Brian's hand reaches out toward its own reflection ... if it *is* a reflection ... and just before flesh contacts screen, just before fingertips
touch anti-fingertips, Carpenter cuts away ... to darkness.

15

Maybe They've Been with Us All Along

They Live

In a short story called "The Ghost Maker," in the *New York Times* of Halloween 1988, John Carpenter fused science fiction with Gothic horror as he had done in *Prince of Darkness*. Parodying both Edgar Allan Poe and H. P. Lovecraft (the mad scientist in the piece is named Howard Necron, hearkening up H. P. Lovecraft's fabled book *The Necronomicon*), Carpenter combines the observational paradox of Schrödinger's Cat with the horror of premature burial and confrontation with one's other self. The short tale climaxes, as *Prince of Darkness* did, with a mirror image.

Four days later, *They Live* opened—as *un*Gothic a film as could be imagined.

At first look, *They Live* is as direct and simplistic as *Prince of Darkness* is subtle and complex. It's more an urban adventure like *Escape from New York* or *Big Trouble in Little China* than a vision of urban horror like *Prince of Darkness*; but its comic book simplicity masks a network of deeply interlacing, sometimes conflicting, ideas and ideologies.

The film's jumping off point is the opposite of the observer-altered reality of Heisenberg and Schrödinger that informed *Prince of Darkness*. It is instead a sender-controlled reality that stresses not the viewer's subjectivity but his victimization by a manipulating force. Where Hitchcock and De Palma focused on the viewer's moral responsibility for what is viewed—as evidenced in the moral ambiguity of *Rear Window* and *Sisters*—Carpenter sees the dilemma of the observer as that of one who cannot trust his senses *not* because they are shaped by his own subjectivity but because they are being shaped by someone (or something) *else*. Carpenter's viewer is an unwilling participant in turning truth into lies, certainty into unknowability.

The spin that Carpenter puts on the observer-controlled reality notion in *They Live* is not an especially new one: Through mass mind control, the alien invaders have been able to alter the perception of their unwitting hosts. It's Orwell's "Freedom Is Slavery," filtered through the alien-induced hypnosis of such films as *It Came from Outer Space*, *Invaders from Mars*, *Invasion of the Body Snatchers*, *I Married a Monster from Outer Space*, *Quatermass II*, and *Village of the Damned*.

Besides echoing motifs from these by-now-familiar Carpenter referents, *They Live*, like *Prince of Darkness*, also rings changes on a variety of Carpenter's own continuing themes: the Hawksian team combating a crypto-political evil; the role of media-assisted (or media-*controlled*) perception in the human idea of self; electronic transmissions as messages from beyond; invasions from space; invasions from *time*; the indistinguishability of the invader from his prey (*The Thing*, *Starman*); contemporary urban psychosis (*Assault on Precinct 13*, *Someone's Watching Me!*, *Escape from New York*, *Prince of Darkness*); and what might be termed California horror (*The Fog, Prince of Darkness, Big Trouble in Little China*).

They Live is more insistently placed in a socioeconomic context than any other Carpenter film. Its hero, ominously named Nada (an echo of the nameless or pseudonymous loners of the spaghetti westerns), is an itinerant worker who moves from short-term job to unemployment line to food bank. With little information on his background, we are asked to accept him not as a dropout but as a victim of the economic system (which is a bit of a stretch). "Computer error," he learns tersely; "Food stamp program canceled." At the unemployment line: "We have nothing for you." He seeks out the hospitality of the ironically named Justiceville, haven for the homeless, a combination tent colony and soup kitchen. To get a job, even for a short time, he finds he needs a union card, and has to put up with the dehumanizing scolding of a tyrannical foreman.

None of this, however, has turned him against the System: "I believe in America," he tells coworker Frank. "I follow the rules ... everybody's got their own hard times these days." Frank, by contrast, has run out of patience—possibly because he has too willingly been the System's victim: Tellingly, *he* is the one who keeps telling Nada to do nothing, to stay out of trouble, toe the line, and he engages in a ridiculously long fistfight just to avoid listening to what Nada has to tell him.

The fact that Frank is black is but one element of a conspicuous multiethnic focus that recalls *Assault on Precinct 13, The Thing, Big Trouble in Little China*, and *Prince of Darkness*. The Asian presence of the latter two films echoes that of the futuristic L.A. of Ridley Scott's *Blade Runner*—though in all of these films, that presence seems more a cultural phenomenon than an economic one, while the black presence, by contrast, deliberately invokes socioeconomic deprivation. The roots of that deprivation are suggested by the film's breathtaking architec-

They Live
Nada (Roddy Piper) teaches Frank (Keith David) how to see.

tural imagery: a small, humble, Spanish-style church dominated by the sterile skyscrapers of downtown L.A.—as potent an image as any imaginable of the heritage of economic oppression from the imperialist colonial days to the liberal capitalism of the present.

That present is described by Carpenter in *They Live* as something bordering on a police state. The law enforcement presence is always ominous and menacing, as it was in the opening massacre in *Assault on Precinct 13* and throughout *Escape from New York* and *Starman*. The film's most compelling and haunting sequence, the brutal bulldozers-and-helicopters night raid on Justiceville, is rivetingly photographed and cut, combining the firelit dark of *Escape from New York* with the fury of outright assault. Carpenter turns again to the helicopter attack, an image of threat that he drew on in *Escape from New York* and later in the climax of *Starman*, and which may well be rooted in the helicopters of the opening scene of *It Came from Outer Space*.

In its moral-equivalent-of-war polarization of oppressors and oppressed, *They Live* apotheosizes Carpenter's affinity for the working class hero, which he had flirted with in the hillbilly heroics of *Elvis*, and effectively parodied in *Escape from New York* and *Big Trouble in Little China*. The atmosphere is further served by Carpenter's music, which taps the black urban blues tradition in its rhythms and its use of harmonica and guitar. The film's street people are an extension of the recognition in *Prince of Darkness* that in the walking mentally ill ("street schizos") we see the alienation and disaffection that are the *true* horrors of our age. But in *They Live*, street people are treated more as the economically downtrodden than as the products of urban dehumanization and crowding psychosis; and they're more sympathetic than scary.

What is going on in all this? "Imagine," Carpenter said of the film, "that the Reagan Revolution is run by aliens from outer space."[1] Is the two-income terror of the yuppie ghouls who turn out to be behind the economic inequity of contemporary America a metaphor for Reaganism? Or is Reaganism itself merely a handy metaphor for the alien horror that Carpenter sees as arising to possess us from within our very selves?

"I think it's a real bad time in America, a real Nazi time,"[2] Carpenter said in an interview. But that overstates the case, tending to trivialize the enormity of what the Nazis did, rather than to say anything meaningful about a perceived failure of Reaganomics. Similarly, the film's characterization of the enemy as "free enterprisers" seems a dangerously simplistic linking of police state fascism to the very consumer-based capitalism that, after all, makes filmmaking (among other things) possible. But Carpenter's use of invader-genre convention and the metaphor of eyesight in *They Live* suggests that the writer-director has not overlooked the irony of his premise.

The science fiction films of the Fifties were characterized by crypto-Communist invaders who threatened the very free enterprise and individual freedom of thought that the United States has stood for for more than two centuries. But since the Sixties, science fiction film has consistently centered on the resistance of good-guy rebels against a repressive, neofascist "empire" that is a thin metaphor for the United States itself. If filmmakers assaying science fiction are no longer inclined to make films in which the established government is not oppressive but benevolent and the *rebels* are the threat, it can only be because some interior self-loathing makes us cheer for those who would destroy the very society we have built in our own image—perhaps another manifestation of Robin Wood's Return of the Repressed.

Or is it simpler than all that? Is it just our indomitable wish to root for the underdog, without regard to meaningful political conviction? Certainly *They Live* reverses the metaphor that Tony Williams and Robin Wood found so offensively reactionary in *Assault on Precinct 13*: The police and the authorities have become the besieging menace; the street people are the victims. But the evolution of the comic book reactionism of *Assault on Precinct 13* into the comic book radicalism of *They Live* is not a midlife radicalization but only a change of imagery in a continuing vision. The message is still that the real enemy is within ourselves and that salvation lies not in a system of thought, belief, or government, but in a pattern of individual heroic action.

Because there's no perceivable malevolence in the aliens' characters or personalities (which is precisely why you can't tell them from us), the threat of the takeover never seems very serious. There's no larger agenda here. If the aliens are successful, our lives are not changed; we simply go on as we have been. Only *resistance* will change our lives utterly ... and most folks don't *like* change. That's why the liberalism of the film fails to speak to today's audience very effectively. We might fight to prevent negative change, to keep ourselves from being unhappy, but we won't fight to bring about positive change, at least not the kind of change that means sloughing off comfortable ways and *working* for something better. So in Carpenter's dystopia à la *Brave New World*—a *1984* with Big Brother as space invader, a *V* with a more economically grounded vision: The enemy is *us*.

If the film's purpose were purely political, Nada's awakening would be more effective, moving, and meaningful if he were the truly

conforming American that his early dialogue suggests, instead of a
transient dropout with a record (like Snake Plissken—our last hope,
maybe, but not, this time, one of our best). As it is, Nada's one-man
crusade—a zombie shoot à la George Romero—is that of a good-
hearted, not very thoughtful avenger. He takes care to shoot only Them,
not Us, and does so with the moral neutrality and self-satisfied glee of a
bounty killer in a spaghetti western. He doesn't realize until Holly betrays him at the climax that They get their strongest support from those
of Us who are willing to work with Them.

Holly Thompson—one of us, one of them, one of us, one of
them—betrays by subterfuge and deception. But the more prevalent
pattern of betrayal in the film is betrayal by persuasion. Drifter, a former transient, now decked out in tuxedo and working with Them,
though not *one* of Them, stupidly shows Nada and Frank around the
aliens' corporate stronghold: "It's business, that's all it is ... There's no
more countries ... no more good guys ... we all sell out every day." He
tries to persuade Frank and Nada to join up, just as the taken-over
townspeople of Santa Mira in *Invasion of the Body Snatchers* try to
persuade their old friends to give in to the invading force ... by going to
sleep.

That sleep is such a critical metaphor in *They Live* is another indication that the message goes to the human consciousness, not to the
political system. On the church wall we spy graffiti: "They Live ... We
Sleep." Non-vigilant human unconsciousness is identified as the
mechanism whereby we are brought low. Our *comfort* is our greatest
vulnerability—which puts the "us" of *They Live* in the same class as the
victims of Michael Myers, too distracted by their own self-indulgence
to look out for the unexpected.

In Justiceville, a transient (Drifter, before his conversion) speaks
of an outbreak of violence in San Anselmo, reported on the television:
"Whole lotta people goin' crazy over some nutty dream they just had."
It's the sleep of reason bringing forth monsters again. Egg Shen described Lo Pan as a dream in *Big Trouble in Little China*, and recog-
nized that "only a dream can kill a dream." In *They Live*, as in *Prince of
Darkness*, dreamlike broadcast transmissions, shot directly to the viewers' unconscious, seek to waken the dreamer to the nightmare of his
own reality. But there is irony here, because in *They Live* a sustained
TV transmission is also the very weapon that the alien invaders use to
subdue us and keep us subdued. As this ambivalent view of the power
of visual communication might suggest, *They Live* is finally a more
potent comment on control by media than on political ideology.

Fully aware of its assault on the reliability of perception, *They
Live* begins by tricking the viewer's eye in its very opening shot. The

film's title becomes a cautionary slogan spray-painted in graffiti (by the hand of John Carpenter); then a leftward movement fools us into taking for a tracking shot what is actually the motion of a departing train. The train moves away to reveal the backpacked transient who becomes the film's hero, in one of Carpenter's many stylistic nods to the western films of Sergio Leone. Having given us an object lesson in the untrustworthiness of our own vision, the film proceeds to elaborate on the metaphor of sight.

Carpenter's notion of the subjectivity of perception being imposed from without, of the viewer being forced to see a different reality than the one that's there, was first treated in *Eyes of Laura Mars*, which combined the problem of perception with the idea of clairvoyance to derive a disturbing metaphor for the artist's vision. The relationship between perception and perpetration was pursued in the visual imagery of *Someone's Watching Me!* and in the subjective camera and chiaroscuro frame composition of *Halloween.*

In *They Live*, ordinary spectacles serve the function of the telescope in *Someone's Watching Me!*—to enhance and clarify the sense of sight, to wake up the viewer to a reality of which he has been unconscious, or at least complacent. Sleep, of course, is not only a surrendering of the conscious will to the unconscious, but also a closing of the eyes and an embrace of the deception of dreams. The blind street-preacher, a mainstay of the resistance movement, inhabits the early part of the film like some modern-day Teiresias, "seeing" in his blindness what the sighted cannot suspect. Putting on the glasses is analogous to awakening from sleep: "How long have they been there?" asks Frank, when Nada finally gets him to look through the truth-lenses. The underlying reality is both black-and-white and print-based: Signs convey subliminal behavior-controlling messages to the unsuspecting viewers.

Only in a filmmaker's vision would monochrome be a code for the real, color for deceptive fantasy. The same imagery was used in *The Wizard of Oz*, making all the more triumphant (or puzzling, depending on your point of view) Dorothy's final preference for dusty-gray Kansas over the lush, unreal, beguiling colors of magical Oz. Somebody in the secret night meeting of the resistance group in *They Live* is overheard to say "colorizing"—a film-on-film joke that, upon reflection, is jarring: The argument against colorization is that it takes beauty and turns it into garishness; but the aliens' colorization takes a harsh reality and glosses it into an acceptable, unquestioned world, promoting sleep. Sleep, of course, was the metaphor of *The Wizard of Oz*, too, Dorothy's trip having turned out to be a dream. The underlying pattern of both films, then, is color/pleasant/fantasy vs. black-and-white/painful/reality.

There are more layers of irony here, however: The black-and-white of *They Live* is not true monochrome, but color film from which the color has been bled in processing. In the objective sequences of the film, what *we* see is also in color, suggesting that our own perception remains deceived even where Nada's and Frank's is not. In a world where seeing ("We've got one that can see," the alien cop says into his wrist-radio) is a synonym for knowing, we're being told that we know nothing. Or at least that we know only what some outside power wants to let us know, which amounts to the same thing.

One of the most striking images in *They Live* underscores this conviction: a man watching a store-window television—spellbound, mesmerized, almost, it appears, lobotomized. The images are the typical montage of American icons commonly shown with the playing of the national anthem at the end of the broadcast day—Mt. Rushmore, a dancing Indian, a bald eagle—not your dazzling TV spectacle, but it has transfixed this guy. Nada glimpses another man entranced by a TV in a rooming house: onscreen, a glamorous soap opera heroine expounds her dream of a really nice lifestyle in which "All I ever have to do is be famous." This is another Carpenter in-joke: The cameo is played by Susan Blanchard, whose character Kelly was taken over by the evil force in *Prince of Darkness*, with distinctly un-glamorous results. But the *Prince of Darkness* reference also makes the shot a kind of cinematic shorthand to link the idea of broadcast suggestion with demonic possession.

The rebels fight the aliens with the aliens' own weapons: A TV commercial for a fingernail product is interrupted by the hackers' garbled broadcast, warning, "Our impulses are being redirected. We are living in an artificially induced state of consciousness that resembles sleep ... signals being sent from ... we are their unwitting accomplices." To the moviegoer watching *They Live*, an important element of the "enemy-is-us" warning may be that the enemy is TV. That recognition may finally justify the film's least justifiable sequence, the protracted fistfight between Nada and Frank as a parody on the broadly theatrical world of television wrestling, from which the film's star, Roddy Piper, emerged. But if a swipe at the numbing effect of television is intended here, it's the sublimest irony of all, for most of the people who see *They Live* will watch it at home on their VCRs.

Film on Film

Though it's a color film, *They Live* is black and white in the memory, and not only because of the black-and-white real world that is masked by the aliens' transmissions. It is also because *They Live*, more than any other Carpenter film, invokes the mood and spirit of so many B-films of the Fifties about invaders, films that adapted the shadowy monochromes of film noir to the purpose of limning the age-old battle of good vs. evil—films with wisecracking heroes and prolonged fist-fights reminiscent of the Saturday matinee serials.

After the hackers' interruption of their TV show, the residents of Justiceville settle back to watching regular programming, despite the headaches induced by the transmission. What they're watching is *The Monolith Monsters*, a late Fifties science fiction film produced and written by Jack Arnold, in which crystalline formations in the desert take on lifelike properties, grow, and move toward the nearby town, crushing or petrifying all in their path. *The Monolith Monsters* was one of a multitude of Fifties films on the theme of invaders threatening the complacent American lifestyle. Sometimes the invaders were crypto-Communists, metaphors for the then-perceived "Red Menace" and "Yellow Peril." Sometimes, as in most of Arnold's films, they were symbolic of the revenge of Nature, outraged by human incursions into things they were not meant to know (namely, the unleashing of atomic energy). And sometimes, as in *Invasion of the Body Snatchers*, the invaders were emblematic of our own complacency and conformity, which may have resulted in prosperity and power but which yielded, on the individual level, the very opposite of life.

The cover-up of a secret invasion was a key metaphor of many science fiction films of the Fifties and early Sixties, on which Carpenter cut his teeth. In *Quatermass II*, which continues to exert a strong influence over his work, giant space creatures are kept hidden in ammonia-atmosphered domes, and a "research station" in the quiet British countryside is actually a factory for fabricating food for the beasts. But *Invasion of the Body Snatchers,* in which sleep was the mechanism by which the aliens took over human beings, seems to have had the profoundest influence on *They Live*.

As evidenced in *Starman*, the *benevolent* invader movie has inevitable associations with the myth of divine intercession into human affairs. The malevolent invader, by contrast, though occasionally associated with the metaphysics of evil (as in *Five Million Years to Earth* and *Prince of Darkness*) is more commonly emblematic of a sociopolitical threat. The invaders of the Fifties—the giant ants of *Them!*, the seed pods of *Invasion of the Body Snatchers*, the parasites of *Invaders from Mars*—all represent imperialist, colonizing, mind-controlling forces not unlike the popular impression of Soviet Communists in the American consciousness of that era, who exploit our lack of vigilance to gain their foothold.

174 *Order in the Universe*

The hunter ... and his prey
Facing page: Alien-hunter Nada (Roddy Piper). Above: The invader and the Real World.

In *They Live*, as in Carpenter collaborator (*Big Trouble in Little China*) W. D. Richter's droll *Adventures of Buckaroo Banzai*, the political menace is located not in a threat to our way of life, but in our way of life itself—a vision at least superficially consistent with Robin Wood's Return of the Repressed. Under the guise of blaming some outside force for the inherent evils of modern life, Carpenter is pointing the accusing finger back at us, fusing the paranoia of the Communist invader movies of the Fifties with the flight from responsibility represented by the "Devil made me do it" horror films of the Seventies.

True to this uneasy marriage of the viewpoints of two different eras, *They Live* plays like *Invasion of the Body Snatchers* with a George Romero solution. Nada's investigation and discovery evoke the inward-turning sense of doom of the film noir; his raid on the aliens' broadcasting station stronghold is more like *Dawn of the Dead*, or the video game Hogan's Alley.

The tough-guy-with-a-gun solution is, of course, also a legacy of the film noir and, before that, the western. In that sense, the contemporary cowboy Nada is an heir of the neo-western heroes of *Assault on Precinct 13*, *Escape from New York*, and *Big Trouble in Little China*, in all of which we see the formation of a Hawksian team. In *They Live* the formation of the team is abortive: Nada, Frank, and a handful of others become the nucleus of a team that is scattered in a night gunfight before it has had a chance to mount its insurgency. The quick elimination of the team keeps the film insistently on the level of the heroism of the lone individual, Nada.

The Dominion of Evil

Nada's awakening to a perception of the realities underlying the socioeconomic evils of the age engenders an analogous existential awakening to self. At one startling moment in this generally broad, half-serious, comic book of a film, he suddenly tells Frank about his childhood at the hands of an abusive father. Nada's story recalls the abused or at least misunderstood youngster of *The Resurrection of Broncho Billy*, Bishop's reminiscence of his father's having delivered him to a police station to be taught a lesson in *Assault on Precinct 13*, and children menaced by their peers and their environment, if not by their parents, in *Halloween*, *Elvis*, and *Christine*.

Nada's revelation of his abused childhood prompts Frank to say, "Maybe they've been with us all along ..." and this is a pivotal intimation in the film. It all but equates the aliens to Nigel Kneale's devilish Martians in *Five Million Years to Earth* (or, for that matter, Satan and his Father in *Prince of Darkness*): architects of pure evil, sowing dis-

cord, enjoying seeing humans hurt one another. But again, the world of
They Live differs in one crucial respect from that of Kneale and of
Prince of Darkness: In the world described in *They Live*, we are collaborators in our own subversion. The aliens are, again, a mirror for
ourselves.

The primordial battle of good vs. evil is conjured up by the film's
play with religious imagery. The blind preacher stands in a Carpenter
tradition of tormented priests: *The Fog*'s Father Malone; the priest who
writes the diary in *Prince of Darkness* as well as the priest who discovers it. The African Episcopal Free Church, which becomes the first
beachhead of the revolution of humankind against possession by an
alien force, recalls the churches that become battlefields in *The Fog* and
Prince of Darkness. (The abandoned church converted to extra-
religious purposes was also a key image in Leone's *For a Few Dollars
More*, a film from which Carpenter has derived many of his motifs and
stylistic gestures.) Carpenter's use of these images of spiritual combat
suggests that the film's socioeconomic elements are relatively small
potatoes compared with what's really at stake.

One traditional mythic-religious motif of evil that is *uncharacter-
istic* of Carpenter also appears in *They Live* and in no other Carpenter
film: the image of the treacherous woman. Holly Thompson is in many
ways the most surprising of Carpenter's women. She's strong and resourceful, but never mannish and, in fact, quite forthcoming in her own
sexuality. She stands in Carpenter's Hawks-influenced tradition of
tough, sexy women: Leigh in *Assault on Precinct 13*; Laurie in *Halloween*; Leigh and Sophie in *Someone's Watching Me!*, Stevie and
Elizabeth in *The Fog*; Maggie in *Escape from New York*; arguably, the
female-voiced computers in *Dark Star* and *The Thing*; Christine but *not*
Leigh in *Christine*; Jenny Hayden in *Starman*; Gracie Law in *Big
Trouble in Little China*; and Catherine Danforth in *Prince of Darkness*.
Holly is, of course, a tough woman with a difference: She turns bad on
us and *stays* bad, unrepentantly. She finally has more in common with
Christine than with Catherine, Maggie, or any of the Leighs.

Holly, having kept us guessing throughout the film, turns out to
be one of Them after all. She shoots Frank and follows Nada to the
roof. Holly and Nada, gun to gun: a potently *noir*ish situation: love and
death, sexuality and self-interest. Nada shoots her.

The decision is the right one and gives him just enough time to
destroy the aliens' signal device. It's hard, of course, to believe that an
alien takeover of these proportions has only one such signal device.
What if the people who learned the truth didn't happen to be just a few
blocks away, but in, say, Brussels? The plot-full-of-holes story idea
puts *They Live* firmly in the realm of the Big Dumb Movie, the comic-

book-inspired serials and programmers of the Fifties that are the film's most solid stylistic and narrative precedent.

In his act of heroism, Nada is shot down—and from a helicopter, ever the image of threat and evil in Carpenter's films. The rooftop climax recalls the abortive escape attempt in *Escape from New York*, but here, even though the protagonist is killed, we have more of a sense of victory than in the dark irony and emptiness of Snake Plissken's last gambit.

It's a limited victory, of course, the most you can expect in the war against evil: We stopped them here, but we know other battles await. Few film directors have taken on so directly and so consistently the battle of good vs. evil. Roman Polanski alone comes to mind as one who has so relentlessly pursued the high-stakes combat toward a universal moral order. But while Polanski's characters finally find themselves the unwitting agents of the very evil they seek to destroy, Carpenter's characters recognize that they can never defeat the evil, only contain it, and in their efforts to do so the best of them remain untainted by it.

Nada dies, but the blow against the empire has been struck. The cloaking device is disabled. Everywhere, earth people begin seeing the aliens for what they really are (though all we can tell about them by looking is that they're ugly), and all is changed utterly. They show up on TV screens—one of them on a talk show, decrying the violence of filmmakers like George Romero and John Carpenter who don't know where to stop—an audacious suggestion that these directors' films are themselves a kind of saving force in a world oppressed.

They show up, too, in conjugal beds. The last shot, of a naked couple making love, and the human woman suddenly seeing for the first time the true face of her alien lover, is a clever sight gag of an ending. But it also makes us wonder about the extent to which the aliens have already inbred with earth people, and recognize that in the future, it may be even *harder* to tell them from us. So we are back to the Nigel Kneale vision that, maybe, we never left in the first place. Maybe we *are* the Martians, after all. It is not we, but They, who live. It may still be a kind of Order, but it's not at all what we had in mind.

Notes

1. In Fischer, Dennis, "John Carpenter's *They Live*," *Cinefantastique* 19:1/2, January 1989, p. 12.
2. In Fischer, "John Carpenter's *They Live*," p. 124.

16

I Can't Believe I Survived That

Notes from a Talk with John Carpenter

On Learning How to Make Movies

Editing movies gives you a lot of perspective on what you can get away with as a director—what you need to tell a story. I think any director who has ever edited a movie is helped enormously. I think it's like learning the camera. You have to learn all the aspects of filmmaking in order to be able to tell a story, at least from my point of view. If you understand the camera and how it works and what you can do with it, and then you understand editing—the process of editing is what you can do to manipulate the film you shot—and then you understand sound mixing, and so on, I think you become a more rounded director.

I've done a lot of different jobs because I was trained at the University of Southern California in film school where a lot of times we did *everything* because we just didn't have any money. I used to have to take responsibility for everything we did—often setting up a camera, then shooting it, directing it, then cutting it, doing the music. And it's a handy way of fighting back, often, because there's a tyranny of professional experts who will come along and tell you what you can or can't do. But, if you *know* how to do it, you can tell them, "No way, pal."

On Storyboarding and Shooting Techniques

I used to storyboard a lot, and on some complicated special effects I think it's really the only way—to sit down and have everybody talk about it. In *Escape From New York* we storyboarded all the special effects extensively so that we could all sit down and say, "Here's what we need. Okay, we need this shot, this shot, this shot, and this shot. And here's what it should look like."

But in general, as I get older in my career and make more and more movies, I storyboard less and less. That's just because after a while you get some kind of fixed image in your mind of what it should look like, and then you arrive on the set and you try to jam it into that image, often destroying the life of a scene. And I also notice a lot of movies that look like they're all storyboarded—every shot looks like it's been drawn out—and it just gets kind of tiresome. It has much more to do with computers than with feeling.

I'm much more influenced by Howard Hawks than, say, the Hitchcock storyboard designing stuff. I'm much more, "Let's stand over here and photograph it from this particular angle." I use certain visual effects, but they don't need to be drawn out. You don't really draw a dolly shot. You know, you can draw the beginning and the end, but it's really like drawing a close-up of a person as well. "Let's get on the set and see what happens"—that's my basic approach.

On Quantum Mechanics and the Art of Observation

In some basic way, according to quantum mechanics, it's not possible for us to be impartial observers. We are participants in reality because we create it as we watch it. In quantum mechanics, this is on a very literal level, and it has to do with wave particle duality and what an object of matter is made up of. Sometimes it's one thing, and sometimes it's another.

The more you get into physics, the more bizarre it gets. I did a lot of studying after *Big Trouble in Little China*; I got into physics pretty heavily, especially quantum mechanics, and read a lot of books on it, and felt that there was something in the philosophy of quantum mechanics that would work in a horror film like *Prince of Darkness*— *Prince of Darkness* being a culmination for me of all the work I'd done in horror movies and of all the horror movies that I've seen, relating them also to science fiction. And I think it finally comes out to *Five Million Years to Earth*, which was the first movie that I know of that dealt with this kind of science fiction horror—this explanation for the occult. I did it on a little bit different basis, the devil coming alive in a church, bringing his father, the anti-God, back from the mirror world, which relates again to quantum mechanics and particle physics in terms of antimatter, reverse world.

But I could only dress up the story of *Prince of Darkness* with particle physics. I really couldn't show what it would be like. I'd love to do that someday, and have a character in a movie who has all the characteristics of the wave in particle physics. It would be really interesting to do. On the other hand, I realize that the audience and most of the public out there has no idea about the Uncertainty Principle. And if they do have an idea about it, they reject it because it's too complicated. You always run into a problem when you're dealing with something like this. It reminds me a lot of the beginning of *Casablanca* when you show a map and have a narrator tell you what's going on in this particular section of the world. You don't necessarily have to do that in a Vietnam story—you *know* you're in Vietnam, and here comes the story.

It's an old-fashioned way of dealing with the lowest common denominator, which is people who don't know anything about where Casablanca is, or what particle physics is, or what the Ark of the Covenant is. And you always run into that if you're going to deal with something that's not common knowledge among the audience like *Love Story*. I have run into those scenes myself, and it's very difficult. I think Nigel Kneale did exposition pretty well in his Quatermass movies. His characters would talk, but they wouldn't insult each other by saying things that the other already knew. And they would come to a conclusion by piecing together evidence. Those movies were always to me a scientific, Sherlock Holmes kind of situation where you had a Watson character who was a little less educated than Holmes: "I don't get it, what are you getting at, Holmes?" ... "I'm getting at this." And that seems to be what Quatermass did pretty well.

On Film Genres

I'd love to do a musical. You know I love westerns because I disguise a lot of my films. They're really westerns underneath. I love all genres of movies—I grew up with them. I was particularly tickled with martial arts when it came in because it's such a fantasy. And, I would love to do all sorts of movies and, fortunately, I got locked into the horror and science fiction genre, which I dearly love, probably more than any other, and really enjoy working in. But I'd love to do *Gentlemen Prefer Blondes*—it would be great.

I'd love to make a western—oh, I'd love it. But what is a western really? A western is a historical drama, or whatever you want to call it, about the West in this country. But it became more than that—it became a symbol for all sorts of things about America, and about the hero, and it became a myth in a sense for a whole generation of people. I think that society has changed so much and life has changed so much with technology in this century that I don't know that myth still holds up quite the way it used to. We've supplanted it with other myths, and they seem to resonate more to the audience.

I think that Sergio Leone's work was, in a sense, the ultimate western and then the end of it because it stylized the western to such an extent, stripping it of its actual locations, stripping it of any kind of real identity—generic backgrounds and generic characters—and yet at the same time, it elevated it to a new height because it became a part of the form. I don't know if you could ever do a western without thinking about Leone's work. And, I don't know that I could do it any better, and I think that one of the reasons I stopped trying for westerns is because there've been so many great ones, and they're such a risk to make, financially.

They're very difficult to make—it takes a lot of work. You have to go out with horses and actors, and horses and actors are hard. You have to put cameras and get horses and actors to hit marks out in the middle of wide open spaces, and often that can be very trying, so the main reason is, I suppose, probably cowardice on my part to come out and do a western. Not only would it be dangerous financially, but hard to compete with so many great directors. But you know, people have been talking about the death of the western for a long time in Hollywood. We'll see. Some daring young man will go out there and make one. But I must say that my admiration for Howard Hawks—not just *Rio Bravo*, but all his works—is very strong, I guess that's obvious.

On Film Music

I usually score my own films because I'm the fastest and the cheapest. ... And I love making music. My dad [Howard Carpenter] was a composer and a musician and a music teacher [University of Kentucky], who earned his Ph.D. in music at the Eastman School in Rochester, New York. I grew up around it, and I grew up around movies and film scores.

I don't do the score first, or while the movie is being made. The musical ideas come after the movie's done. Basically, it's all improvised. I get a cut of the movie in pretty close shape, and then I transfer it to video tape, synchronize videotape with the synthesizers and basically just play along, and out it comes. And it supports what's going on, hopefully. That's the idea—to make sometimes very dead scenes come alive and often to lead the audience slightly. It's a lot of fun to do.

I can play anything on a synthesizer, and I can play the violin, guitar, and so forth. But mainly all my work is in synthesizer—that's just keyboard, which is easy. Alan Howarth owns the recording studio that we work in. We've worked together since *Escape from New York*, and our personalities fit so well. He's an old rock 'n' roller from way back, and he used to play with Weather Report, kind of a jazz-rock group. We just have a good time together, and it's a relaxing atmosphere—there's not a lot of competition that goes on—and it's out of that atmosphere that the best work gets done. That's why I've stayed with him.

On Writing

[I'm working on] a book on my experiences in Hollywood, and it's a little avant-garde at this time. Popular books on directors tend to be more about the politics and, you know, "How was Clint Eastwood to work with?" And if that's going to be the basis of a book, I'd rather do my own. The book that I have been working on is much more about gossip and the politics of Hollywood as opposed to what goes on the screen.

I would love to write novels, and I've got several of them under way here in my drawer. It's just that writing is very hard. Writing for movies is very easy, but writing to be read is different.

On Independence, Integrity, and Hollywood

Comparing my independent work with my studio work in terms of quality: You know, there's a kind of duality here because what you say about independent films having less money but more freedom is absolutely true, which is the reason for my choice in returning to independent films after *Big Trouble in Little China*. But there is one thing that you must always keep in mind when you're talking about studio films: They offer the opportunity to work with lots of money backing you up, with the best that money can buy, and also working in the Hollywood system.

You know, all of us grew up watching movies. And I grew up watching Hollywood films, and I dearly love them, even when they're bad I love them. And, I've always wanted to be a Hollywood director. I thought that when I got into the movie business that I *would* be, and wanted to take a certain amount of freedom with me. Unfortunately—in the Eighties especially—it's the death of the auteur theory and the destruction of the director as a creative authority.

I found that out when I got into studio filmmaking—and I consider my first studio film to be *The Thing*. I did *The Fog* and *Escape from New York* for Avco-Embassy, but they weren't a studio. They were basically a distribution company. Universal was the first company that I worked for that was a traditional Hollywood studio. And it was during this particular time—'81 to '82—where the director began to lose his creative authority on the set, mainly due to, believe it or not, *Heaven's Gate*. There was a director who was lauded with an Academy Award and called an artist, and then he turns around and makes a movie that the *New York Times* said was about as exciting as touring your own living room. Well, you know, that casts a giant pall on the idea of the director as the creative captain of the ship.

And also, a lot of filmmakers who got a lot of praise had made films that critics didn't like. And, all of a sudden, you find yourself as a director that in order to have a lot of creative freedom, you have to constantly get good reviews. In order to get good reviews, you have to start playing to the critics, and that way lies death because the critics can often be very stupid. The whole point of it—the whole point of what it was about—was exploited in Hollywood by a lot of directors who decreed themselves artists. And now in Hollywood, one of the credits that's being thrown around all the time is "A Film By ...," which I find enormously overused, and it doesn't mean anything anymore. It doesn't mean *anything*. Everybody has a "Film By" credit. My dog does.

In independent studio work, often you're out for a different purpose, and you can take more chances because you have less money at risk. Whereas, when you're making a big studio film, even a medium one, you're talking about 12 to 15 million dollars—well, the risks have to stop because you need to make money back. It's just a fact of life in Hollywood. You have to please your investors. And that's part of the wonderful and ongoing clash between business and art: When somebody invests money in you as a filmmaker, do your damnedest to pay it back.

I have different standards. I always look at the independent films and say, "My God, I can't believe we *did* that," just because I remember being out in the middle of the night with a camera and a bunch of rubber. But, in terms of the big studio films, I usually think, "I can't believe I *survived* that."

We all get seduced into show business, intoxicated by the money and the proximity to big stars. I've seen it happen to every other career around me, I can't imagine that I was somehow fortunate enough to miss it. I think you are seduced by Hollywood—and often, the early films in your career seem to focus more of your ideas, and you tend to be more bold because you're trying to make a name for yourself. Then all of a sudden, when you become established, then you become more conservative because you're trying to protect it. So after a while, you just sort of say, "Well, as long as I can survive, I'm doing all right." That's really the name of the game—survival.

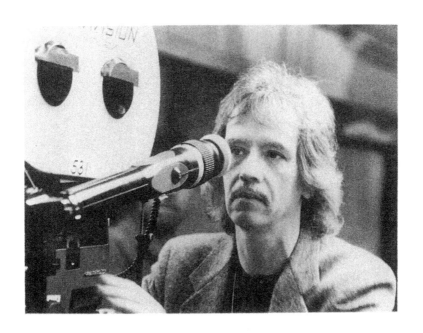

John Carpenter
1987

17

High Noon

El Diablo

The would-be cowboy finally bought himself a horse. John Carpenter made his western.

He didn't direct, and he only shared production credit. But the film, *El Diablo*, was based on a "Gothic western" screenplay Carpenter had drafted more than a decade earlier. In a finished version cowritten by Tommy Lee Wallace and Bill Phillips, it was aired over Home Box Office in July, 1990, and subsequently became available on videotape.

In his coscenarists and in director Peter Markle, Carpenter clearly found kindred spirits: The love and understanding for the icons of the western that is omnipresent in Carpenter's own films is equally pervasive in *El Diablo*. It is a good-spirited film that combines startling violence with coarse comedy and a timeless sense of poetry—the elements that also characterize the westerns of Carpenter's admired masters Howard Hawks, John Ford, and Sergio Leone.

The plot of the tale is much like an amalgam of Ford's *The Searchers* and his *The Man Who Shot Liberty Valance*—the former centering on the tireless search for the desperado-kidnapper of a virginal white girl, the latter on a frontier lawyer's eye-opening discovery of the difference between truth and legend. In *El Diablo*, legends—whether from books or from told tales—loom larger than life, just as western icons and gestures dominated the contemporary landscape of *The Resurrection of Broncho Billy*. Where *The Resurrection of Broncho Billy* is about mythologizing the present, *El Diablo* is about demythologizing the past. Billy Ray Smith, the small-town school teacher in *El Diablo*, has his starry-eyed notions of western heroism turned back on him as he confronts "the way it really is."

Though Billy Ray succeeds in his quixotic quest of pursuing El Diablo and rescuing his kidnapped student Nettie, he wins only by learning the lessons of *The Man Who Shot Liberty Valance*: If you want somebody shot, do it yourself and shoot him in the back; and when the legend becomes fact, print the legend. Billy Ray comes out of his adventure as a *writer*. A generation later he'd have been a filmmaker.

The misadventures of Billy Ray and the anti-Hawksian team of misfits he gathers around him are spun out against a background of western iconography new and old. The music is part American folk, part Ennio Morricone, and part samurai. A singing of "Gather at the River" accompanies a hanging, from which a victim is freed when the rope is severed by a rifle shot. A dog comes yipping out of a house into a dusty street. A gang of bandits thunders across the screen. The dictum that you should watch a gunman's eyes is debunked: "Watch his *hands*, not his eyes. Man don't draw a gun with his *eyes*." Billy Ray learns—or fails to learn—to shoot by firing at a row of bottles set up on a fence. He moves closer and closer. Finally his friend tells him the truth: "You're gonna need bigger bottles."

People, even legends, grow old: "Fast don't mean a lot these days," says Thomas Van Leek, from whom Billy Ray learns about watching hands as well as about shooting people in the back, at least when they deserve it. The phrase "these days," recalling what MacReady said about trust in *The Thing*, and what Brian said about faith in *Prince of Darkness*, conveys that sense of changing times, of lost innocence, of humanity slipping away that haunts all of Carpenter's work. No wonder that Sam Peckinpah's *The Wild Bunch* is as strong a reference in the film's climax as anything from Ford or Hawks.

No wonder, either, that the arch-criminal, the agent of rude awakening in Billy Ray's otherwise idyllic world, is named "El Diablo," making him kin to the world-threatening anti-force of *Prince of Darkness*. Once again, the order was not quite what we had in mind: The finale has that characteristically Carpenterian sense of missed connections, of postponed destiny. "*Some* day ..." says Billy Ray to the admiring Nettie, as—like old Jack Burton—he rides off into the sunset *without* the girl. *El Diablo* is not about ending, but about keeping on.

A year after *El Diablo* aired, another John Carpenter western finally saw the light of day. Early in his career, Carpenter sold John Wayne a screenplay entitled *Blood River*. Wayne died in 1979, and his company never produced the film, but on March 17, 1991, a made-for-television version aired, with Rick Schroder in the lead role as a young man who avenges the killing of his parents, then goes into hiding under the aegis of an old mountain man who has his own reasons for sheltering him. After its initial airing, the film has rarely, if ever, reappeared, and as of this writing remains unavailable on videotape or disk.

It was not until 1998, however, that John Carpenter finally exorcised his Western demon altogether by directing *Vampires*, a visually poetic battle between good and evil set in the American Southwest and owing more to Sergio Leone and Sam Peckinpah than to Bram Stoker.

18

You're Not Alone Anymore

Memoirs of an Invisible Man

Memoirs of an Invisible Man shares much with *Starman*. Both were major studio productions that John Carpenter directed as a "hired gun"—not the more personal, independent projects with which he is more commonly associated. Both, therefore, are subject to the deceptively simple accusation of not being true Carpenter films. Nevertheless, Carpenter found in each project a thematic connection to the thread that ties up his more personal body of work: the recognition and reluctant acceptance of an order different from what was expected.

Interestingly, both films center on protagonists who live outside the rest of humanity, who struggle to cope with a body that, because of a transforming event, is new to them, who are sought by forces that would put to ill uses the very qualities that make them unique, and who ultimately escape those forces and accept new life through the love of a woman. It's a pattern that is readily identifiable as Dantesque or Faustian, and each has its Mephisthophelean nemesis as well as its redeeming angel.

Dante? Goethe? This is a pop movie based on a literarily well-received but comparatively lightweight pop novel, and it stars Chevy Chase for gosh sake! Actually, H. F. Saint's novel received some good notices for its skillful fusion of a fantasy thriller plotline with a darkly satirical portrait of the professional life in the Eighties. Its dubious hero was a stock trader whose literal invisibility was a perfect metaphor for the virtual invisibility that already enveloped his life. With no real relationships and no apparent past or future, he did business by telephone, never making any real connection with any real human being, and the novel's penetrating central point was how easily he could continue his life and his career despite the burden of invisibility.

A sinking feeling greeted the announcement that ex-*Saturday Night Live* pratfaller Chevy Chase would play the Wall Street whiz kid forced to undergo a brutal self-reexamination with the recognition that his invisibility inconvenienced him, but made no difference to anyone else, or their perception of him. It looked as if Harry Saint's pretty good novel about Self in the Eighties would be turned into a dopey showcase for Chase's increasingly tiresome shtick, much as Gregory Mac-Donald's pretty clever mystery *Fletch* had been seven years earlier.

Not to worry. We were in good hands with John Carpenter—and with Chase, who turned in what is arguably his most controlled film performance. While the film may lack the satiric edge of Saint's novel, it manages to make a pretty decent John Carpenter movie.

There are, to be sure, vast differences in plot and concept between novel and film, but the film is often faithful in spirit to the novel, especially in its recognition that Nick Halloway "was invisible before he became invisible," which was much of the point of Saint's novel. Invisibility, ironically, occasions self-confrontation. The novel's Nick saw himself as a nonentity already, so invisibility was a metaphor for what he had really become, a wake-up call to real life. This tried to happen in the film as well; but the special effects and the inherent comedy of Nick's dangerous situation kept the film so upbeat that it never seemed as serious or important as Saint's novel.

Chase's performance is an uneasy marriage of comedy and seriousness. His abandonment of his usual slapstick mode is heroic, but in his restrained, self-limiting approach to the role, none of Nick's painful self-awareness comes out, only his sense of enraged victim. The accident that drives the film's action is made to seem Nick's fault, in a way: A technician spills coffee on his keyboard while pointing the way to the men's room for Nick, precipitating the event that causes Nick to become invisible. This suggestion that Nick indirectly authors his own misfortune focuses the metaphor on what Nick has made of his life, rather than on a capricious fate that forces him to look at himself and see nothing. But despite the spilled coffee, Nick's ordeal is always something the government has done to him, is doing to him, not something he has done to himself. In this way, the film eschews Harry Saint's dark night of the yuppie soul to become a political parable, like *They Live*, using altered perception as metaphor for dehumanization and loss of freedom. In both films, sight can't be trusted: in *They Live*, because what we see isn't what's really there; in *Memoirs of an Invisible Man* because we can't see what *is* really there. In both films, it is a "They" that is to be feared, not the confrontation with, and acceptance of, an undeniable "I."

The film's pre-title use of helicopters underscores this by summoning up an image that Carpenter developed in *Escape from New York*, *The Thing*, *Starman*, and *They Live*. In each, the helicopter is a harbinger of foreboding, paranoia-inducing evil, and in all except *The Thing*, it is emblematic of the terrors of the police state.

The helicopters are looking for Nick and, after a main title sequence that eschews Carpenter's usual simple black-on-white titles for
an urban nightscape, we get a brief prologue that adopts the narrative
voice of the novel, while at the same time recalling the prologue to *Big
Trouble in Little China*. An invisible man seated opposite us across a
desk performs "magic" to persuade us of the truth of the outlandish tale
he is about to tell. Look: No strings. We see bubblegum chewed, but
we don't see the chewer. This is a story about what happens when a
man's bubble bursts, and as in *Little China*, it begins "very small."

The link with *Big Trouble in Little China* continues in the use of a
voice-over narration to take us into the story, reminding us that this is,
after all, the "memoirs" of an invisible man, but the film echoes the
first-person ruminations of the novel only sparingly. John Carpenter is
more interested in turning Harry Saint's modern parable into a John
Carpenter film—one that connects not only to other Carpenter films but
also to the broader matrix of horror and science fiction films of which
the Carpenter oeuvre is inexorably a part.

The accident that renders Nick invisible, for example, occurs in
Santa Mira—the name of the mythical California town that spawned
the body snatchers of Donald Siegel's 1956 classic and that Carpenter
earlier resurrected in the script for *Halloween III: Season of the Witch*.
In both cases, the town is home to a sinister company where dark-sided
research is the order of the day. Within his own mythos, then, Carpenter draws a parallel between Conal Cochran's insidious Silver Shamrock toy company and the only apparently more benign Magnoscopic
research company, whose secret experimentations lead to Nick's life-
altering catastrophe.

But the villain of the piece is not some Cochran-like arch-nemesis
at the head of the corporation—it's David Jenkins, amoral CIA operative who sees in Nick the opportunity to recruit the perfect spy. Nick
catches on to the operatives' motive and, in another movie reference,
slows them up by identifying himself only as "Harvey" (the man-sized
invisible rabbit friend of alcoholic Elwood P. Dowd in *Harvey*). He
then makes his escape from Santa Mira to San Francisco (in the tracks
of Miles Bennell in *Invasion of the Body Snatchers*)—by becoming the
voice of an unconscious drunk whom he manipulates like a puppet.

Carpenter took a big risk in approaching the problem of representing Nick's "molecular flux"—the name given the state of invisibility in
the film's technology (an explain-nothing MacGuffin like the sunspots
of *Assault on Precinct 13*). In James Whale's ground-breaking *The
Invisible Man* (1933), an objective point of view was maintained
throughout the film. The invisible man was never seen until the end of

the film, and his presence was limned only by the effect he had on the visible objects around him. Carpenter decided on the riskier approach of alternating two points of view: sometimes we see Nick, sometimes we don't. Remarkably, Carpenter makes it work. When we can see Nick, we never forget that no one else can, and the alternations among a real Chevy Chase, a special effect, and nothing at all never seem jarring. When Nick tries to put on his clothes without being able to see himself, we see him (and, perhaps, connect him with the Starman's efforts to get used to an unfamiliar body); when he tries to *take off* clothes that everyone else *can* see, we see the clothes and not him; and when he tries to flag down an oncoming truck, we see (from the trucker's point of view) nothing at all.

The alternation of viewpoints is not simply arbitrary. The scene in which a street crook snatches a woman's purse, only to have it re-snatched from him and returned to the woman by an invisible Nick, could have been shot with Nick unseen. Instead it gains worlds of impact (and becomes one of the film's best shots) by the inclusion of a visible Nick, with Chevy Chase miming Nick's tired, bored, self-absorbed indifference to the potentially critical realization that he can use his invisibility to do good. His sense of right and wrong is intact, and perhaps he feels a nascent a sense of responsibility to his fellow citizens; but a superhero he is not.

Jenkins recognizes that Nick has the "perfect profile: He was invisible before he was invisible." But Nick will have none of being an intelligence agent or a secret weapon, and defies Jenkins: "Whatever I become it's gonna be my choice, not yours." The film, in its light-hearted way, is about Nick Halloway's discovery (and empowerment) of himself.

In another oblique reference to *Invasion of the Body Snatchers*, Nick leaves San Francisco in a produce truck—and he *is*, like Miles Bennell, trying to escape a dehumanizing conspiracy. He's not afraid, though—he's bitter: "I would make them pay," he narrates. There is a problem in the film's frequent return to Nick's voice-over narration. While Carpenter solved the problem of varying seen and unseen points of view of Nick, he seems indifferent to the fact that, although Nick is narrating the film, we frequently see and know things that he doesn't. The novel is all from Nick's viewpoint, and we never see, know, or learn anything except through his invisible eyes. The film's changes between subjective and objective views *are* jarring, and one can't help wondering how it might have been if Carpenter had stuck strictly to what Nick sees and knows. The few scenes outside of Nick's ken— exchanges between Jenkins and Singleton, or George and Richard, or

Alice waiting for Nick at the lunch date he misses—could have been disclosed as Nick discovered them, or omitted altogether. Such an approach would lend emphasis to one of the most effective conceits of both novel and film: Nick's invisibility gives him the gift of being able to see himself as others see him—to hear how people talk about him when he isn't around. It's an important gift, of course, because through it, he discovers there's nothing there.

He seems to sense this even before its full impact strikes him. Revealing his invisibility to Alice, he wisecracks, "For years women have been telling me they could see right through me." In one of Carpenter's more inspired visual jokes, the revelation is treated as a kind of sexual act. His disrobing leaves her prostrate in a faint, and afterward he is discovered smoking a cigarette.

The compelling question is, Does Nick's discovery that he is a cipher come in time for him? In a moment that might as well be subtitled "Author's Message" he tells Alice, "I never realized how important it is to be seen ... to be acknowledged." But which "author" is delivering the message? While it's a sentiment that certainly emerges from Harry Saint's novel, it's expressed in the kind of terms that would appeal particularly to a filmmaker: "to be *seen*." It is precisely the visual dimension that has been lost to Nick—but not the ability to *see*, which is important to a viewer; instead, it's the ability to *be seen*, which is important to an artist—or an artist's creation. In children's fantasies and games, the loss of the ability to see is a handicap (one must cover one's eyes and not peek while the others hide themselves); while the loss of the ability to *be seen* is imagined to be a treat, an adventure, an opportunity to get away with who knows how many japes and gambols absolutely denied to those who can be seen. ("If you were blind," says Carpenter's Nick to Alice, "we'd make the perfect couple." She'd be unable to see his unseeability.) It was Harry Saint's achievement to suggest—in a way that never seemed to occur to H. G. Wells—that the inability to be seen is more a curse than a convenience. In the end, though, it is a curse that makes the cursed one morally whole.

To John Carpenter, who from even his earliest films has made each of his works comment not only on its own characters and themes but also on the filmmaker's art itself, this recognition must have been at least as appealing as the technical challenge of "showing" invisibility on the motion picture screen—of allowing audiences to "see" something that, by its own definition, cannot be seen. Indeed, the problem of filming the unfilmable is, in many respects, the same as the problem of expressing (and perhaps redeeming) a character who is by his own recognition a zero. It is, finally, albeit in comic terms, an exploration of the fragility of personal identity not so far removed from the icy bleakness of *The Thing*.

Salvation for Nick comes from without rather than within—and this, too, is a recurrent theme in Carpenter's work. Alice tells Nick: "Trust me. You're not alone anymore." Trust is a tough thing to come by these days, and the difference between the uncompromising open-ended doubt of *The Thing* and the upbeat comedic ending of *Memoirs of an Invisible Man* depends upon the willingness of one human being to trust in another. We recall the connection of another idealized, near-angelic woman with another freakish man on the run from evil government agents in *Starman*, and the reaching out of Brian to Catherine in *Prince of Darkness*.

The redemption of Nick is crystallized in one gorgeous scene that, again, combines the wit and vision of a well-written story with the cleverness and inspiration of innovative special effects technology. Nick is ready to leave Alice, more for her own safety than for his— finally, a genuinely unselfish act from him. The critical moment occurs outside a train station in the rain, recalling Rick Blaine left waiting at the station in *Casablanca*. Here, though, both lovers are present and they kiss in the rain, the water outlining his body with a shimmering luminescence, a moment of transfiguration that seems to change everything. Evidently, even though Alice is not blind—or maybe precisely *because* she is not—they make the perfect couple anyway.

Or do they? There is a curious touch of dark ambiguity in Carpenter's transposition of Jenkins's face on Alice's on the window of the train-car door when he catches up with them. A neat bit, but is it meaningful? In what sense, if any, is Alice like Jenkins? None at all. The image could simply suggest Jenkins's domination of Alice, his use of her to get to Nick. But a transposition of physical image is a bit extreme to describe that kind of relationship. It may be intended to suggest only the precarious difference between seeing and seeing through. Nevertheless, it's a troubling moment that suggests a resurgence of the open-endedness of *The Thing*—all may not, after all, be entirely well.

But dark or light, Alice is the one whose intercession makes Nick whole. She quite literally "gives him a face" when she hits upon the idea of using makeup to make him appear normal (well, *near*-normal). This cuts both ways when, forced to shed his clothes to escape, he becomes a disembodied running head—which also provides a visual metaphor of his incompleteness as a human being. Of course, the

Trust and Distrust in *Memoirs of an Invisible Man*
Above: Alice (Daryl Hannah) and Nick (Chevy Chase). Below: Nick, invisible, has Jenkins (Sam Neill) as a hostage—for the moment.

use of makeup as a way of discovering himself through playing a role is yet another of the film's oblique references to the world of theatre and film—of created art.

Like *They Live*, the film climaxes on a rooftop, and the image of a Carpenter character looking down from on high at a crisis-point recalls not only his early films *Dark Star* and *Someone's Watching Me!*, but also Hitchcock's *Vertigo*, which echoes throughout the film in shots of a spiraling staircase, the streets of San Francisco, the protagonist's obsession with a stunning blonde, and other incidental motifs.

In the event, Nick and Alice escape in a way that enables Nick to make the rest of the world think he is dead. Now they can be left alone, and the finale of the film is an upbeat epilogue in which Nick in a ski mask, faceless underneath, embraces a now-pregnant Alice. She has accepted him as he is, like Jenny Hayden accepted the Starman, and that helps Nick accept himself—and know himself for the first time.

The film differs in tone, however, from the transfiguring resignation that ends the novel. There Nick finally accepts the new order, like Scott Carey at the finale of Jack Arnold's *The Incredible Shrinking Man*: "To God, there is no zero. I still exist!" Carpenter's film is of lighter weight: Here, ironically, Nick's new order is to embark on a happy life with Alice, with nothing heavier on his mind than keeping out of other people's way and being left alone. Just like he always did.

19

<u>These Guys Crack Me Up</u>

Body Bags

In a turn at a *Tales from the Crypt* style anthology, John Carpenter indulged the flair for comedy that has enriched even his most serious films since the beginning of his career. *Body Bags* is an enjoyable diversion, not among his best work, and not really intended to be.

Steven Spielberg's *Amazing Stories* sought to revitalize the television "weird tale" anthology series, spawning, over the next few years, shows like *Monsters*, *Tales from the Dark Side*, and new versions of *The Twilight Zone* and *The Outer Limits*. Carpenter's *Body Bags* is a "pilot film" comprising three tales made for Showtime and designed to compete with HBO's *Tales from the Crypt*.

The horror anthology has an honorable place in film history, beginning, perhaps, with Fritz Lang's moody 1921 silent film *Der Müde Tod* (*Weary Death*), a collection of atmospheric tales about Death's grim duties on earth. The most celebrated horror anthology on film is still Ealing Studios' multidirectored *Dead of Night* (1945). But it was the EC horror comics of the Fifties ("Tales from the Crypt," "The Vault of Horror" and others) that proved the main inspiration for a series of British anthology films produced by Amicus, Tigard and others—the best of which is still Kevin Connor's *From Beyond the Grave* (1973). The horror anthology cycle burned itself out in the mid-Seventies, but enjoyed a brief revival in the 1983 George Romero-Stephen King collaboration *Creepshow*—more spoof than spook.

Carpenter's film, though it owes (and acknowledges) a debt to earlier cinematic horror anthologies, is most like *Creepshow* in that it is played largely for laughs. Not that the goings-on aren't fairly grim, with an occasional serious thematic gesture. But the black comic tone imparted by the "Coroner"—Carpenter's version of the Keeper of the Crypt—sets the atmosphere and spirit for the entire film. Even though

John Carpenter as the "Coroner"

we may fear for Anne in "The Gas Station" and start at its surprises, recoil at the hair-growing device in "Hair," and empathize with the loss and agony of ruined baseball star Brent Matthews in "Eye," it's the comic book gags that we remember. Carpenter leaves us laughing; nothing in the film gets us in the guts the way *Assault on Precinct 13*, *Halloween*, *The Thing*, *Prince of Darkness*, and *In the Mouth of Madness* do. This one is strictly for fun.

Each of the three short tales echoes themes and situations that Carpenter has visited before. "The Gas Station," the first of the film's three tales, was directed by Carpenter, and plays like *Halloween* at an all-night service station. The haunted gas station is an idea Carpenter had already briefly explored in *The Fog*, partly as an *hommage* to Alfred Hitchcock's *The Birds*. Here, the station becomes the target not of supernatural forces but of a very real serial killer, with Anne, the new night attendant, becoming a young woman in peril like the babysitters of Haddonfield.

In "Hair," the best of the three (if only because it is also the funniest), we find a recurrence of the Unholy Corporation image embodied earlier in Silver Shamrock in *Halloween III: Season of the Witch*, the television station in *They Live*, and the Magnoscopic Corporation in *Memoirs of an Invisible Man*. Once again the corporation is the means whereby a destructive force intrudes upon our civilization, but here, Carpenter has more of a sense of humor about the idea. The story tells of the disastrous results of a vain, middle-aged loverboy's obsessive efforts to reverse his baldness.

The third story, "Eye," was directed by Tobe Hooper, and is the most ambitious of the three in its adoption of a more lofty theme—the desperate desire of an injured baseball player to restore himself to star status. The predictable climax of the tale borrows a page from Roger Corman's *X—The Man with X-Ray Eyes* (1963)—which itself owed a debt to Flannery O'Connor's more serious *Wise Blood*. But in the scheme of Carpenter's career, "Eye" seems to be a revisit to the world of *Eyes of Laura Mars*, a reworking of the theme of seeing with the eyes of another—specifically, of a murderer.

In addition to paying homage to earlier film traditions in the three tales of *Body Bags*, Carpenter adds to the fun with casting jokes, employing as cameo actors fellow directors, classic stars, and pop culture has-beens. The appearance and style of Deborah Harry's portrayal of the Nurse in "Hair" appears deliberately calculated to pun on her name as well as to spoof the style of Carpenter's by-then ex-wife Adrienne Barbeau. Horror directors Wes Craven and Sam Raimi turn up (Raimi as a corpse), and Roger Corman, director of *X—The Man with X-Ray Eyes*, is one of the doctors who officiates over the eye implant in

"Eye." His companion is John Agar, mainstay of numerous Fifties horror films, playing a character named Dr. Lang—bringing the horror anthology full circle back to its creator. Unaccountably, British pop stars Sheena Easton and Twiggy do supporting turns in the film, and acquit themselves nicely in "didn't you used to be—?" roles.

Carpenter has mixed comedy with high theme in most of his films—another Hawksian characteristic of his work. Even the relentlessly dark *The Thing* has its comic gestures. Yet the two films that most deliberately adopt a comic view—*Big Trouble in Little China* and *Memoirs of an Invisible Man*—still reflect Carpenter's continuing view of the world (and the world of film) by building on his characteristic tension between an expected, redeeming classical order and an unexpected, invasive alien order right next door. *Body Bags* alone among Carpenter's films seems never to touch more than lightly on this notion. Still, Carpenter's continuing interest in this theme is evident in the choice of stories. "Bill," the night manager of "The Gas Station," is not the "Bill" he seems to be; Dr. Lock's hair restoration formula is certainly not what it was expected to be; and Brent Matthews's "Eye" imposes an entirely unanticipated new order on its recipient. These are ultimately, of course, mere devices, not explored in thematic depth because such exploration is not the intent of this made-for-cable-TV comic book. But with his next film, Carpenter would regain his unique skill at combining dark, offbeat comedy with chilling horror, and emerge into a new golden era of his career.

20

We've Only Just Begun

In the Mouth of Madness

John Carpenter has called *In the Mouth of Madness* the third film in his "Apocalyptic Trilogy"—the other two being *The Thing* and *Prince of Darkness*. Each film proposes the genuine possibility of the end of the world, but an end that is, however temporarily, held off by the courage and defiance of truly heroic people. The same motif was treated light-heartedly in *Big Trouble in Little China*, but *In the Mouth of Madness* is perhaps Carpenter's most complex and challenging film. It echoes the Lovecraftian theme of an apocalypse brought about by the incursion of unspeakable beings from a universe next door, bleeding subtly, then horrifically, into our own. It counterpoints that theme, however, with an even more provocative suggestion: The world that we see destroyed may be that of a single deteriorating mind.

The possibility that John Trent may be delusional is one that we entertain, reject, and entertain again throughout the film. Indeed, we are encouraged to do so by Carpenter's decision to begin the film with Trent's admission to a mental institution, followed soon afterward by his interview with a psychiatrist, Dr. Wrenn (portrayed by David Warner, the insidious Dr. Lock of *Body Bags*'s "Hair"). The film proper unfolds as a flashback—Trent's memory of the events of the last few days. Even at the end of the film we are not satisfied as to whether Trent really is the last man on Earth, or only believes he is. For the compleat filmgoer, the experience of questioning what is real and what is hallucinatory in Trent's story inevitably conjures up the spectre of an earlier cinematic psychiatrist-patient relationship, that of Robert Wiene's *The Cabinet of Dr. Caligari* (1919).

This classic masterwork of the Gothic cinema, hailed by many as the first horror film, begins as an old man finishes telling his story to a younger man seated with him in a garden. As a seemingly entranced woman walks past them, the younger man, Francis, reveals that he has an even stranger tale to tell, an experience he has had with the woman,

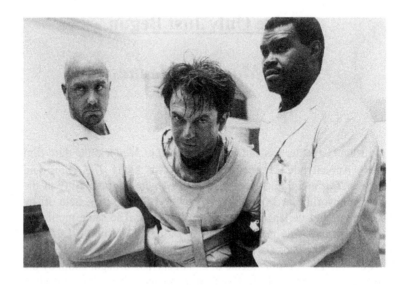

In the Mouth of Madness
John Trent (Sam Neill) enters the institution.

Jane. He tells of a festival in his hometown, to which came one Dr. Caligari, seeking permission to exhibit at the fair his protégé, a somnambulist who acts in a trance and foretells the future. The town clerk grants the permission, but only after treating Caligari abusively. Later, the clerk is killed under mysterious circumstances. Francis, Jane, and a friend, Alan, visit Caligari's cabinet at the fair, and ask questions of the somnambulist, Cesare, who predicts that Alan will die before dawn. That night, Alan is murdered. Francis suspects that the murderer is Cesare himself, under Caligari's control. He learns that Caligari is in reality the director of a nearby insane asylum, but Caligari has already dispatched Cesare to murder Jane. Unable to kill the beautiful sleeping woman, Cesare abducts her instead and is pursued by the townspeople through a surreal landscape of alleyways and rooftops, hounded finally to his death. When Francis presents Cesare's dead body to Caligari at the asylum, Caligari becomes violent and has to be restrained in one of his institution's own straitjackets.

The original story, "an indictment of Germany's ruling class,"[1] ended there. But director Robert Wiene added an epilogue that to this day remains the object of debate among film critics and historians. Francis and the old man are revealed to be seated in a garden on the grounds of that very asylum, and when the director appears (none other than Caligari himself), Francis becomes violent and must himself be restrained. But the doctor announces that, now that he understands the nature of the young man's delusions, he can cure him (a line echoed half a century later in the finale to Philip Roth's novel *Portnoy's Complaint*: "So. Now vee may perhaps to begin. Yes?"). Cesare and Jane are seen to be other inmates of the asylum.

The controversial tacked-on epilogue actually sacrifices none of the ambiguity in the asylum director's character, and at the same time brings the somewhat preposterous horror burlesque down to a more immediate and realistic possibility. Although it is strongly implied that the Caligari story exists solely in the mind of Francis, it is at least possible that Francis, rather than being delusional, is making the story up as he goes along (a device that also informs a more recent dissection of cinematic narrative, *The Usual Suspects*). Is he trying to invent a story that will "top" that of the old man whose own tale is ending as the film begins? Francis naturally incorporates into his fantasy-tale the things closest to him: his fellow inmates, the asylum director, his childhood hometown, and a friend, Alan, who has died—perhaps killed by Francis himself? It is natural that the villain of the piece is the very man Francis sees as his oppressor—the director of the institution in which he is confined.

The final, ambiguous shot of Caligari's face glowering out at us spits a question at the viewer. Is Francis inventing? Telling the truth? Or raving with paranoid fantasy? The point is that the film is as much about the nature of narrative as it is about the horror of mind control.

Another great cinematic psychiatrist-patient interview—and another controversial tacked-on ending—are found in Donald Siegel's 1956 *Invasion of the Body Snatchers*. After objections from the studio to his downbeat, "you're all doomed" ending, Siegel changed the film to frame it as a flashback: In the beginning, Dr. Miles Bennell is brought hysterical into a police station, aware that his story of alien vegetable pods taking over local communities seems far-fetched, but insisting that he is not crazy. The film proper is his story as he tells it to the police psychiatrist. The ending brings the revelation of evidence supporting the truth of his story and promising deliverance from the invading evil.

Elements of both of these classics of film narrative are present in John Carpenter's *In the Mouth of Madness*. But Carpenter makes this presentation of the "madman's subjective narrative" uniquely his own. He even brands it with a self-referential in-joke: "Not the Carpenters!" cries John Trent, newly admitted to the institution, as the archetypal mellow Seventies duo intones "We've only just begun"—and we have. It is still the very beginning of the film and the deterioration that its narrative describes. The fact that a deranged man—who is possibly the only sane one left—is placed at the mercy of the soothing influence of someone named Carpenter is just one of many ironies awaiting us.

The conceit of *In the Mouth of Madness*, for all its debt to both H. P. Lovecraft and Nigel Kneale, is, of course, the Stephen King phenomenon. It takes as its premise the best-selling horror novelist who is so phenomenally popular that readers build their lives and their consciousness around his work, and wait with barely controlled patience for the appearance of his next novel. The popularity and influence of Sutter Cane is only slightly exaggerated over that of sound-alike Stephen King. But does Cane, like his biblical namesake, embody an evil influence? Is he under some other power that, through his writing, induces itself into the minds of his readers, permitting them to be overtaken by the maddening reality waiting to creep into our dimension?

The ability of art to harm is, of course, a social issue that has been addressed throughout the ages. The makers of horror films, more than any other group of artists (except perhaps pornographers), have seen that accusation directed at their work, and a few of them have, in turn, analyzed it themselves—most notably in *Wes Craven's New Nightmare* (1994). Certainly Carpenter, perhaps more than any other maker of horror films, has wrestled with this issue. As the creator of *Halloween* he unwittingly fathered the entire "stalk and slash" genre that became synonymous with the term "horror film" during the Seventies, and gave rise to questions about misogyny, sexuality, and violence, as well as the sensational treatment of violence and its purportedly desensitizing effect on contemporary youth.

In a 1998 interview, Carpenter said, "People who direct horror movies are often looked at as pornographers: 'How can you do this?' It's unseemly, do you know what I mean, it's not correct to do it. ... People wonder 'Why are you making these terrible movies about scary things and death?' Because I'm reminding everybody that there are things to fear."

Certainly there is a sense in which *In the Mouth of Madness* is "John Carpenter's New Nightmare"—his own reflection on his work and vision, and on its cultural and market impact. Can an artist's work corrupt others? Can an artist, without intending to, be the medium through which corrupting influences are transmitted to others? John Trent, in the course of his skeptical investigation into Sutter Cane, apparently discovers that the answer is yes, and that Sutter Cane, both literally and literarily, is the means by which an alien evil corrupts and destroys our civilization.

But that's what John Trent knows—or thinks he knows. What if Trent really is mad? *In the Mouth of Madness* piles ambiguity upon ambiguity, not unlike its grandfather, *The Cabinet of Dr. Caligari*.

Art as a medium for the emergence of things from beyond has been a recurring theme in horror literature, most notably that of Lovecraft, who frequently relied on the device of a forbidden book as the source of unspeakable evils. While the possibility of a truly evil book becoming the means by which destructive forces enter and demolish our universe seems preposterous, the literal destruction of our world and our bodies is certainly a compelling metaphor for the destruction of our moral and philosophical order by the incursion of "forbidden ideas"—things, perhaps, that man was not meant to know—the "anti-Promethean" theme of horror literature from Mary Shelley's *Frankenstein* onward, and of horror and science fiction film from their very beginnings.

In the Mouth of Madness is, as much as *Prince of Darkness*, a definitive Carpenter film, bearing the most important hallmarks of his vision and style. Its elusive town of Hob's End stands in for Stephen King's Castle Rock while pointing backward to both the London district haunted by primordial unearthly invaders in Nigel Kneale's *Five Million Years to Earth* (*Quatermass and the Pit*) and the little New

In the Mouth of Madness
Facing page: Above: Styles with the cursed manuscript. Below:
Sutter Cane (Jürgen Prochnow). This page: John Trent (Sam Neill)
and Linda Styles (Julie Carmen) in Hob's End.

England towns that become doorways to unspeakable worlds in the stories of H. P. Lovecraft. Hob's End is not easily reached; to do so requires a passage like the fulfillment of certain rituals required before a particular evil spirit may be invoked. First you need to figure out where it is—and the way Trent does so, constructing a map from clues hidden in the cover illustrations to Cane's books, is one of the greater frustrations of the film, since we don't share in the discovery ourselves. The audience isn't allowed to know what it is he sees in the covers that provides clues that may be assembled into a map. We just have to take his—and Carpenter's—word for the fact that something was there that gave the game away. Thus it becomes a mere device rather than an integral part of the film's journey into horror and madness. Indeed, the audience should be, throughout the film, more of a participant and less of an observer, if the film's black comic message is to have its full effect, and it is here that a certain apparent unwillingness to fully trust the viewer takes a toll.

It is possible, of course, that the audience is excluded from sharing in Trent's process of reasoning and discovery precisely in order to separate us from Trent. The more distanced we are from him, the more objectified he becomes, the more likely we are to see him as mad; whereas the more we see things with his eyes, the more we identify with him, the more likely we are to see him as the only sane one left. Carpenter wishes to sustain this ambivalence in the way we perceive Trent, and that tends to explain why sometimes we are trapped inside Trent's own perceptions (as when the world suddenly turns blue on him), while other times we are left out of them entirely.

This tendency to shift points of view is signaled near the beginning of the film proper—the story Trent tells the psychiatrist—when Trent and a friend are chatting at a café. Behind Trent, through the café's picture window, seen by us but not by him, a crazed man with an axe strides single-mindedly through a panicked crowd, headed straight for Trent. Now if the "story" is being told by Trent, we'd be seeing only what he saw; we'd know only what he knew. The fact that we see the marauding axeman before Trent notices him imparts a certain objectivity; it suggests that what we are seeing and hearing is not just a product of Trent's own disordered mind.

There are many more instances of this throughout the film, most notably when we are shifted from Trent's viewpoint to that of Linda Styles, the aptly named book editor and publicist who is assigned to accompany Trent on the investigative mission that leads him to Hob's End. Though Trent is the focus and the narrator from start to finish, these little shifts in point of view bleed into the film just as the tentacled, Lovecraftian creatures from the next dimension bleed into Trent's world, provoking us to ask, Whose story is this anyway?

Once the map is in place, Hob's End is still reached only by passage through a dreamlike zone in which time and perception go haywire. Things happen twice, or happen in reverse. A bicyclist seems to come at us from another decade, is hit by Trent's and Styles's car, but disappears unharmed (cf. the first appearance of Lo Pan in *Big Trouble in Little China*).

And once found, Hob's End is not easily escaped. In one horrific sequence, every road that Trent takes leads him back to the point from which he started—the endless loop hearkening back to the most remarkable sequence in the little seen and less appreciated 1979 film *The Legacy*, directed by Richard Marquand. In that film, as in this, someone trying to escape a haunted and haunting place by simply driving away from it finds that, no matter what direction one goes, what turns one takes, all routes lead straight back to the inescapable horror.

The device is repeated when Trent, finally departing from Hob's End with the manuscript of Cane's next—and cataclysmically final—novel, realizes that by not delivering the novel to the publisher, he can save the world. But then, no matter what he does to lose it, the manuscript keeps coming back to him. The entrapping recursion suggests the ineluctable power of the novels of Sutter Cane, and the alien reality that underlies them and acts through them. It is a fitting emblem for the insistent Return of the Repressed, the inescapability of one's own personal horrors. In that sense it also suggests the degree to which Trent is limited, trapped by his own perception. And so, Carpenter seems to say, are we all trapped by the limits of perception (both as movie viewers and as human beings).

So if John Trent is mad, then we must be, too.

What's the role of Jackson Harglow and his publishing company in all of this? They seem to have known more, all along, than they were willing to impart to Trent. When he returns from his hallucinatory excursion, he learns that the book he thought he was saving the world from has already been delivered and published long since. Apocalypse is already here.

In this, the film indicts corporate greed, the socially unconscious amorality of Cane's publisher, for bringing about the moral and literary collapse of the culture—as well as, perhaps, the literal collapse of the world. Thus *In the Mouth of Madness* reiterates from *They Live* the distrust of corporate and commercial endeavors that Carpenter shares

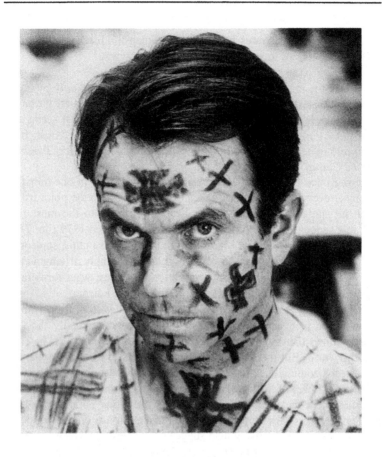

John Trent fortified against evil.

with virtually all independent filmmakers who have gone mainstream. It's what's behind the Unholy Corporation theme that also underscores *Halloween III: Season of the Witch, Memoirs of an Invisible Man,* and the "Hair" episode from *Body Bags.* The attack on that all-purpose cinematic villain "corporate greed"—certainly an anachronism now that the "owners" of most corporations are no longer deep-pocketed fat cats, but the investment plans and mutual funds that carry with them every American's hopes for a comfortable retirement—is not really a political world view. It's just the independent filmmaker's only way of expressing his resentment of the business necessities that make his particular art form (and most others) possible. It's the love-hate relationship between the paid piper and the sponsor whose hand feeds him. Of course, the finale of the film suggests that what it has all really been about is only the making of a movie. An order, after all—but not the one we, or John Trent, had in mind.

So now that we know, we may perhaps to begin, yes? But we already have begun. Only just. The psychiatrist slips insignificantly out of the film, and Trent is left to treat himself—inexorably, terrifyingly, wondrously alone.

The "corporate greed" motif and its dovetail into the "film on film" motif finally amount to comparatively little in light of the film's more enormous and urgent themes—the reality of evil, the willingness of people to embrace what will destroy them, and the entrapping power of the subjective mind. These are big ideas, and if Carpenter does not seem always certain, clear, and consistent in the way he addresses them, that only reaffirms the final, awful power of moral and intellectual subjectivism. Whether the disruption of order in the film is the literal incursion of an ultimate evil into our lives, or the collapse of Trent's own mind, or simply the imposition of a filmmaker's will upon the subject matter of his art, we are left with this: If nothing is certain, then anything is possible—which is at once the most promising thought and the most horrifying.

Note

1. Clarens, Carlos, *An Illustrated History of the Horror Film* (New York: Capricorn, 1967), p. 15.

21

There Are Going to Be Changes

Village of the Damned

When it first appeared in 1960, Wolf Rilla's *Village of the Damned* was, in a way, the epitome of the Age of Anxiety film. It came at the end of a decade that had seen an explosion of films in which invading monsters metaphorically crystallized the nightmares of the era—nuclear destruction, autocracy, dehumanization, increasing government control, rampant conformism. John Wyndham's 1957 novel *The Midwich Cuckoos*—named for the fact that cuckoos lay their eggs in other birds' nests—chose as its metaphorical monster perhaps the most terrifying of all: our own children. If horror films are essentially about loss of control, then certainly loss of control over our own children—and thus over ourselves and our destiny—is one of the most compelling of horror themes.

By the time Rilla made Wyndham's novel into *Village of the Damned*, Jack Arnold had already made *The Space Children* (1958), in which normal human children fell under an alien influence that caused them to sabotage the nation's nuclear defense systems. The notion that children could be the instrument of invasion was perfectly suited to an age in which the emergence of rock 'n' roll, "juvenile delinquents," motorcycle rebels, and the Beat Generation in the United States was counterpointed by stories of an increasingly autocratic Soviet Union in which children were brainwashed and encouraged to inform on their dissenting parents.

The theme, which undoubtedly springs from the most fundamental fears of parents about being inadequate to the task of raising their children, and perhaps from long-buried resentments of the way in which children irretrievably change the lives of their parents has, of course, emerged in other horror films in other eras, most notably *The Exorcist* (1973). *Village of the Damned* itself spawned a sequel, Anton Leader's *Children of the Damned* (1963), held by some critics to be superior to the original.

In Rilla's film, the rural English town of Midwich suddenly becomes unaccountably paralyzed, its inhabitants—and anyone within a
certain sharply defined radius—rendered unconscious. The condition
dissipates after a short time, but soon afterward every woman in the
town is discovered to be pregnant. The children—blond, bright-eyed,
intelligent automata who resemble one another more than they resemble their ostensible "parents"—gradually and increasingly assert their
collective will over the residents of the town, to unknown purpose. Ultimately the threat must be destroyed by one man willing to sacrifice
his own life in a battle of wills against the children.

To a young John Carpenter, *Village of the Damned* certainly
stood in the proud tradition of eerie, icy, monochrome British horror
films he admired: *X—The Unknown* (1956) and the Nigel Kneale-
scripted Quatermass films *The Creeping Unknown* (1956) and *Enemy
from Space* (1957). Making an updated American version was a long-
time dream of Carpenter's (as was a proposed remake of Jack Arnold's
1954 *Creature from the Black Lagoon*, which thus far has not seen the
light of day).

In a sense, Carpenter's remake of *Village of the Damned* is also a
remake of (or at least a revisit to) his own *The Fog*—which was itself
to some degree a remake of Wolf Rilla's original *Village of the
Damned* (1960). In each, there's a little town with a secret, a power
failure signals an invasion, something goes terribly wrong, the towns-
folk deny the problem and go forward with a festival that celebrates
their pride in their village, and things seem to return to normal when in
fact they are changed utterly. *The Fog*'s Antonio Bay is a lot like
Rilla's Midwich, and Carpenter's Midwich is more like Antonio Bay
than it is like its British prototype.

Did this film need to be remade? a lot of critics asked, when Carpenter's version appeared in 1995. But Carpenter surely brought his
own touch to the film, characterized by the haunting montages of crisp,
clean compositions that have characterized his work since *Halloween*
and that reached a pinnacle in *Prince of Darkness*. A true filmmaker—
certainly more so than the more literarily inclined Rilla—Carpenter
tells much of his story by elision and allusion, eschewing expository
dialogue, telling his story by not telling it, revealing by suggesting,
trusting the viewer to draw conclusions that remain unarticulated for
much of the film.

The story is still Wyndham out of Rilla, but Carpenter has
branded it with some of his own recurring themes and devices: A pivotal character is a priest, as in *Prince of Darkness* and *The Fog*. A

Village of the Damned
The Children
in Wolf Rilla's 1960 film (above)
and in John Carpenter's 1995 remake (below).

reference to a Lovecraftian "Book of the Damned" looks back to *Prince of Darkness* and *In the Mouth of Madness*; distrust of the government, and of any enterprise in which it takes an interest, echoes the repressive government agencies of *Starman* and *Memoirs of an Invisible Man* and the crypto-Nazi alien government of *They Live*. The theme crescendos with the depiction of martial law—not the benevolent, likeable, saving militia of Wolf Rilla's film, but a menacing force whose purpose is to conceal and condemn. The imagery—soldiers in safe suits and masks, jeeps taking over the town—recalls George Romero's little-seen but haunting 1973 film *The Crazies* (*Code Name: Trixie*). Ultimately we will learn (another divergence from the original) that the government plans to destroy the village, as it has similar villages in other parts of the world—and no evacuation can be efficiently carried out without alerting the children. Thus, in true Carpenter ambivalence, the film's paranoia is split between fear of the alien invasion and fear of the very government that seeks to protect us from it. If the repressive government vs. benevolent alien of *Starman* reversed the dialectic of *The Thing*, then *Village of the Damned* combines both, leaving us nowhere to turn but inward. Thus *Village of the Damned* makes more sense as the work of the John Carpenter of *In the Mouth of Madness*.

The original film and novel's coy turn on Christianity—a plethora of miraculous births, some of them to virgins, resulting in a dozen Anti-Christs—gets a new spin in Carpenter's version. The possibility of abortion is raised early on, when the government-associated research scientist Susan Verner offers to pay the Midwich mothers to go through with having their babies so they can be studied. "The choice is yours," she says, emphatically—and the suggestion is that we do have control over what befalls us. It is the government, in its eagerness to exploit the phenomenon, that indirectly causes the Midwich cuckoos to come to full term and emerge as a threat to human survival. This theme echoes the structure of the vast majority of the monster movies of the Fifties, in which the monsters created by Promethean technology (usually the bomb) could finally be destroyed only by recourse to that same technology. Here, oppressive government acts as both midwife and executioner to the alien Children.

As in the traditional model of the anti-intellectual, anti-Promethean science fiction film, *Frankenstein* and its progeny, it is the simple folk who rise up to hound both the monster and its creator to their destruction. Here, though, it doesn't work: a lynch mob led by Sarah Miller—wife of the village minister, killed by the children after his desperate attempt to pick them off with a hunting rifle—is defeated by the Children's superior will. Only a single, heroic individual can save us now. Who would have thought that the mild-mannered, gentle, withdrawn Dr. Chaffee would end up being the last best hope of mankind? (But then, who would have thought that of the strutting, ineffectual Jack Burton in *Big Trouble in Little China*, or the classroom intellectual Howard Birack in *Prince of Darkness*?)

The ambivalent role of government as both creator and destroyer of the menace is crystallized in Dr. Verner, who places the burden of "choice" in the hands of the mothers, but uses the powers of government to perpetuate the menace until it is too late. It is she who removes and conceals the one stillborn baby (whose death reduces the Children to an odd number, leaving one partnerless), the better to understand what this thing is that has come among us. She knows early on, but does nothing to warn Midwich until the children have grown to a treacherous preadolescence.

Carpenter retains some of Rilla's devices, most notably the cutting-in of pictorial representations of the thoughts of various characters as they either resist or give in to the influence of the Children. As in the original film, thinking of a wall is Dr. Chaffee's strongest weapon against the Children's mind control. But Carpenter uses the technique more expansively, adding the thought of an ocean earlier on, and he applies it to several characters, not just Chaffee.

Similarly, the visual image of the Children is adopted from the earlier film, but spectacularly enhanced. They are white-haired, as in Rilla's film; but in this color version the device tends to evoke less the Children of the original than the white-haired, hyperintelligent alien Essex in *This Island Earth* (1954). Indeed, David—the one sensitive, feeling soul among the Children—looks as if he could be Essex as a child (or one of Essex's children?). Moreover, when the children use their power to influence human action, we can see the configuration of their alien faces showing through their human ones—a device not from the original Village of the Damned but from Gene Fowler's evocative *I Married a Monster from Outer Space* (1958).

The universal experience of American parents is captured in another device: a shot of a line of cars at twilight bringing the Midwich mothers to the clinic to deliver their babies is echoed later in a similar shot of a line of cars, now at night, bringing the children to the barn outside of town, to be dropped off at their new communal headquarters—surely the most ominous kids' sleepover in history.

By the time the Children demand to be removed to the barn to mount their strategies together, without human interference or the inconvenience of physical separation, they have already changed utterly the order of things in middle-American Midwich. Like Santa Rosa in Hitchcock's *Shadow of a Doubt*, or Bodega Bay in *The Birds*, or the little towns of David Lynch's *Blue Velvet* and *Twin Peaks*, or, indeed, Antonio Bay in *The Fog* and Hob's End in *In the Mouth of Madness*, Midwich is small-town America utterly subverted by evil—not the neatly trimmed lawns but the corruption-feeding worms writhing just below the surface.

The onset of the new order is announced when Mara—leader of the Children, "daughter" of Dr. Chaffee, and murderer of her host-mother—tells Chaffee, "There are going to be changes." Carpenter's stylistic emphasis on this moment underscores its importance. Mara's is the only line in a brief scene that begins as we discover Chaffee brooding over a photograph of himself and his now-dead wife. In the preceding scene, the children have telekinetically engineered the suicide (by a leap from a high place, just as with Chaffee's wife) of the school building custodian who, in his cups as always, dared to challenge them. Chaffee now wordlessly connects the two deaths. As he does so, Mara enters the room. She waits until he has sensed her presence and has looked up to give her his attention. Then she announces, "There are going to be changes." For all the world like a new officer taking charge of an undisciplined military unit, or a petty martinet of a politician taking over a hamlet in need of "re-education," she lets the message stand, turns, and leaves the room.

Mara's cryptic message signals an apocalyptic disturbance in the order of things. We recall Egg Shen's recount of a previous era of disruptive change in *Big Trouble in Little China*: "Huge earthquakes turned the world upside down. Many normal people were killed. Many unnatural people roamed free to commit great offenses ..." Or the ancient diary at the beginning of *Prince of Darkness*, with its forbidding words, "The Sleeper wakens. I have witnessed his stirrings." Or Brian Marsh's analysis of the same phenomenon in the same film: "A life form ... self-organizing ... becoming something," and later, describing the force as "reaching out ... influencing ... changing things." The children are agents of change, fatal, final change, change that strikes at the heart of the very order of things. As in *They Live*, the sense of the order of the universe is disrupted by uninvited visitors who only seem to be like us, and who bring changes undreamed of. Like the desperate resistance of Nada and his colleagues, Dr. Chaffee's self-sacrifice is a reaffirmation, for now, of the proper order of things—a darker version of Professor Birack's "We stopped it here." We have the sense not of victory but of a beachhead, the temporary containment of an evil that can never be altogether defeated.

Jill MacGowan, the host-mother of David, her husband having been the first victim of the invasion, would seem likely to be the most adamant against the children; but that role falls to Sarah Miller (Pippa

Pearthree, in a ferocious performance evocative of Mercedes McCambridge's unforgettable mob leader Emma Small in Nicholas Ray's 1954 *Johnny Guitar*). Jill, by contrast, clings to her belief that there is something good in David, something salvageable. Of her, a woman impregnated by a godlike force, we wonder, as William Butler Yeats did of Leda, "Did she put on his knowledge with his power?"

Indeed, David, her son, the odd one (the stillborn baby was to have been his "partner"), is the one who becomes most human as he develops. In a plot development unconnected to anything in the original film, David begins to stray from the group and thus becomes someone—something—Dr. Chaffee can reach. The boy broods on his dead partner, as if, knowing something of death (unlike the other children, who have been untouched by it), he is affected by it, and becomes able to feel.

But there is a distinct ambiguity in David's survival at the end of the film. Is this another case of "evil never dies," as in the final shots of *Halloween, The Fog, Christine, Big Trouble in Little China, Prince of Darkness*? Or does this thing that survives still have a chance of becoming good or evil, as in the open ending of *The Thing*, or the black comic finale to *In the Mouth of Madness*? The film turns back on itself and, without saying so, readdresses the Christian (or anti-Christian) suggestion of its original source. The question we are left with is another one asked by Yeats when looking at the Millennium from a few decades farther off:

> ... twenty centuries of stony sleep
> Were vexed to nightmare by a rocking cradle,
> And what rough beast, its hour come round at last,
> Slouches toward Bethlehem to be born?

Escape from L.A.
Above: The President (Cliff Robertson).
Below: Snake Plissken in L.A.

22

Sooner or Later They Get Everybody

Escape from L.A.

"Basically, sequels mean the same film," John Carpenter had said in 1989, commenting on the string of *Halloween* sequels and his sale of his rights in the property to Moustapha Akkad.[1] It must have amused him to make a sequel of his own in *Escape from L.A.*—and, of course, to make it the same film as *Escape from New York*.

More a remake than a sequel, *Escape from L.A.* updates the events and milieu of *Escape from New York*. Each character and episode in the original film has an analogue in the new one (Malloy as Bob Hauck, Map to the Stars Eddie as Cabbie, Hershe Las Palmas as Brain, Cuervo Jones as Duke). Once again the scruffy, irreverent Snake Plissken is the last best hope of mankind (or unkind), and once again, owing to the compromising position of a President with awesome, world-destroying power, the stakes are nothing less than the survival of the human race. Finally, as in *Escape from New York*, Snake saves us by being less concerned about whether we survive than about what it is that survives.

The allegations that Tony Williams made about use of the imagery of political dissent in *Assault on Precinct 13*[2] seem more applicable to *Escape from L.A.*, a film that, unlike *Assault on Precinct 13*, does aspire to political comment. But here again, Carpenter is not engaging in political dialectic, but is simply stereotyping two extremes of evil, in a style consistent with the comic book approach of his film. The beret of the political revolutionary, on the head of Cuervo Jones, is mere cover for a sick mind, an unequivocally evil nemesis.

With neo-Nazi cops, "Moral America," and a Religious Right dictator-President on the one side, and a beret-wearing, womanizing, stop-at-nothing Che Guevara look-alike on the other, how can we not put our faith in the nihilistic Snake Plissken? Snake is reminiscent not only of the earlier Snake of Escape from New York but also of Nada in *They Live*, walking the line between the living death of sheepish, submissive conformism and the real death meted out by malevolent alien oppressors.

What Tony Williams called the "radical alternative" in his analysis of *Assault on Precinct 13* is no better than the oppressive system it opposes. If we wonder how, in the course of Carpenter's ideological development, the heroic police of *Assault on Precinct 13* have become the figures of political repression of *They Live* and *Escape from L.A.*, we have only to recognize that even as early as *Assault on Precinct 13*, it was never "the police" that were heroic—only individual policemen. There were more repressive and abusive police in *Assault on Precinct 13* than there were heroic ones.

If there is one key to Carpenter's work, it is the perennial struggle to balance Hawks's commitment to the professionalism of the team with Leone's devotion to the pared-down behavior code of the lone, self-interested individual. In this regard, it is worth noting that Kurt Russell—the one actor who has mattered most in the iconography of John Carpenter—mimicked a Hawksian John Wayne in *Big Trouble in Little China*, where he played a member of a team, but in his Snake Plissken portrayals he mimics a Leonean Clint Eastwood—evident especially in *Escape from L.A.*'s game of "Bangkok Rules." (Also, near the end of Escape from L.A., Carpenter manages a close shot of Snake in which Kurt Russell, even with only one eye visible, looks for all the world like the Charles Bronson of *Once Upon a Time in the West*.)

So after all, the film—like *Assault on Precinct 13*—suggests that salvation lies not in attachment to any one political view or order of belief, but to a code of personal honor and heroism in the face of evil. Make no mistake about it: Even in the wacky world of *Escape from L.A.*, the face of evil is very real.

Where New York became a prison, Los Angeles has become a microcosm of the world. Evil is laid at the doorstep of the city itself. Even the self-styled anarchist Cuervo Jones says without glee, "This fucking city can kill anybody." The attitude is pressed in a twist on the original film's oft-echoed "I heard you were dead" tagline. When Snake is asked, "You are Snake Plissken, aren't you?" his reply is "I useta be." And later there's this exchange with Taslima:

> "What are you doing in L.A.?"
> "Dyin'."

Of course, Snake is referring to the device (also adopted from the original film) of a doomsday bug implanted in Snake that will kill him if he doesn't fulfill his mission and return in time for the antidote to be administered. But he is also characterizing the corrosive influence of the city itself. L.A. is a "Dark Paradise" emblematic of a system—or a world—that is indefatigable.

"So they got you too."
"Sooner or later they get everybody."

Dialogue like this fills the film with a sense of hopelessness that is crucial to setting up Carpenter's finale. Indeed, if the film weren't otherwise filled with offbeat comedy and over-the-top thrills, it would run the risk of being too depressing to bear. Nowhere is that more apparent than the darkly comic timing and raw emotional punch of the moment in which Taslima, whom Snake, and we, have grown to like, half-defends L.A., saying, "Once you figure out this place, it's really not so bad." *Bang!* Almost before she finishes the sentence, she's shot dead. The city doesn't take kindly to being figured out.

It does, however, love a winner. That, at least, is what Map to the Stars Eddie tells Snake after Snake's victory at lethal basketball, the film's analogue to the gladiatorial combat of *Escape from New York*. It's clear that, characteristically for Carpenter, L.A.'s Dark Paradise epitomizes not only a corrupt and corrosive socioeconomic system but also the Movie Business itself: Eddie describes himself as Cuervo Jones's agent, and in effect becomes Snake's; the film's dark L.A. is like a subverted movie theme park; the President's tirades against L.A. echo the Moral Right's war against the movies in the early Nineties. So much of the film's dialogue and dialectic operate as a dark satire on the world of Hollywood and the movie industry that *Escape from L.A.* seems to be John Carpenter's hate letter to the industry and the whole Southern California lifestyle (plastic surgery included) that it has engendered.

There are, of course, moments of redemption—the most satisfying and justly beloved of which is the self-effacing performance of B-movie icon Peter Fonda, parodying himself at a time when B-movies have become A-movies, surfing a tsunami with Snake through L.A.'s storm drains. But even this sequence, with its sense of bonding and liberation, is underscored with mutual distrust. Trust is a tough thing to come by these days, and the world of *Escape from L.A.* is a world where distrust is the rule. Though the film is peopled with many characters and massive, crowded action sequences, *Escape from L.A.*'s basic composition is the one-on-one confrontation: It's Snake against everybody else, one at a time.

The confrontational world of *Escape from L.A.*
Snake Plissken (Kurt Russell) vs.:
Facing page: Above: Pipeline (Peter Fonda). Below: the Surgeon
General of Beverly Hills (Bruce Campbell). This page: Above: Her-
she Las Palmas (Pam Grier), with Map to the Stars Eddie (Steve
Buscemi) looking on. Below: Malloy (Stacy Keach).

In the worlds of both *Escape from New York* and *Escape from L.A.*, so many of the characters—Snake especially—seem to make the right gestures for the wrong reasons. Ironically, Snake ends up doing exactly the same thing that Cuervo Jones threatened to do. But when Snake pushes the button and plunges mankind into a world lit only by stick matches, it isn't evil. It's as if he's doing us a favor. Is *Escape from L.A.* ultimately cynical about the human race? Or only about the mediocre people who purport to run it, and the technological tyranny their power enables them to exercise?

The film's ending suggests another case of something surviving that may not be evil at all, but may indeed be of value. Like *The Thing*, the film ends with a shutdown of technology and the subjection of humankind to the forces of nature. This might be a fourth installment in what may now have become Carpenter's "Apocalyptic Tetralogy." Here, though, the apocalypse is less an end than a new beginning. Not an easy one, to be sure, but one that carries the hope that human beings will, in starting over, rediscover something of value, something that has, until now, been terribly lost.

It is an odd message for an essentially comic action thriller, and as anti-Promethean a message as any ever embraced in the long tradition of science fiction film: Our hope lies not in mastering the earth through technology, but in rediscovering what it is to be human.

Notes

1. See p. 65.
2. See discussion in Chapter 3, pp. 35-41.

23

<u>Sunset</u>

Vampires

After nearly a year in the can, John Carpenter's *Vampires* opened on Halloween, 1998, to almost universally denigrating reviews. I had always found much to like in even the somewhat disappointing Carpenter films, and anticipated that *Vampires* would be no different. In fact, however, far from finding *something* to like in the film, I found it an easy film to like as a whole, even admire.

Though not a lot of John Steakley's novel *Vampire$* remains in John Carpenter's *Vampires*, it's easy to see what attracted Carpenter to the project in the first place. It must have seemed as Hawksian a project as any Carpenter had ever taken on, centered as it is on a Hawksian team with a mission consisting of nothing short of saving the world from complete infection at the hands of an apocalyptic menace. It offered the opportunity to visit, once again, the Hawksian dynamics of *Assault on Precinct 13*, *The Thing*, *Big Trouble in Little China*, *Prince of Darkness*, and *They Live*, and to bring a new treatment to the theme of the small team of professionals playing for the highest stakes of all. At the same time, it focused on a tough Leonean antihero who is able to be a team unto himself, who out-Snakes even Snake Plissken, who never hesitates to slap someone around in the service of his mission and his professionalism in achieving it—stranger, friend, woman, priest. Brutality in the battle against evil is no vice, it seems, and it may be no accident that Jack Crow, besides having the same initials as Jesus Christ, also shares the monogram of John Chance—and of John Carpenter.

The setting of the American Southwest must have been the frosting on the cake. If any project ever afforded Carpenter the opportunity to make the western he always wanted to direct, combining horror and heroism, Hawks and Leone, *Vampire$* was it. It was an opportunity to revisit (perhaps to culminate?) his career-long flirtation with the western. He'd written at least two westerns (*El Diablo* and *Blood River*), arguably three (the parodistic urban western *The Resurrection of Broncho Billy*), produced one, but as a director contented himself with infusing Western elements into tales of urban horror (*Assault on Precinct 13, Escape from New York, They Live, Escape from L.A.*). In an interview in late 1998 he commented, "in essence, I've always loved westerns, and one of the reasons I'm doing this movie is that this is the closest I've come to being able to do a western."[1]

Certainly he has risen to the challenge, as evidenced in the film's commitment to primordial male confrontation, paucity of dialogue, abundance of close-ups, and emphasis on horizontal composition. An insistence upon sunsets is also critical. That traditional image of the western as the end of a way of life for a certain type of hero here takes on a second meaning. Nightfall is daybreak for the living dead, and it is the ability to live by day as well as by night that informs Valek's ultimate quest for power. "The hour's gettin' late," says Crow to the Padre, pointedly paraphrasing a key line from Leone's *Once Upon a Time in the West* to new purpose and urgency. The film's evocation of the western (and specifically the Italian western) also affords Carpenter the opportunity to mimic, in his music, the electric guitar underscoring that helped make that film genre so compelling. The music for *Vampires* is Carpenter's best, an amalgam of country blues, surf music, and hard rock, with rhythms that recall the stylish appeal of Leone's first films, but with a growling lead guitar that gives voice to the bestiality of the film's confrontations.

Novel Into Film

Vampires retains some of the novel's most inventive ideas and riveting sequences, such as the opening attack on the house, the motel room massacre, and the raid on the abandoned jailhouse, with Crow's use of an old elevator as a means of delivering the vampires into the hands of the slayers. But in most other ways, little remains of Steakley's novel.

The first thing to disappear from *Vampire$* was the dollar sign. Unlike the team of Steakley's novel, the slayers in Carpenter's film are not mercenaries. Devotion to their cause, not to profit, is what gives the slayers their incentive—that and pride in their own professionalism. They thus remain poor and even less appreciated than they are in the novel, where the anti-vampire campaign is carried out on a strictly for-hire basis, and there is always the chance of walking away (though even there the capitalistic angle is far less important than the novel's title makes it seem).

Another thing that disappeared in the transformation of *Vampire$* into *Vampires* is eroticism. Steakley's novel features a much more compelling female character than the film's Katrina, the prostitute who becomes the bride of both Valek the Master Vampire and Montoya, the vampire slayer. The novel's Davette, a reporter who joins the team ostensibly to tell their story to the world ends up telling her own story to the team—a story of seduction by evil that evolves from the most beguiling eroticism to the most horrific perversion of sexuality and violence, and is the most powerful passage of a novel filled with remarkably affecting writing.

Truth to tell, John Carpenter has always been a director more of Mars than of Eros. While he worked romantic magic with Karen Allen and Jeff Bridges in *Starman*, he remains less interested in sexual attraction than in the ability of women to prove themselves to be at least as tough and resourceful as the men around them. Yet even Annabelle, the novel's crusty housemother to the team, did not survive into the film, and some of the most interesting subordinate characters in the novel, the team members themselves, are wiped out early in the film in Valek's riveting one-man attack on the team's motel suite. Carpenter wastes no time in getting Steakley's panoply of literary characters honed down to something as spare as a Sergio Leone western: an arch-villain, a bunch of bad guys, no more than three good guys, and a lot of desert.

But what remains is the raw power, impossible strength, and unrelenting evil of Steakley's vampires—the objectivity of evil. Valek is like The Shape in *Halloween* in more than his stature and his seeming indestructibility. It has always been essential to the Carpenter vision that evil exists. It is part of the Order of things. There was no excusing the gang members of *Assault on Precinct 13*; notwithstanding their adoption of the trappings of disadvantaged youth and political dissent, they were cold-blooded agents of evil who would shoot down a kid from an ice cream truck. There was no excusing Michael Myers, nor even any understanding him (notwithstanding the lame psychological and occult "explanations" for his behavior in the string of sequels). He really was the Bogey Man. There was no excusing the Thing, the vampiric Lo Pan, the Dark Father of *Prince of Darkness*, the aliens of *They Live*, nor the Children of *Village of the Damned*. Make no mistake: These are beings that mean us harm. They're not here to propose alternatives, they're here to destroy us all and take over, like the Lovecraftian beings from beyond in *In the Mouth of Madness*.

John Carpenter and his characters have no patience with efforts to "understand" the other side. The bad guys are pure evil, to be unsympathetically rooted out and destroyed. In the film, Jack Crow admonishes his wanna-be apprentice, Father Adam, to forget all he's read or heard or seen in movies about vampires. These guys are "not romantic." In an interview, Carpenter said:

> I've never liked victim stories. In other words, Vampires as victims ... they're victims of a curse, they can't help themselves. That sounds like a movie of the week, it sounds like a TV movie, you know what I mean? I want my vampires to be really grim and terrifying and seeking power and seeking eternal life. Well they have eternal life and if you think about it, if I had a chance to have eternal life I might go for it. I might sell out and go for it. So I wanted Valek, my main character, to be a very powerful and unapologetic vampire. He's no victim.

As I have attempted to show in the preceding chapters, most of Carpenter's films involve a struggle between two orders—an existing one and a usurping one. In most of his films, this tension arises from one of two metaphoric incursions: an invasion of beings from another planet, who seek, for good or ill, to establish a presence on Earth (*The Thing, Starman, They Live, Village of the Damned*); or the upsurge of an already-present but dormant evil in our own world (*Assault on Precinct 13, Halloween, The Fog, Christine, Big Trouble in Little China, Prince of Darkness, In the Mouth of Madness*). Sometimes the invading force is the force of good and human beings are the authors of evil (as in *Starman*). Sometimes good is nowhere to be found (as in *The Fog*, in which a supernatural evil arises to punish an even more evil human community). But more commonly the invading or resurgent force is an evil both inherent in and a direct challenge to our concept of the order of our universe, and good subsists, if at all, in our ability and willingness to fight to ensure the survival of what is truly human. Carpenter is ultimately less interested in which side wins, because evil always survives. What interests him is the conflict itself, and the way it illuminates and transforms the human character.

What also remains from Steakley is the strength of Crow and his team. Indeed, if anything, this is the element of the novel that Carpenter has most enhanced in the film, because it is at the core of what is most essential to Carpenter's vision.

Assault on Precinct 13 involved the assembly, from unexpectedly disparate elements, of a Hawksian team that was good enough to defeat the evil forces marshaled against it. *The Thing*, despite its obvious debt

Vampires
... and Slayers

to Hawks, was in a way an anti-Hawksian film, since it began with a Hawksian team of professionals and mercilessly observed its disintegration at the hands of an evil too powerful for the team to withstand. Spirit and conviction energize the Hawksian team. They are sustained by mutual trust (the lack of which is exactly what breaks down the team of Carpenter's *The Thing*) and by certainty of right, as in Carpenter's loose trilogy of independent films in the late Eighties in each of which a Hawksian team faces hell with somewhat more success. *Big Trouble in Little China* is perhaps Carpenter's most Hawksian film, concerned with professionalism, teamwork, and masculinity, but also gently comic, willing to brook failings in even its strongest characters in order to give them something to rise above. The nerdier academic team assembled by Prof. Howard Birack in *Prince of Darkness* is less decisively victorious, and *They Live*'s team of two ends up destroyed for the sake of saving the earth—or at least of making us see.

Several individual-centered films intervened before Carpenter again addressed the theme of the Hawksian team in *Vampires*. Nick Halloway could not, ultimately, survive and surmount his affliction without the commitment of a loving partner. John Trent, alone, could do nothing but watch (and unwittingly participate in) apocalyptic destruction. Dr. Chaffee left at least one of the alien Children alive in Midwich. Even Snake Plissken, resourceful as Odysseus, was dependent upon the kindness of strangers to fulfill his mission—strangers who gave their lives to see him through.

But *Vampires* gives us in Jack Crow a Hawksian hero who remains good enough to draw others to himself, command loyalty, and see the job through. Crow, like Snake, has the power to draw to himself the best and the strongest; and in the course of the film his crack team is utterly destroyed, then slowly reconstituted by the sheer force of Crow's own will. Where Carpenter's framing in *The Thing* stressed the isolation of the individual from the group, and in *Escape from L.A.* emphasized one-to-one confrontation, his compositions in *Vampires* underscore this reconstitution—disparate individuals coming together after disastrous disjunction.

A Problem with Women

What are we to make of this unlikely Leonean hero dropped into Carpenter's Hawksian world? Much has been made—by viewers and critics—of Crow's misogyny. Too much, perhaps, since to my mind Crow is pretty egalitarian—he abuses not just women but everyone. Moreover, it's hard to say anything meaningful about his attitude toward "women" when there is only one woman in the film for him to have any attitude toward. But it's worthwhile to remember that the same approach to women was characteristic of James Woods's character in *Once Upon a Time in America* (and, come to think of it, a few other Woods characters as well). Carpenter, in *Vampires*, cross-references Leone as much with the casting of Woods as he does with his approach to music and cinematography. In Leone's last film, the misogyny of Woods's character, Max—and arguably of all the members of the gang portrayed in that difficult gangster epic—is a reaffirmation of their all-male universe. It is, again, a Hawksian theme that women—and men's too-soft attitude toward them—harms the strength and professionalism of the team. That is why, in Carpenter's films as in Leone's, only the toughest women belong, and only they survive.

In Valek's hair-raising attack on the motel room party and his single-handed slaughter of most of the slayers, the members of the team are killed while (and arguably because) they are whoring. The women die in nakedness—a slasher-movie motif that became de rigeur in the "dead teenager" movies that followed in the wake of *Halloween* where, as we have seen, it had some semblance of meaning beyond the moralistic subtext so many read into it. The suggestion is of a condemnation not of women, nor of sex, but of promiscuity, of the kind of self-indulgence that causes the Hawksian professional to lose control and become vulnerable.

But of equal importance is the way in which Crow's misogyny (if that is, after all, the appropriate word for his suspicion, resentment, and abuse of the vampire-infected Katrina) counterpoints a certain crypto-homosexual baiting of Father Adam. Crow's interest in sexuality seems inextricably intertwined with violence between males. After administering a beating to the young priest, Crow probingly asks if being a victim gave him "wood." The use of the term "wood," punning on the actor's name as well as on the wood of the penile stake used to penetrate and destroy vampires, is not just an idle throwaway. It's important enough to be the note that the film ends on. Father Adam is silent on the question whether he felt a sexual thrill at being the victim of physical abuse; but he gives as good as he gets in the banter that ends the film. His acknowledgement that being on the slayer end is what really gives him "wood" makes near-explicit the homosexual sub-motif of the film and of Crow's character. Naturally he has a problem with women.

Finally, not to put too fine a point on it, recall that vampirism is characterized in *Vampires* as an "infection"—the same metaphor that was adopted by F. W. Murnau for his *Nosferatu* (1922), and that John

John Carpenter and James Woods on the set of *Vampires*.

Carpenter had himself used in *The Thing*, which appeared just at the beginning of the growing awareness of AIDS. There is a sense in which, whether by accident or design, Team Crow's zeal in the merciless slaying of vampires becomes metaphoric of the ferocity of a homosexual community's response to the new, apocalyptic, universal killer—an infection that ultimately, tragically, cannot be separated from its victims.

Brothers under the Skin

Interestingly, Valek's victims match those of Crow, who beats up on Katrina, the priest, and Montoya, even as Valek attacks Katrina, kills her sister whores, slashes priests and monks, and turns on the members of Crow's own team. Does this curious parallel suggest that the slayers, and Crow in particular, in their zealous commitment to eradicating evil, ultimately become like the very evil they aim to destroy? Are Crow and Valek brothers after all? Or is Crow's abusive physicality a kind of "Tough Love," brutalizing others in order to save them—and to save something bigger?

If these hired guns of the Catholic Church are Christian, they are among the most unlikely Christians ever to grace the silver screen. Yet their battle is, as noted before, fought from conviction and dedication. Montoya tells one of the whores, "We know vampires are stalkin' the earth. We also know there's a God." His colleague Cat (one of the novel's most intriguing characters, who survives only a few minutes of the movie) chimes in, "We just don't understand Him."

Certainly the film, like the novel, is fueled by the tension between the pretense, empty ritual, and oppressive power of an organized religion and the urgent necessity of the battle to save the values that religion upholds. Here, as in *Prince of Darkness*, priests guard an ancient talismanic object until its time comes round and it may be turned once again to its intended use. The Church in this sense is burdened with both creating and destroying the evil, much like the government-funded scientists of the monster movies of the Fifties. We recall also another priest-with-an-old-book in *The Fog*, in which, again, like the Repressed, the evil returned to its point of creation to do final battle with what spawned it.

Oblique references to religion, and specifically to Christianity, abound in the film. There is a rendezvous at the Sun God Motel. The towns have the names of saints, and the scene of the final battle is San Miguel, which bears the same name as the town cleaned up by The Man with No Name in Leone's landmark *A Fistful of Dollars*. Jack Crow is crucified, and it is a cross that will ultimately fulfill Valek's

Vampires
The Passion of Valek before the Cross

unholy quest. When Valek is finally destroyed in a monumental explosion, Crow ambiguously utters a single word: "Jesus."

The uneasy relationship between Father Adam Guiteau and Jack Crow gives the film the objective correlate to the tension between religious faith and nihilistic cynicism in the face of violence and horror. It is not Crow but the members of his new team—the half-formed vampire Montoya and the half-formed slayer Father Adam—who foil the ceremony that would enable Valek to walk in light. After the final battle has been won, Father Adam says, "He was with us." Crow, whether out of physical exhaustion or the beginning of a true transformation of character, is willing to concede the point: "Fair enough."

Despite his name, Crow does, finally, represent light, and Valek darkness. Valek at last goes down, and Crow faces Montoya, like MacReady and Childs at the end of *The Thing*—two professionals brought to frozen stalemate because of an inability to trust each other and an unwillingness not to.

The film's ambiguous denouement recalls the ending to *Village of the Damned*: Just as Jill MacGowan and her alien "son" David survived Armageddon and headed out for "a place where no one knows who we are," Montoya and Katrina head down to Mexico, knowing they have both been infected—and Jack, who also knows, lets them go. Some people have complained that Jack Crow's willingness to let them escape is incredible and inconsistent. They haven't been paying attention—either to Crow or to his alter-ego John Carpenter. It is part of the order of the universe—perhaps the most important part—that evil never dies.

Note

1. Interviewed on Radio Canada, transcribed at:
http://radio-canada.ca/infoculture/speciale/fantasia/carpenter.html and cited in an article by Sean Axmaker on Film.com, *http://www.film.com*. The notion of a vampire Western was the subject of a fair amount of joking among reviewers of the film, and a few critics and fans mockingly recalled *Billy the Kid v. Dracula*, William Beaudine's goofy 1966 merger of the two classic film genres (to the detriment of both). No one, on the other hand, seems to have recalled *Curse of the Undead*, Edward Dein's genuinely eerie and atmospheric 1959 film, as far as I can tell the first vampire western, with haunting cinematography and a truly scary performance by Michael Pate as a vampire gunslinger.

John Carpenter
1997

See What Happens

I'm in the middle of an extended vacation. At the end of *Vampires* last January I realized that if I didn't take some time off I was going to burn out. I've been doing this too long. You can't just keep doing it, you have to get away from it. And I thought about Howard Hawks; he's the director I most feel is my mentor. In the Fifties he stopped for three years and he evaluated movies and his place in movies and what he wanted to do. I'm in the process of that. I don't think I'll take three years, but I need to step back—I have a family that I haven't seen—and see what happens.

—John Carpenter, 1998

Chronology

[D=director; W=writer; M=music composer; CM=music, shared credit; E=editor; CW=co-writer; P=producer; CP=co-producer; CXP=co-executive producer; A=actor]

1970	*The Resurrection of Broncho Billy*	CW, E, M
1975	*Dark Star*	D, CW, CP, M
1976	*Network*	A
1976	*Assault on Precinct 13*	D, W, M, E
1978	*Zuma Beach*	CW
1978	*Eyes of Laura Mars*	CW
1978	*Halloween*	D, CW, M
1978	*Someone's Watching Me!*	D, W
1979	*Elvis*	D
1980	*The Fog*	D, CW, M, A
1981	*Escape from New York*	D, CW, CM, A
1981	*Halloween II*	W, CP
1982	*The Thing*	D, CM
1983	*Christine*	D, CM
1983	*Halloween III: Season of the Witch*	CP
1984	*The Philadelphia Experiment*	CW, CP
1984	*Starman*	D
1985	*Black Moon Rising*	W
1986	*Big Trouble in Little China*	D, W, CM
1987	*Prince of Darkness*	D, W, CM
1988	*They Live*	D, W, CM
1988	*Halloween 4: The Return of Michael Myers*	CM
1989	*Halloween 5: The Revenge of Michael Myers*	CM
1990	*El Diablo*	CW, CXP
1991	*Blood River*	W
1992	*Memoirs of an Invisible Man*	D, A
1993	*Body Bags*	D, CM, CP
1993	*Darkness*	E
1994	*The Silence of the Hams*	A

1995	*In the Mouth of Madness*	D, CM
1995	*Village of the Damned*	D, CM
1995	*Halloween:*	
	The Curse of Michael Myers	CM
1996	*Escape from L.A.*	D, CW, CM
1998	*Halloween H20:*	
	Twenty Years Later	CM
1998	*Vampires*	D, CW, M

Filmography

THE RESURRECTION OF BRONCHO BILLY

University of Southern California, 1970

Direction: James Rokos. *Story*: **John Carpenter**, Nick Castle,[1] Trace Johnston, John Longnecker, James Rokos. *Cinematography*: Nick Castle. *Editing*: **John Carpenter**. *Music*: **John Carpenter**. *Production*: John Longnecker.
(21 minutes)

Players

Broncho Billy	Johnny Crawford
Artist	Kristen Nelson
Landlady	Nancy Wible
Old Timer	Wild Bill Tucker
Stockboy	Lee Hammerschmitt
Boss	Ray Montgomery
Businessman	Bill Lechner
Bartender	Bob Courtleigh
Counter Girl	Merry Scanlon

The Action

Billy gets through the boredom and adversity of 20th century urban life by adopting the manner of a B-movie cowboy. His one regret is that he can't afford a horse. In the end, if only in fancy, he gets the horse *and* the girl.

DARK STAR

Jack H. Harris Release,[2] 1975

Direction: **John Carpenter**. *Screenplay*: **John Carpenter**, Dan O'Bannon. *Cinematography*: Douglas Knapp. *Camera Assistant*: Nick Castle. *Special Effects*: Dan O'Bannon. *Visual Effects Consultant (opticals)*: Bill Taylor. *Production Design, Special Effects Supervision, and Editing*: Dan O'Bannon. *Animation*: Bob Greenberg. *Animation (computer effects)*: John Walsh. *Miniatures*: Greg Jein, Harry Walton. *Associate Art Director*: Tommy Lee Wallace. *Spaceship Exterior Design*: Ron Cobb. *Matte paintings*: Jim Danforth. *Music*: **John Carpenter**. *Song "Benson, Arizona" by*: Bill Taylor. *Production*: **John Carpenter**. (83 minutes)

Players

Doolittle	Brian Narelle
Talby	Andreijah (Dre) Pahich
Boiler	Cal Kuniholm
Pinback	Dan O'Bannon
Powell	Joe Sanders
Voice of Talby	John Carpenter
	(uncredited)

The Action

After losing their commander to a radiation leak, the crew of the scout-ship Dark Star continue their deep space mission to seek out and destroy uninhabited "unstable" planets. With little support from Earth, the crewmen begin to succumb to boredom and claustrophobia. The situation is worsened when a recalcitrant alien loose on the ship causes an electrical malfunction to the computer-controlled bomb system. Doolittle, the acting commander, tries to talk the bomb into ignoring the computer's orders, but the bomb ultimately destroys itself and the ship, and the crew members take their place in the heavens.

ASSAULT ON PRECINCT 13[3]

C.K.K. Productions, Turtle Releasing,[4] 1976

Direction: **John Carpenter**. *Screenplay*: **John Carpenter**. *Cinematography*: Douglas Knapp. *Music*: **John Carpenter**. *Editing*: John T. Chance.[5] *Special Effects*: Richard Albain, Jr. *Art Direction, Sound Effects*: Tommy Wallace. *Assistant Director*: James Nichols. *Assistant Editor, Script Supervisor*: Debra Hill. *Production Manager*: John Syrjamaki. *Production*: J. S. Kaplan. *Executive Production*: Joseph Kaufman.
(91 minutes)

Players

Ethan Bishop	Austin Stoker
Napoleon Wilson	Darwin Joston
Leigh	Laurie Zimmer
Lawson	Martin West
Wells	Tony Burton
Julie	Nancy Loomis
Starker	Charles Cyphers
Sgt. Chaney	Henry Brandon
Kathy	Kim Richards
"Ice Cream Man"	Peter Bruni
Warden	John J. Fox
White warlord	Frank Doubleday
Chicano warlord	Gilbert de la Peña
Oriental warlord	Al Makauchi
Black warlord	James Johnson
Patrolmen	Marc Ross
	Alan Koss

The Action

In Anderson, a ghetto of Los Angeles, a street gang swears a blood oath of vengeance after police kill six gang members. A nearby police precinct house is reduced to minimum staff, headed by young Lt. Ethan Bishop, as officers and equipment are relocated to a new station some distance away. Meanwhile, three dangerous convicts are loaded aboard a prison bus headed for the maximum security prison in Sonora. When one of the prisoners becomes ill, the bus must make an unscheduled stop at the nearly abandoned Anderson precinct house. When a gang member kills a little girl, her father, Lawson, pursues the gang, kills the killer, then flees to the precinct house for protection. Left in charge of the station's skeleton crew, Lt. Bishop—who grew up in Anderson— finds himself with his hands full as the marauding gang mounts a relentless offensive on the precinct house. With all outside communication cut off, Bishop commands precinct employees and the Sonora-bound prisoners in a desperate defense of the little station.

ZUMA BEACH

NBC Television, 1978

Direction: Lee H. Katzin. *Teleplay*: **John Carpenter** & William Schwartz. *Story by*: John Herman Shaner & Alvin Ramrus. *Cinematography*: Hector Figueroa. *Art Direction*: Al Manser. *Editing*: Robert L. Swanson and Bobbie Shapiro. *Music*: Dick Halligan. *Executive Production*: Edgar J. Scherick & Daniel H. Blatt. *Production*: Bruce Cohn Curtis & Brian Grazer.
(100 minutes)

Players

Bonnie Catt	Suzanne Somers
Jerry McCabe	Steven Keats
David Hunter	Mark Wheeler
J.D.	Michael Biehn
Norman	Gary Imhoff
Beverly	Rosanna Arquette
Nancy	P. J. Soles
with:	Perry Lang
	Kimberly Beck
	Biff Warren
	Les Lannom
	Leonard Stone
	Steve Franken
	Richard Molinare
	Tanya Roberts
	Timothy Hutton
	Joshua Daniel
	Susan Duvall
	Bobby Doran
	Ben Marley

                                                    Shelley Johnson
                                                    Gary Prendergast
                                                    Victor Brandt
                                                    Pater Kowalski

The Action

Singer/songwriter Bonnie Catt faces her midlife crisis a little early
when her recording contract is canceled after she has gone a year and a
half without a Top 40 hit. Uncertain where to turn, or how to reorganize
her life, she finds herself drawn to Zuma Beach, where she used to
hang out in high school. Spending the day there helps her separate what
matters from what does not. During a day spent among high schoolers,
building sand castles, playing games, and giving advice, Bonnie officiates at the coming of age of David, helps Sandy choose between earnest
but erring David and overbearing, arrogant J.D., inspires some self-
assessment on the part of middle-aged dropout Jerry McCabe, and
helps catalyze the rebellion of brutalized Norman and David against the
bully J.D. She leaves the beach determined to resume her career with a
reaffirmed sense of self-worth, and satisfaction at having been able to
touch the lives of others.

EYES OF LAURA MARS

Columbia Pictures, 1978

Direction: Irvin Kershner. *Screenplay*: **John Carpenter** & David Zelag
Goodman. *Based on a story by*: **John Carpenter** (& Jon Peters, un-
credited). *Cinematography*: Victor Kemper. *Production Design*: Gene
Callahan. *Art Direction*: Robert Gundlach. *Costumes*: Theoni V. Al-
dredge. *Gallery Photographs*: Helmut Newton. *Other Photographs*:
Rebecca Blake. *Editing*: Michael Kahn. *Music*: Artie Kane. *Production*:
Jon Peters.
(103 minutes)

Players

Laura Mars   Faye Dunaway
John Neville   Tommy Lee Jones
Donald Phelps   Rene Auberjonois
Tommy Ludlow   Brad Dourif
Michael Reisler   "R.J." [Raul Julia]

Detective Sal Volpe	Frank Adonis
Michelle	Lisa Taylor
Lulu	Darlanne Fluegel
Bert	Michael Tucker
Elaine Cassell	Rose Gregorio

The Action

Fashion photographer Laura Mars begins suffering "blackouts" in which she sees murders committed as if she had the killer's eyes. She continues her controversial, violence-tinged work in photography, as the unseen murderer continues to stalk and slay, choosing victims from Laura's circle of friends and associates. Detective John Neville, investigating the killings, is initially repulsed and later fascinated by Laura and her work. His ambivalent attitude toward her ripens into love—but its true roots are revealed when Laura discovers that Neville himself is the murderer.

HALLOWEEN

Compass International, 1978

Direction: **John Carpenter**. *Screenplay*: **John Carpenter** and Debra Hill. *Cinematography*: Dean Cundey. *Panaglide Camera Operation*: Ray Stella. *Production Design*: Tommy Lee Wallace. *Music*: **John Carpenter**. *Editing*: Tommy Lee Wallace and Charles Bornstein. *Production*: Debra Hill. *Executive Production*: Irwin Yablans.
(93 minutes)

Players

Dr. Sam Loomis	Donald Pleasence
Laurie Strode	Jamie Lee Curtis
Annie Brackett	Nancy Loomis
Lynda	P.J. Soles
Deputy Leigh Brackett	Charles Cyphers
Lindsey Wallace	Kyle Richards
Tommy Doyle	Brian Andrews
Bob	John Michael Graham
Marion	Nancy Stephens
Michael Myers, age 23[6]	Tony Moran
The Shape	Nick Castle

The Action

Halloween 1978: Fifteen years after brutally murdering his own sister on Halloween night, psychopathic Michael Myers escapes from the mental institution where he has been confined and returns to his old neighborhood, pursued by his psychiatrist, Dr. Loomis. Stalking teenage girls who are like his sister, Michael fixes on Laurie, who is babysitting for the evening. With the help of Dr. Loomis, Laurie is able to rid herself of Michael; but the killer's superhuman strength leaves her and Dr. Loomis believing that he may not be dead and that, indeed, he may be a supernatural figure of indestructible evil, "the Bogey Man."

SOMEONE'S WATCHING ME!

Warner Bros. Television Productions, for NBC Television, 1978

Direction: **John Carpenter**. *Screenplay*: **John Carpenter**. *Cinematography*: Robert Hauser. *Art Direction*: Phil Barber. *Music*: Harry Sukman. *Editing*: Jerry Taylor. *Executive Production*: Richard Kobritz. (100 minutes)

Players

Leigh Michaels	Lauren Hutton
Sophie	Adrienne Barbeau
Paul	David Birney
Hunt	Charles Cyphers
Steve	Grainger Hines
Burly man	Len Lesser
Frimsin	John Mahon
Mr. Leone	James Murtaugh
Inspector	J. Jay Saunders
TV Anchor	Michael Laurence
Herbert Stiles	George Skaff
Wayne	Robert Phalen
Groves	Robert Snively
Waitress	Jean LeBouvier
Slick man	James McAlpine
Charlie	Edgar Justice
Eddie	John Fox

The Action

Trying to get over the collapse of a romantic relationship, New York TV director Leigh Michaels accepts a job in Los Angeles and moves into a luxury high-rise apartment. She begins receiving menacing phone calls as well as a series of mysterious gifts in the mail. As the situation intensifies, she gets help from Sophie, a coworker; Paul, a man she is dating; and Hunt, a police detective. Deducing that Leigh's nemesis is a man who lives in the apartment tower just opposite hers, the police pressure the man into leaving town. Shortly afterward, the calls resume. Leigh discovers that the man is operating out of a different apartment than that of the previous suspect. When the police will not believe her story, she ventures into her tormentor's apartment herself, leaving Sophie behind to keep watch. Looking back at her own apartment through the suspect's telescope, Leigh sees the man enter her apartment and kill Sophie. With no trace of a body or a crime, she is unable to persuade the police that a murder has been committed. With Paul's help she finds the true identity of the menace, an apartment building inspector who has access to the power, communications, and security systems of both apartment buildings, and who temporarily occupies the apartments of vacationing tenants as a base of operations from which to terrorize and kill single women. Leigh visits her enemy's house and finds evidence that he is the killer, then returns to her apartment to face him alone in a final confrontation.

ELVIS

NBC Television, 1979

Direction: **John Carpenter**. *Screenplay*: Anthony Lawrence. *Cinematography*: Donald M. Morgan. *Supervising Editor*: Tom Walls. *Editing*: Ron Moler. *Art Direction*: Tracy Borsman, James Newport. *Production*: Anthony Lawrence. *Supervising Production*: Tony Bishop. *Executive Production*: Dick Clark.
(Original version: 150 minutes; short version: 119 minutes)

Players

Elvis Presley	Kurt Russell
Mama	Shelley Winters
Elvis's father	Bing Russell
Priscilla Beaulieu Presley	Season Hubley

Bonnie   Melody Anderson
Col. Tom Parker   Pat Hingle
with: Robert Gray
                                              Ed Begley, Jr.
                                              Charles Cyphers
                                              Dennis Christopher
                                              James Canning
                                              Peter Hobbs
                                              Les Lannon
                                              Elliott Street

The Action

Young outcast Elvis Presley mourns the death of his brother and turns
to music to escape the teasing and ridicule of his schoolmates. Fighting
his fear, he enters a talent show, then makes a recording, and rockets to
success. Along the way, he continues to search for meaning in his life,
and is sustained by his devotion to his mother. When his mother dies,
Elvis seeks to start a new kind of life with his young wife, Priscilla, but
he is unable to balance his career, his growing need for audience acceptance, his marriage, and fatherhood. Against the wishes of his wife,
whose affections are increasingly estranged, he embarks on a concert
engagement in Las Vegas in a last-ditch effort to revive his career and
find new meaning in the strange role fate has decreed for him.

THE FOG

Avco-Embassy, 1980

Direction: **John Carpenter**. *Screenplay*: **John Carpenter** and Debra
Hill. *Production Design*: Tommy Lee Wallace. *Cinematography*: Dean
Cundey. *Editing*: Tommy Lee Wallace and Charles Bornstein. *Music*:
John Carpenter, electronic realization by Dan Wyman. *Special Effects*: Dick Albain, Jr. *Special Make-Up Effects*: Rob Bottin. *Production*: Debra Hill.
(91 minutes)

Players

Stevie Wayne   Adrienne Barbeau
Elizabeth Solley   Jamie Lee Curtis
Nick Castle   Tom Atkins

Kathy Williams	Janet Leigh
Father Malone	Hal Holbrook
Mr. Machen	John Houseman
Dick Baxter	James Canning
Dave O'Bannon	Charles Cyphers
Sandy Fadel	Nancy Loomis
Andy	Ty Mitchell
Al Williams	John Goff
Tommy Wallace	George "Buck" Flower
Mrs. Kobritz	Regina Waldon
The Dockmaster	Jim Hayne
Blake	Rob Bottin
Ghosts	Ric Moreno
	Lee Sacks
	Tommy Wallace
Dr. Phibes	Darwin Joston
Bennett	John Carpenter[7]

The Action

A strange fog rolls in off the ocean toward the town of Antonio Bay, California, coinciding with the town's celebration of its centennial. Horror and mayhem take hold, as out of the fog come the walking spirits of seamen murdered 100 years earlier by the original settlers of the town. The creatures wreak revenge, forcing the townspeople to face their heritage of evil.

ESCAPE FROM NEW YORK

Avco-Embassy, 1981

Direction: **John Carpenter**. *Screenplay*: **John Carpenter** and Nick Castle. *Production Design*: Joe Alves. *Cinematography*: Dean Cundey. *Editing*: Todd Ramsay. *Music*: **John Carpenter** and Alan Howarth. *Makeup*: Ken Chase, Ben Douglas. *Costumes*: Stephen Loomis. *Special Effects*: Roy Arbogast. *Special Visual Effects*: Newworld/Venice. *Production*: Larry Franco, Debra Hill. *Associate Production*: Aaron Lipstadt.
(99 minutes)

Players

Snake Plissken	Kurt Russell
Bob Hauck	Lee Van Cleef
Maggie	Adrienne Barbeau
Brain	Harry Dean Stanton
Cabbie	Ernest Borgnine
President	Donald Pleasence
Duke of New York	Isaac Hayes
Girl in Chock Full o' Nuts diner	Season Hubley
Rehme, security controller	Tom Atkins
Secretary of State	Charles Cyphers
Romero	Frank Doubleday
Dr. Cronenberg	John Strobel
Taylor	Joe Unger

The Action

The city of New York has been turned into a penal colony where convicted criminals are allowed to roam freely. The President's plane, en
route to a summit meeting, is hijacked by terrorists, and crashes inside
the city. Carrying with him a cassette tape containing information vital
to world peace, the President must be rescued within a matter of hours.
Warden Bob Hauck engages renegade war-hero-turned-criminal Snake
Plissken to enter the city and bring the President and his precious cargo
back to safety. Plissken reluctantly takes on the mission, persisting in
his antiauthoritarian attitude. Inside the city, he meets up with an old
crony, Brain. With his sweetheart Maggie, Brain joins forces with
Snake and a taxicab driver to rescue the President from the clutches of
the Duke of New York and his brutal henchmen. Snake's allies are
killed, but he escapes with the President. However, moments before the
President's announcement of the information on the cassette, Snake
gets his revenge and vents his resentment, by destroying the tape.

HALLOWEEN II

Universal, 1981

Direction: Rick Rosenthal. *Screenplay*: **John Carpenter** and Debra
Hill. *Production Design*: Michael Riva. *Cinematography*: Dean Cundey. *Editing*: Mark Goldblatt. *Music*: **John Carpenter** and Alan Howarth. *Special Effects Supervision*: Larry Cavanaugh. *Special Effects*:

Frank Munoz. *Executive Production*: Irwin Yablans, Joseph Wolf. *Production*: Debra Hill and **John Carpenter**.
(92 minutes)

Players

Laurie Strode	Jamie Lee Curtis
Sam Loomis	Donald Pleasence
Leigh Brackett	Charles Cyphers
Graham	Jeffrey Kramer
Jimmy	Lance Guest
Karen	Pamela Susan Shoop
The Shape	Dick Warlock

The Action

Michael Myers vanishes after being shot six times by his psychiatrist, Dr. Loomis. Convinced that Myers is a supernaturally evil force that must be destroyed, Loomis dragoons local law enforcement authorities into an all-out manhunt. Meanwhile, in shock from her knife wound and her terrifying encounter with Michael, Laurie is taken to the nearby hospital. After killing several people, Michael makes his way to the hospital, where he wreaks further mayhem, finally seeking out Laurie and once again attacking her. In a desperate effort to rid the world of the evil, Dr. Loomis sacrifices himself in a monumental explosion—from which Michael Myers emerges, burning, but still alive.

THE THING

Universal, 1982

Direction: **John Carpenter**. *Screenplay*: Bill Lancaster, based on the short story "Who Goes There?" by William M. Campbell, Jr. *Production Design*: John L. Lloyd. *Art Direction*: Henry Larrecq. *Cinematography*: Dean Cundey. *Editing*: Todd Ramsay. *Music*: Ennio Morricone. *Special Effects*: Roy Arbogast. *Special Visual Effects*: Albert Whitlock. *Special Make-Up Effects*: Rob Bottin. *Associate Producer, First Assistant Director*: Larry Franco. *Executive Production*: Wilbur Stark. *Production*: David Foster, Lawrence Turman.
(108 minutes)

Players

MacReady	Kurt Russell
Blair	Wilford Brimley
Nauls	T. K. Carter
Palmer	David Clennon
Childs	Keith David
Norris	Charles Hallahan
Bennings	Peter Maloney
Clark	Richard Masur
Windows	Thomas Waites
Garry	Donald Moffat
Doc Copper	Richard Dysart
Fuchs	Joel Polis
Norwegian	Norbert Weisser
Norwegian with rifle	Larry Franco

The Action

An American research station in Antarctica is disrupted by the discovery of an alien organism, long buried in ice, that can assume the shape of any other living being. One by one the members of the crew are killed hideously, and no one can be sure that the other guy is really himself and not the alien. The horror turns the men against one another, and finally only two are left, uncertain whether by sacrificing themselves they can really keep the creature from reaching—and destroying—civilization.

CHRISTINE

Columbia Pictures, 1983

Direction: **John Carpenter**. *Screenplay*: Bill Phillips, based upon the novel by Stephen King. *Production Design*: Daniel Lomino. *Cinematography*: Donald M. Morgan. *Editing*: Marion Rothman. *Music*: **John Carpenter**, in association with Alan Howarth. *First Assistant Director*: Larry Franco. *Executive Production*: Kirby McCauley, Mark Tarlov. *Production*: Richard Kobritz.
(110 minutes)

Players

Arnie Cunningham	Keith Gordon
Dennis Guilder	John Stockwell
Leigh Cabot	Alexandra Paul
Will Darnell	Robert Prosky
Officer Rudolph Junkins	Harry Dean Stanton
Regina Cunningham	Christine Belford
George LeBay	Roberts Blossom
Buddy Repperton	William Ostrander
Mr. Casey	David Spielberg
Moochie Welch	Malcolm Danare
Richard Trelawney	Steven Tash
Doc Vandenberg	Stuart Charno

The Action

Outcast and ridiculed by his high school classmates, Arnie undergoes a personality change when he buys a used car from an eccentric named LeBay. After a refreshing improvement in his self-confidence, Arnie begins to show signs of a treacherous arrogance, gradually alienating his girlfriend Leigh and his best buddy Dennis. The car, Christine, takes over his life; he becomes obsessed—especially when he discovers that the car has a will of her own and will help him get even with his enemies. When the situation reaches disastrous proportions, Leigh and Dennis take desperate action to destroy the cursed car—but is Christine destructible?

NOTE: The film is dedicated to Bob Dawn, a make-up artist who died of natural causes during the filming of *Christine*.

HALLOWEEN III: SEASON OF THE WITCH

Universal, 1982

Direction: Tommy Lee Wallace. *Screenplay*: Tommy Lee Wallace (re-vision of an uncredited original draft by Nigel Kneale). *Production Design*: Peter Jamison. *Cinematography*: Dean Cundey. *Editing*: Millie Moore. *Music*: **John Carpenter** and Alan Howarth. *Special Make-Up Effects*: Tom Burman. *Executive Production*: Irwin Yablans, Joseph Wolf. *Production*: **John Carpenter**, Debra Hill.
(96 minutes)

Players

Dr. Daniel Challis	Tom Atkins
Ellie Grimbridge	Stacey Nelkin
Conal Cochran	Dan O'Herlihy
Buddy Kupfer	Ralph Strait
Rafferty	Michael Currie
Betty Kupfer	Jadeen Barbor
Little Buddy	Bradley Schachter
Marge	Garn Stephens
Linda Challis	Nancy Kyes
Starker	John Terry
Technician	Patrick Pankurst
Harry Grimbridge	Al Berry
Teddy Bryant	Wendy Wessberg
Assassin	Dick Warlock
Red	Norman Merrill
Bella Challis	Michelle Walker
Willie Challis	Joshua Miller

The Action

Investigating the death of a patient, Dr. Daniel Challis and the patient's daughter visit the Silver Shamrock plant, where the country's biggest-selling Halloween masks are manufactured. They discover that Conal Cochran, the owner of the plant, has implanted computer chips in the millions of masks already sold. A television transmission activating these chips will call up supernatural powers from rock chips taken from Stonehenge, causing those wearing the masks to die hideously. After being captured by Cochran, Challis fights against time to escape the factory and stop the fatal broadcasts.

STARMAN

Columbia Pictures, 1984

Direction: **John Carpenter.** *Screenplay*: Bruce A. Evans and Raynold Gideon.[8] *Production Design*: Daniel Lomino. *Cinematography*: Donald M. Morgan. *Editing*: Marion Rothman. *Music*: Jack Nitzsche. *Special Effects Supervision*: Bruce Nicholson. *Special Effects Coordination*: Roy Arbogast. *Special Visual Effects*: Industrial Light & Magic. *Starman Transformation*: Dick Smith, Stan Winston, Rick Baker. *Visual*

Consultation, Second Unit Direction: Joe Alves. *Executive Production*: Michael Douglas. *Coproducer*: Barry Bernardi. *First Assistant Director, Production*: Larry J. Franco.
(115 minutes)

Players

Starman	Jeff Bridges
Jenny Hayden	Karen Allen
Mark Sherman	Charles Martin Smith
George Fox	Richard Jaeckel
Major Bell	Robert Phalen
Sergeant Lemon	Tony Edwards

The Action

Young widow Jenny Hayden, still mourning her husband's death, is frightened when a visitor from another world assumes her husband's shape and forces her at gunpoint to drive him across the country. While a ruthless government official seeks to capture and kill the alien, and a government scientist tries to get a chance to talk with the creature, Jenny softens toward the "Starman," as she learns to understand his feelings and strange abilities. He learns the ways of earth, too, and he and Jenny fall in love. On the way to the point of rendezvous, where he will be met by a rescue ship sent to take him home, Starman gives the hitherto infertile Jenny the gift of a child who will be "like his father." The scientist, in defiance of the government official's orders, helps Jenny and Starman escape, and Starman departs for his own world, leaving Jenny transformed.

THE PHILADELPHIA EXPERIMENT

New World Pictures, 1984

Direction: Stewart Raffill. *Screenplay*: William Gray & Michael Janover. *Story*: Wallace Bennett and Don Jakoby.[9] *Cinematography*: Dick Bush. *Editing*: Neil Travis. *Music*: Kenn Wannberg. *Special Visual Effects, Second Unit Director*: Max W. Anderson. *Executive Production*: **John Carpenter**. *Production*: Joel B. Michaels & Douglas Curtis.

(102 minutes)

Players

Mike Herdeg	Michael Paré
Alison	Nancy Allen
Jimmy Parker, 1943	Bobby diCicco
Pam Parker, 1984	Louise Latham
Professor Longstreet	Eric Christmas

The Action

In 1943, an experiment to make ships invisible to radar generates a powerful and complex magnetic field that sends an entire ship into a Limbo-like vortex in the space-time continuum. When shipmates Herdeg and Parker jump overboard they drop through the vortex and come out the other end, emerging in Nevada in 1984, where a similar experiment in radiation shielding has criss-crossed the energy produced by the 1943 experiment. After Parker is pulled back into the vortex, Herdeg enlists the help of Alison, a 1984 woman, to find out what has happened—and what's going to happen. Entering the vortex, he turns off the ship's generators, allowing the ship to return to 1943—but not before he leaps overboard again, opting to stay with Alison in 1984.

BLACK MOON RISING

New World Pictures, 1985

Direction: Harley Cokliss. *Screenplay*: **John Carpenter**, Desmond Nakano, William Gray, story by **John Carpenter**. *Cinematography*: Misha Suslov. *Editing*: Todd Ramsay. *Production Design*: Bryan Ryman. *Special Visual Effects*: Max W. Anderson. *Music*: Lalo Schifrin. *Production*: Joel B. Michaels, Douglas Curtis.
(100 minutes)

Players

Quint	Tommy Lee Jones
Nina	Linda Hamilton
Ryland	Robert Vaughn
Earl	Richard Jaeckel
Ringer	Lee Ving
Johnson	Bubba Smith
Billy	Dan Shor

Tyke   William Sanderson
Iron John   Keenan Wynn

The Action

Quint, a freelance dealer in information and risk-taking, steals for government agents a tape containing information on a corporation under
investigation. Pursued by his old nemesis, Ringer, he hides the cassette
in the Black Moon, a futuristic car destined for a luxury automobile
show. Nina, a high-class car thief, steals the car, and Quint must recover it within two days to deliver the tape to the government agents on
time. Alienated from her boss, car-theft czar Ryland, Nina flirts with
Quint and finally allies with him and the Black Moon's designers to
raid the Ryland Building and rescue the car.

BIG TROUBLE IN LITTLE CHINA

Twentieth Century Fox, 1986

Direction: **John Carpenter**. *Screenplay*: Gary Goldman & David Z.
Weinstein, adaptation by W. D. Richter. *Production Design*: John J.
Lloyd. *Cinematography*: Dean Cundey. *Editing*: Mark Warner, Steve
Mirkovich, Edward A. Warschilka. *Music*: **John Carpenter**, in asso-
ciation with Alan Howarth. *Special Visual Effects*: Richard Edlund.
Executive Production: Paul Monash, Keith Barish. *First Assistant Di-
rector, Production*: Larry J. Franco.
(99 minutes)

Players

Jack Burton   Kurt Russell
Gracie Law   Kim Cattrall
Wang Chi   Dennis Dun
Lo Pan   James Hong
Egg Shen   Victor Wong
Margo   Kate Burton
Eddie Lee   Donald Li
Thunder   Carter Wong
Rain   Peter Kwong
Lightning   James Pax
Miao Yin   Suzee Pai
Uncle Chu   Chao Li Chi

The Action

Freelance trucker Jack Burton and his friend Wang Chi are swept into a storm of action and mystery when a young Chinese woman, arriving to join Wang, is kidnapped by forces unknown. The appearance of a trio of warriors with supernatural abilities leads the sage Egg Shen to conclude that the legendary Lo Pan is behind the kidnapping. Investigating an underground world beneath the streets of Chinatown, Jack and Wang discover the empire of Lo Pan, an immortal who plans to sacrifice the kidnapped woman in order to regain his lost youth. Mounting a raiding party, Jack, Wang, and Egg stage a daring rescue assault on Lo Pan's stronghold, overcoming forces both natural and supernatural to win the day.

PRINCE OF DARKNESS

Universal/Alive, 1987

Direction: **John Carpenter**. *Screenplay*: Martin Quatermass.[10] *Production Design*: Daniel Lomino. *Cinematography*: Gary B. Kibbe. *Editing*: Steve Mirkovich. *Music*: **John Carpenter,** in association with Alan Howarth. *Special Make-Up Effects*: Frank Carissosa. *Executive Production*: Shep Gordon, Andre Blay. *Production*: Larry Franco.
(101 minutes)

Players

Priest	Donald Pleasence
Brian Marsh	Jameson Parker
Prof. Howard Birack	Victor Wong
Catherine Danforth	Lisa Blount
Walter	Dennis Dun
Kelly	Susan Blanchard
Susan	Anne Howard
Lisa	Ann Yen
Lomax	Ken Wright
Mullins	Dirk Blocker
Calder	Jessie Lawrence Ferguson
Dr. Paul Leahy	Peter Jason
Wyndham	Robert Grasmere
Etchinson	Thom Bray
Bag Lady	Joanna Merlin

Street Schizo	Alice Cooper
Nun	Betty Ramey
Dark Figure	Jessie Ferguson

The Action

A dying priest leaves a diary containing disturbing information about a long-dormant evil spirit that is imprisoned in a small church in urban Los Angeles, and that is about to reawaken with dire consequences for the world. Messages from a future race invade the dreams of contemporary human beings, cautioning them of the danger and seeking their help in destroying the menace. Approached with the information by a zealous priest, college physicist and metaphysicist Prof. Howard Birack chooses a crack team of his best students, including Brian and Catherine, and sets up a field lab in the church, seeking to study the strange force and, if possible, to stop it. One by one, the members of the team are possessed or destroyed by the being. Finally, in order to hurl the creature back into its own universe and save our world, Catherine makes an awesome self-sacrifice, and Brian is left haunted by the knowledge that evil is always present and waiting.

THEY LIVE

Universal/Alive, 1988

Direction: **John Carpenter**. *Screenplay*: Frank Armitage,[11] based on the short story "Eight O'Clock in the Morning," by Ray Nelson. *Art Direction*: William J. Durrell, Jr., Daniel Lomino. *Cinematography*: Gary B. Kibbe. *Editing*: Gib Jaffe, Frank E. Jimenez. *Music*: **John Carpenter**, Alan Howarth. *Executive Production*: Shep Gordon, Andre Blay, for Alive Pictures. *Production*: Larry Franco. *Associate Production*: Sandy King.
(95 minutes)

Players

Nada	Roddy Piper
Frank	Keith David
Holly	Meg Foster
Drifter	George "Buck" Flower
Gilbert	Peter Jason
Street Preacher	Raymond St. Jacques

Family Man	Jason Robards III
Bearded Man	John Lawrence
Brown-haired Woman	Susan Barnes
Black Revolutionary	Sy Richardson
Family Man's Daughter	Wendy Brainard
Female Interviewer	Lucille Meredith
Ingenue	Susan Blanchard
Foreman	Norman Alden
Black Junkie	Dana Bratton
Well-dressed Customer	John F. Goff

The Action

Nada, a vagrant worker down on his luck, settles in with a colony of the poor and unemployed in Los Angeles. Strange activities in a nearby church arouse his suspicion. Unexplained television transmissions and boxloads of unusual sunglasses pique his curiosity. Putting on the glasses, he discovers that the world is not what it seems, that aliens are among us and have hypnotized us into seeing only what they want us to imagine we see. In reality, we are being subjected continually to a subliminal reality that conditions our behavior as willing consumers and complacent political followers. With the glasses on, Nada can tell which of us are aliens, and he begins a one-man crusade to destroy the conquering evil. Through repeated efforts, he manages to win a few supporters to his side, and joins forces with a resistance group already mounting an offensive against the aliens. The aim is to destroy the transmission tower that keeps the illusory world alive by the energy it relays. Nada loses his allies, and is betrayed by a woman he thought he could trust, but he manages to destroy the tower, sacrificing himself in the process. With the aliens' energy source destroyed, human beings begin to see the aliens for what they really are.

HALLOWEEN 4: THE RETURN OF MICHAEL MYERS

Trancas International Films, 1988

Direction: Dwight H. Little. *Screenplay*: Alan B. McElroy. Story by Ohani Lipsius, Larry Rattner & Benjamin Ruffner, and Alan B. McElroy. *Cinematography*: Peter Lyons Collister. *Editing*: Curtiss Clayton. *Music*: Alan Howarth. "Halloween Theme" by **John Carpenter**. *Executive Production*: Moustapha Akkad. *Production*: Paul Freeman. (88 minutes)

Players

Dr. Loomis	Donald Pleasence
Rachel Carruthers	Ellie Cornell
Jamie Lloyd	Danielle Harris
Michael Myers	George P. Wilbur
Dr. Hoffman	Michael Pataki
Sheriff Meeker	Beau Starr
Kelly Meeker	Kathleen Kinmont
Brady	Sasha Jenson
Earl	Gene Ross

The Action

Nine years after the night of horror in which he killed 16 people, Michael Myers awakens from sedation while being transferred from a state to a federal sanitarium, and begins to kill again. He comes to Haddonfield, Illinois, in search of his only living relative, a niece, Jamie Lloyd (daughter of Laurie Strode, Michael's sister). Both haunted and possessed by Michael, and taunted by her classmates ("Your uncle is the Bogey Man!"), Jamie sees the killer in her nightmares, and is stalked by him in real life on Halloween night, 1988. Local police, Dr. Loomis, and a mob of townsmen with shotguns all try to find Michael and avert a second night of carnage. Jamie's adoptive sister, Rachel, seeking to protect her, brings about the apparent end of Michael in a barrage of state police gunfire. But the torch of evil is passed, and to Loomis's horror, Jamie, dressed in a clown costume like the one young Michael wore on the night he murdered his sister, attacks her stepmother with a knife.

HALLOWEEN 5: THE REVENGE OF MICHAEL MYERS

Trancas International Films, 1989

Direction: Dominique Othenin-Girard. *Screenplay*: Michael Jacobs & Dominique Othenin-Girard and Shem Bitterman. *Production Design*: Brent Swift. *Cinematography*: Robert Draper. *Editing*: Charles Tetoni, Jerry Brady. *Music*: Alan Howarth. "Halloween Theme" by **John Carpenter**. *Executive Production*: Moustapha Akkad. *Line Production*: Rick Nathanson. *Production*: Ramsey Thomas.
(96 minutes)

Players

Dr. Loomis	Donald Pleasence
Rachel Carruthers	Ellie Cornell
Jamie Lloyd	Danielle Harris
Michael Myers	Donald L. Shanks
Sheriff Meeker	Beau Starr
Tina	Wendy Kaplan
Samantha	Tamara Glynn
Spitz	Matthew Walker
Michael (Tina's boyfriend)	Jonathan Chapin
Billy	Jeffrey Landman

The Action

Michael Myers survives the police gunfire and, after a year's recupera-
tion, rises to claim victims again on Halloween in Haddonfield. His
niece, Jamie, muted by the horror of her earlier encounter with Michael, and her imitation of his own knife-wielding violence, is in a
children's clinic, but knows Michael's every move through a telepathic
link that joins the two. Michael kills Rachel, her friends Tina and
Samantha, and their boyfriends, Michael and Spitz. Increasingly obsessed with destroying Michael, Dr. Loomis decides to use Jamie as
bait for a trap to capture the psychopathic killer once and for all. Michael seems briefly to soften to gentleness when the psychiatrist, and
later, Jamie, appeal to something human still living within him, but he
can't conquer the rage within and finally must be subdued by gunfire
and a net of chain. Held in the local jail for transfer to a maximum security installation, Michael is set free by a heavily armed stranger in a
dark cape and silver-tipped boots.

EL DIABLO

HBO Pictures, 1990

Direction: Peter Markle. *Screenplay*: Tommy Lee Wallace & **John
Carpenter** and Bill Phillips. *Production Design*: Vincent J. Cresciman.
Cinematography: Ron Garcia. *Editing*: Stephen E. Rivkin. *Music*: William Olvis. *Executive Production*: Joe Wizan; Debra Hill and **John
Carpenter**. *Production*: Mickey Borofsky & Todd Black. *Coproduction*: Peter Burrell.
(110 minutes)

Players

Billy Ray Smith	Anthony Edwards
Thomas Van Leek	Louis Gosset, Jr.
Preacher	John Glover
Truman Feathers ("Kid Durango")	Joe Pantoliano
"El Diablo"	Robert Beltran
Bebe	M. C. Gainey
Zamudio	Miguel Sandoval
Nettie Tuleen	Sarah Trigger
Dancing Bear	Branscombe Richmond
Spivey Irick	Jim Beaver
Mrs. Tuleen	Kathleen Erickson
Chak Mol	Geno Silva
Pitchfork Napier	David Dunard

The Action

Foppish Bostonian Billy Ray Smith teaches school in a struggling western frontier town, and dreams of the exploits of his hero, Kid Durango, the subject of a series of "dime novels." A gang led by El Diablo, a sadistic bandit, raids the town and carries off one of Billy Ray's students, Nettie Tuleen. When the pursuing sheriff returns mutilated, his posse wiped out, Billy Ray determines to hunt down the outlaw himself. Knowing neither horsemanship nor marksmanship, Billy Ray makes his way uneasily until he is joined by Van Leek, an unprincipled gunman whom Billy Ray hires to help him run El Diablo to earth. The two are joined by a motley crew of drifters, including an itinerant preacher and an eccentric novelist who, it turns out, is the author of the "Kid Durango" books and bases them on the adventures of none other than Van Leek! The misadventurous band finally tracks El Diablo to his hideaway for a final reckoning, from which Billy Ray emerges victorious, and with a new understanding of the difference between reality and legend.

BLOOD RIVER

CBS Entertainment, 1991

Direction: Mel Damski. *Screenplay*: **John Carpenter**. *Production Design*: Brian Eatwell. *Cinematography*: Robert M. Baldwin, Gary B. Kibbe. *Editing*: Bernard Gribble. *Music*: William Goldstein. *Executive*

Production: Mel Damski and Merrill H. Karpf. *Production*: Andrew Gottlieb.
(100 minutes)

Players

Jimmy Pearls	Rick Schroder
Winston Patrick Culler	Wilford Brimley
Henry Logan	John P. Ryan
Jake	Mills Watson
Sheriff	Henry Beckman
Squints	Dwight McFee
Georgina	Adrienne Barbeau
Congressman	Don S. Davis
Hotchner	Jay Brazeau
Laurie	Venus Terzo
Storekeeper	J. C. 'Jim' Roberts
Smiling Knife	Gordon Tootoosis
Parson	Stephen Hair
Parson's Wife	Maureen Thomas
Deputy	Jordi Thompson

The Action

After learning that they were responsible for the deaths of his parents, Jimmy Pearls kills three men—one of them the son of the powerful Henry Logan. On the run to protect himself against Logan's own vengeance, Pearls falls in with Culler, a crusty old mountain man who, it turns out, has reasons of his own for hiding the young man.

MEMOIRS OF AN INVISIBLE MAN

Warner Brothers, 1992

Direction: **John Carpenter**. *Screenplay*: Robert Collector & Dana Olsen and William Goldman, based on the novel by H. F. Saint. *Production Design*: Lawrence G. Paull. *Cinematography*: William A. Fraker. *Visual Effects Supervision*: Bruce Nicholson. *Editing*: Marion Rothman. *Music*: Shirley Walker. *Executive Production*: Arnon Milchan. *Production*: Bruce Bodner and Dan Kolsrud.
(99 minutes)

Players

Nick Halloway	Chevy Chase
Alice Monroe	Daryl Hannah
David Jenkins	Sam Neill
George Talbot	Michael McKean
Warren Singleton	Stephen Tobolowsky
Dr. Bernard Wachs	Jim Norton
Morrissey	Pat Skipper
Richard	Gregory Paul Martin
Ellen	Patricia Heaton
Gomez	Paul Perri
Tyler	Richard Epcar
Clellan	Steven Barr
Drunk Businessman	Barry Kivel
Cab Driver	Donald Li
Cathy DiTolla	Rosalind Chao
Roger Whitman	Jay Gerber
Patrick the Bartender	Shay Duffin
Edward Schneiderman	Edmund L. Shaff
Chairman of the House Committee	Sam Anderson
News Anchor	Elaine Corral
Mrs. Coulson	Ellen Albertini Dow
Delivery Boy	Jonathan Wigan
Maitre'd	I. M. Hobson
Helicopter Pilot	Rip Haight
	(John Carpenter)
Man who hails taxi	Chip Heller
Technician	Aaron Lustig

The Action

Things are going well for Wall Street analyst Nick Halloway. Despite being vaguely discontented with his job and his boss, he is successful and popular—and he's just met Alice Monroe, a comely blind date he's been introduced to by his coworker George Talbot. Alice and Nick fall for each other. But Nick's world collapses when, on the scene of a scientific experiment, a mishap occurs leaving Nick invisible. Government intelligence operative David Jenkins and his boss Warren Singleton try to keep to themselves the information that an invisible man exists, hoping to capture Nick and convert him to their service. A truly invisible man could be the most valuable weapon international espionage has ever seen—or rather, not seen. Nick is having none of it, however. In hope of having his freakish condition reversed, Nick presents himself to Dr. Bernard Wachs, the scientist in charge of the ill-fated experiment. But this puts Jenkins on Nick's trail—and Wachs in Jenkins's hands. As Jenkins becomes increasingly obsessed with capturing Nick, Singleton breaks faith with his operative, but Jenkins continues in dogged pursuit of the invisible man. Holing up in the summer home of his friend George, Nick finds he can eke out a living by ordering groceries by phone and charging them. When George holds a weekend party at the house, Alice reenters Nick's life. Nick reveals himself and his condition to her; Alice continues to love him and decides to help him. Time and again Nick eludes Jenkins, but when Alice falls into Jenkins's hands, Nick must take drastic action. He offers to exchange himself for Alice, but once Alice is free, the "Nick" seized by Jenkins's men proves to be George—Nick has escaped with Alice. Jenkins pursues Nick to a nearby rooftop, where Nick engineers a final ruse that leaves Jenkins dead and Nick presumed dead. He and Alice escape to the mountains to begin an unusual but happy married life.

BODY BAGS

Showtime, 1993

Direction: **John Carpenter** ("The Gas Station"; "Hair"), Tobe Hooper ("Eye"). *Screenplay*: Dan Angel, Bill Brown. *Production Design*: Daniel A. Lomino. *Set Decoration*: Cloudia. *Cinematography*: Gary B. Kibbe. *Special Effects*: Howard Jensen. *Coroner's Make-Up*: Rick Baker. *Editing*: Edward A. Warschilka. *Music*: **John Carpenter** and Jim Lang. *Executive Production*: Sandy King. *Coproduction*: **John Carpenter**. *Production*: Dan Angel.
(93 minutes)

Players

Coroner	John Carpenter
Man #1	Tom Arnold
Man #2	Tobe Hooper
"The Gas Station"	
"Bill"	Robert Carradine
Anne	Alex Datcher
Gent	Peter Jason
Divorcée	Molly Cheek

Pasty Faced Man	Wes Craven
Bill (dead attendant)	Sam Raimi
Pete	David Naughton
Stranger	Buck Flower
Peggy	Lucy Boyrer
TV Anchorman	Roger Rooks

"Hair"
Richard	Stacy Keach
Dr. Lock	David Warner
Megan	Sheena Easton
Dennis	Dan Blom
Woman	Kim Alexis
Man with dog	Gregory Nicotero
Nurse	Deborah Harry

"Eye"
Brent Matthews	Mark Hamill
Cathy	Twiggy
Dr. Lang	John Agar
Dr. Bregman	Roger Corman
Manager	Charles Napier
Player	Eddie Velez
Librarian	Betty Muramoto
Nurse	Bebe Drake-Massey
Minister	Sean McClory
Man	Robert Lewis Bush
Technician	Gregory Alpert

The Action

In a framing device, the Coroner cracks both wise and gross, and introduces a trilogy of tales, each ostensibly tied to one of the bodies that have arrived at the morgue zipped into body bags that bespeak death by violence rather than by natural causes. In the first tale, "The Gas Station," Anne, a new employee on her first night shift at a 24-hour gas station, is besieged by a maniacal mass murderer. The second tale, "Hair," involves a vain, obsessive man whose willingness to try anything to restore his thinning hair delivers him into the hands of Dr. Lock, an illusory savior who turns out to have an unexpectedly different agenda. "Eye" tells the story of Brent Matthews, a minor league baseball player on the way up who suddenly loses his right eye in a car accident. He agrees to an eye transplant, which is initially successful but soon causes him to have visions, "seeing" with the eye's previous owner, John Randall, a recently executed, child-abused serial killer. Increasingly possessed by the dead murderer, Matthews fixes upon his own pregnant wife as his next victim. The tales having been told, the Coroner reveals himself to be not a coroner at all but an inhabitant of one of the body bags, and the film ends as two assistant coroners begin his autopsy.

IN THE MOUTH OF MADNESS

New Line, 1995

Direction: **John Carpenter**. *Screenplay*: Michael De Luca. *Production Design*: Jeff Steven Ginn. *Art Direction*: Peter Grundy. *Cinematography*: Gary B. Kibbe. *Visual Effects Supervision*: Bruce Nicholson. *Special Make-Up Effects*: Robert Kurtzman. *Editing*: Edward A. Warschilka. *Music*: **John Carpenter**, Dave Davies, and Jim Lang. *Executive Production*: Sandy King. *Production*: Michael De Luca. (94 minutes)

Players

John Trent	Sam Neill
Linda Styles	Julie Carmen
Sutter Cane	Jürgen Prochnow
Jackson Harglow	Charlton Heston
Robinson	Bernie Casey
Saperstein	John Glover
Dr. Wrenn	David Warner
Paul	Peter Jason
Mrs. Pickman	Frances Bay
Robinson	Bernie Casey
Paul	Peter Jason
Simon	Wilhelm von Homburg
Guard #1	Kevin Rushton
Guard #2	Gene Mack
Axe Maniac	Conrad Bergschneider
Reporter	Marvin Scott
Receptionist	Katherine Ashby
Young Teen	Ben Gilbert
Cop	Dennis O'Connor
Scrawny Teen	Paul Brogren

Homeless Lady	Sharon Dyer
Bicycle Boy	Sean Ryan
Little Boy	Lance Paton
Little Girl	Jacelyn Holmes
Paper Boy	Hayden Christensen
Truck Driver	Garry Robbins
Desk Clerk	Sean Roberge
Hotel Man	Robert Lewis Bush
Old Lady	Louise Beaven
Bus Driver	Cliff Woolner
Municipal Woman	Deborah Theaker
Customer	Chuck Campbell
Nurse	Carolyn Tweedle
Farmer	Thom Bell
Window Teen	Mark Adriaans
Simon's Son (Johnny)	Jack Moore-Wickham
Kids	David Austerwell
	Richard Kohler
	Kieran Sells
	Laura Schmidt
	Kyle Sheehan
	Daniel Verhoeven
	Kevin Zegers
	Katie Zegers

The Action

Insurance investigator John Trent is admitted, raving, to a mental institution managed by Saperstein. At first desperately wanting to be released, he soon changes his mind and comes to view his cell as the last safe refuge against a mania that has overtaken the outside world. Dr. Wrenn arrives to examine Trent, ostensibly to determine whether the new patient is "one of them." The astounding story that Trent tells Wrenn begins when Trent and his colleague Robinson witness a man run amok with an axe at an urban café. The crazed man attacks Trent, shouting, "Do you read Sutter Cane?" and is shot dead by police. Later, called to the office of publishing executive Jackson Harglow to be given a special assignment, Trent learns that the man was the literary agent of popular horror novelist Sutter Cane. Cane, who is Harglow's top-earning author, has disappeared, leaving the publisher with the unfinished manuscript of his latest novel, *In the Mouth of Madness*. Harglow hires Trent to locate Cane, and orders his promotion director,

Linda Styles, to accompany Trent. Trent smells a rat: He is certain that he is being drawn into an elaborate publicity stunt designed to boost Cane's aura of mystery (and his marketability). Researching the Cane phenomenon, Trent learns that the author commands a fanatically devoted and growing readership, and that many people are persuaded that, at some level of consciousness, the things Cane writes about are "real."

Reading a few Cane novels to bone up, Trent finds certain of the novelist's events and images haunting his dreams and even creating waking hallucinations. He discovers in the cover art to recent Cane books a cryptic clue to Cane's hiding place, and he and Styles set out to find the small New England town of Hob's End, setting of Cane's novels, which appears on no map. After a couple of hallucinatory encounters, Styles becomes increasingly frightened that they have somehow left reality and entered the fictional world of Sutter Cane—that they are actually "in" the novel *In the Mouth of Madness*. Trent is surer than ever that he is being duped by an elaborate publicity scam—until a series of violent and unexplainable occurrences, culminating with a meeting with Cane himself, force him to believe otherwise, and to doubt his own sanity.

Directed by Cane to take back to the real world the now-finished manuscript of the novel, Trent refuses, knowing that the novel is somehow the channel whereby unspeakable creatures from the next world will destroy humanity and claim the earth for their own. Trent finds his return to reality haunted by growing evidence that Cane is manipulating him as an author manipulates his characters. From Harglow he learns that, in fact, the finished manuscript had reached the publisher long before, and has now been published, creating waves of unaccountable, unmotivated violence among both its readers and would-be buyers who learn that the stock is sold out. To make matters worse, the film version of the novel is about to be released. Arming himself with an axe, Trent sets out to destroy those who are infected by Cane's novels and thwart the insidious creatures who wait to inherit the earth—but this only precipitates his confinement to Saperstein's asylum.

Having heard Trent's astonishing story, Dr. Wrenn leaves; but soon afterward the asylum erupts in an orgy of violence, whose aftermath Trent discovers when he escapes from his cell to find himself, apparently, the only human being left. Wandering the devastated city, Trent happens upon a movie theatre advertising the film *In the Mouth of Madness*, "starring John Trent" and "directed by John Carpenter." Entering the empty theatre, Trent watches the film that he is in, the very one "we" have just watched, and collapses in hysterical laughter.

VILLAGE OF THE DAMNED

Universal, 1995

Direction: **John Carpenter**. *Screenplay*: David Himmelstein, based on a screenplay by Stirling Siliphant and Wolf Rilla, from the novel *The Midwich Cuckoos* by John Wyndham; Steven Siebert (uncredited). *Production Design*: Rodger Maus. *Cinematography*: Gary B. Kibbe. *Visual Effects Supervision*: Bruce Nicholson. *Mechanical Visual Effects Supervision*: Roy Arbogast. *Editing*: Edward A. Warschilka. *Music*: **John Carpenter** and Dave Davies. *Executive Production*: David Chackler, James Jacks, Michael Preger, Ted Vernon. *Co-Executive Production*: Shep Gordon, Sandy King. *Coproduction*: Sean Daniel. *Production*: Andre Blay.
(94 minutes)

Players

Dr. Alan Chaffee	Christopher Reeve
Dr. Susan Verner	Kirstie Alley
Jill McGowan	Linda Kozlowski
Frank McGowan	Michael Paré
Melanie Roberts	Meredith Salenger
Rev. George Miller	Mark Hamill
Sarah Miller	Pippa Pearthree
Ben Blum	Peter Jason
Callie Blum	Constance Forslund
Barbara Chaffee	Karen Kahn
David	Thomas Dekker
Mara	Lindsey Haun
Robert	Cody Dorkin
Julie	Trishalee Hardy
Dorothy	Jessye Quarry
Isaac	Adam Robbins
Matt	Chelsea DeRidder Simms
Casey	Renee Rene Simms
Lily	Danielle Wiener
Mara, age 1	Hillary Harvey
David, age 9 months/1 year	Bradley Wilhelm
Mara/David, age 4 months	Jennifer Wilhelm
Carlton	George "Buck" Flower
The Sheriff	Squire Fridell
CHP	Darryl Jones

Older Deputy	Ed Corbett
Younger Deputy	Ross Martineau
Deputy	Skip Richardson
Dr. Bush	Tony Harey
Eye Doctor	Sharon Iwai
Mr. Roberts	Robert Lewis Bush
Technician	Montgomery Hom
Trooper #1	Steven Chambers
Trooper #2	Ron Kaell
Scientist	Lane Nishikawa
Station Attendant Harold	Michael Halton
Eileen Moore	Julie Eccles
Doctor at Clinic	Lois Saunders
Labor Room Physician	Sidney Baldwin
Nurse #5	Wendolyn Lee
Nurse #3	Kathleen Turco-Lyon
Nurse #1	Abigail Van Alyn
Oliver	Roy Conrad
Young Husband	Dan Belzer
Young Wife	Dena Martinez
Woman at Town Hall	Alice Barden
Man at Town Hall	John Brebner
Villager	Ralph Miller
Man at Phone Booth in Gas Station	Rip Haight
	(John Carpenter)

The Action

An unexplained presence does a "flyover" of the quiet rural town of Midwich. Later, during a church bazaar, every living creature within a specific area around the town falls unconscious for a period of six hours. The government takes an interest in the phenomenon and continues its research even after everyone regains consciousness and life goes on. Interest intensifies—especially for geneticist Dr. Susan Verner—when several women in the town are discovered to be pregnant, conception seeming to date from the time of the "blackout." The government offers the women financial incentives to bring the babies to full term, provided the government is allowed to make periodic tests and conduct studies. All of the children except one are born alive. Soon afterward, genetic similarities are noted among the children, and strange powers begin to be revealed, including high intelligence, a seeming ability of the children to communicate subliminally with one another, and the power to influence the minds of others. After his wife is prompted to suicide by the influence of their child Mara, the town's doctor, Alan Chaffee is identified by the town as the man most likely to be able to teach the children, learn more about them, and perhaps enable the townspeople to figure out how to control the growing terror among them. Chaffee begins to form a bond with David, the one child who is not matched with another (his partner having been the one who was stillborn). The children, under the control of Mara, meet any perceived threat with increasingly violent reaction, causing the injury or death of anyone they suspect may be trying to stop them. Chaffee learns from Dr. Verner that other communities, elsewhere in the world, have experienced a similar phenomenon, and that the generation of telekinetically linked pseudo-siblings is the first wave of an alien colonization of Earth. Finally Mara confirms this, and as the government plans to annihilate the village, as it has done with others elsewhere in the world, Chaffee combines an appeal to the vulnerability he sees in David's tendency toward human feelings with a contest of mental strength with Mara, in a last-ditch effort to stop the menace.

HALLOWEEN: THE CURSE OF MICHAEL MYERS

Miramax, 1995

Direction: Joe Chappelle. *Screenplay*: Daniel Farrands, based on characters created by **John Carpenter** and Nick Castle. *Production Design*: Bryan Ryman. *Cinematography*: Billy Dickson. *Editing*: Randy Bricker. *Music*: **John Carpenter** and Alan Howarth. *Executive Production*: Paul Freeman. *Associate Production*: Moustapha Akkad. *Production*: Malek Akkad.
(88 minutes)

Players

Doctor Sam Loomis	Donald Pleasence
Tommy Doyle	Paul Stephen Rudd
Kara Strode	Marianne Hagan
Dr. Wynn	Mitchell Ryan
Debra Strode	Kim Darby
John Strode	Bradford English
Tim Strode	Keith Bogart
Beth	Mariah O'Brien
Barry Simms	Leo Geter

The Action

This fifth sequel to *Halloween* takes place once again on Halloween
night—this time six years after the last Halloween night on which Michael Myers tormented Haddonfield. During the intervening time, Michael has been under the protection of a Druidic cult, along with his
niece, Jamie Lloyd, who seems to have inherited Michael's propensity
for evil from her mother, Laurie Strode (revealed in an earlier sequel to
have been, unknowingly, Michael's blood sister). After bearing Michael's child, Jamie escapes the cult and seeks out Michael's original
psychiatrist, Dr. Loomis, to help her combat the horror that has possessed her and Michael. The Myers house has been occupied, ever
since *that night*, by the family that had adopted Laurie Strode. Now it is
once again targeted by Michael. Jamie, Dr. Loomis, and the inveterate
Tommy Doyle unite in an effort to rid the world of an evil that now
appears even worse than the Bogey Man.

ESCAPE FROM L.A.

Paramount, 1996

Direction: **John Carpenter**. *Screenplay*: **John Carpenter**, Debra Hill,
and Kurt Russell, based on characters created by **John Carpenter** and
Nick Castle. *Production Design*: Lawrence G. Paull. *Costume Design*:
Robin Michel Bush. *Special Make-Up Effects*: Rick Baker. *Special
Effects Coordination*: Marty Bresin. *Art Direction*: Bruce Crone. *Set
Design*: Nathan Crowley. *Cinematography*: Gary B. Kibbe. *Visual Ef-
fects Supervision*: Dale Ettema. *Editing*: Edward A. Warschilka. *Music*:
John Carpenter and Shirley Walker. *Executive Production*: Harrison
Ellenshaw. *Production*: Debra Hill and Kurt Russell.
(101 minutes)

Players

Snake Plissken	Kurt Russell
Malloy	Stacy Keach
Brazen	Michelle Forbes
The President	Cliff Robertson
Cuervo Jones	George Corraface
Map to the Stars Eddie	Steve Buscemi
Pipeline	Peter Fonda
Hershe Las Palmas	Pam Grier

Taslima	Valerie Golino
Utopia	A. J. Langer
Skinhead	Robert Carradine
Official	Paul Bartel
Saigon Shadow	Jeff Imada
Hooker	Ina Romero
Duty Sergeant	Peter Jason
Police Anchor	Jordan Baker
Woman on freeway	Caroleen Feeney
Congressman	Paul Bartel
Officer	Tom McNulty
Surgeon General of Beverly Hills	Bruce Campbell
Surfer	Breckin Meyer
Skinhead	Robert Carradine
Cloaked Figure	Shelly Desai
Test Tube	Leland Orser
Female Narrator	Kathleen Blanchard
Mescalito	William Luduena
Mescalito	Gabriel Castillo
Jacket Mescalito	William Peña
U.S. Cleric Justice	David Perrone
Hershe's Bodyguard	Al Leong

The Action

In 1997 a devastating earthquake makes Los Angeles an island. The nation's religious-right President declares the island a deportation point for all of the undesirables expelled from a new "Moral America." In 2013, the President's daughter, Utopia, flees to L.A. to join rebel forces headed by Cuervo Jones, taking with her a "black box" that holds the key to activating a weapon capable of destroying all power sources on a global scale and returning earth to the Dark Ages. Snake Plissken, newly arrived at the point of embarkation for L.A., is coerced by the President and the governmental police into undertaking a mission into L.A. to recapture the black box and execute Utopia. Plissken's cooperation is assured once they tell him he has been infected with Plutoxin 7, a virus certain to kill him horribly within 10 hours; an antitoxin awaits him if he returns with the black box in time. A series of misadventures awaits Snake in L.A., roughly tracking the episodes of *Escape from New York*, and including a battle with plastic-surgery mutants and a gladiatorial ordeal involving basketball and machine guns. With the unreliable help of Map of the Stars Eddie, Snake gets the black box from Cuervo. Encountering an old partner in crime, Carjack, who after a sex change has become the goddess-like gangleader Hershe, Snake learns that Plutoxin 7 is a fake. He enlists the help of her minions in staging a raid on Cuervo Jones and his armies, who are massing for an assault on the mainland of the United States, already under seige by a Third World invading force from Cuba and Brazil. During the battle, Map of the Stars Eddie attempts to switch the black box's remote control trigger with a similar one of his own. Cuervo is killed and his army decimated, as Snake escapes L.A. with both remotes and Utopia. Arriving on the mainland, Snake and Utopia are captured. When the President attempts to thwart the Third World invasion by using the remote taken from Utopia, only to discover that it is Eddie's spoken guide to the homes of Hollywood stars, he orders the summary execution of Snake and the seizure of the real remote triggering device. Snake, however, can't be killed; he is only a hologram, projected by the holographic camera weapon given him before his sortie into L.A. The real Snake, some distance away, pushes the Doomsday button, disempowering the entire world, and intones, "Welcome to the human race."

HALLOWEEN H20: TWENTY YEARS LATER

Miramax, 1998

Direction: Steve Miner. *Screenplay*: Robert Zappia and Matt Greenberg, story by Robert Zappia and Kevin Williamson (uncredited), based on characters created by **John Carpenter** and Nick Castle. *Production Design*: John Willett. *Cinematography*: Daryn Okada. *Special Effects Supervision*: John Hardigan. *Editing*: Patrick Lussier. *Music*: **John Carpenter**, Maerco Beltrami, John Ottman. *Executive Production*: Paul Freeman, Cary Granat. *Co-Executive Production*: Bob Weinstein, Harvey Weinstein, Kevin Williamson. *Associate Production*: Moustapha Akkad. *Production*: Malek Akkad.
(85 minutes)

Players

Laurie Strode/Keri Tate	Jamie Lee Curtis
Will	Adam Arkin
John	Josh Hartnett
Molly	Michelle Williams
Charlie	Adam Hann-Byrd
Sarah	Jodi Lyn O'Keefe
Norma	Janet Leigh

Ronny   LL Cool J
Dr. Samuel Loomis (voice)   Donald Pleasence

The Action

Twenty years after Michael Myers's first attack on babysitter Laurie
Strode and her circle of friends, Laurie is living a new life as Keri Tate,
headmistress of a school. She has buried her identity under the story
that Laurie Strode died in a car crash some years before. She's haunted,
though: she drinks, and the drink doesn't keep her from having nightmares. Her son, John, a teenager with whom she has a turbulent relationship, won't believe that Michael is still alive. At a Halloween party
she reveals the truth to her boyfriend and fellow teacher Will. Meanwhile, information about Laurie's identity and whereabouts has been
mysteriously removed from the papers of the recently dead Dr. Loomis.
Michael returns once again, and begins claiming victims during the
party, working his way toward Laurie—who, as she did 20 years ago,
finds she has no choice but to face the evil.

VAMPIRES

Columbia, 1998

Direction: **John Carpenter**. *Screenplay*: **John Carpenter**, Don Jakoby, Dan Mazur, based on the novel *Vampire$* by John Steakley. *Pro-
duction Design*: Thomas A. Walsh. *Cinematography*: Gary B. Kibbe.
Special Effects Supervision: Darrell Pritchett. *Editing*: Edward A. Warschilka. *Music*: **John Carpenter**. *Executive Production*: Barr B. Potter.
Coproduction: Sandy King. *Production*: Don Jakoby.
(107 minutes)

Players

Jack Crow   James Woods
Tony Montoya   Daniel Baldwin
Katrina   Sheryl Lee
Valek   Thomas Ian Griffith
Father Adam Guiteau   Tim Guinee
Cardinal Alba   Maximilian Schell
Deyo   Cary-Hiroyuki Tagawa
Thomas Rosales   Mark Boone, Jr.
Man with the Buick   Frank Darabont

Female Master   Anita Hart
Father Henry Kingi   Gregory Sierra

The Action

In a remote section of southwestern desert, Jack Crow and his crack team of vampire slayers locate a nest of "goons"—newly created vampires under the telepathic control of a Master. Puzzled by the fact that the Master was not at the nest, Crow nevertheless drops his guard, and while his men celebrate in drunken ribaldry, Valek, a Master vampire, attacks. The only surviors are Crow, his trusted adjutant Tony Mon toya, and Katrina, a whore who has been infected with Valek's bite. Knowing that Katrina's growing telepathic link with Valek will enable the slayers to find the Master, Crow tells Montoya to take her to a hotel and wait for Crow, who has an appointment to keep with Cardinal Alba, an emissary from the Vatican. Crow's meeting with the Cardinal adds a new member to his decimated team, Father Adam Guiteau, and also leaves Crow with the conviction that Valek is the original Master vampire he has been seeking, the sole source of the entire vampiric infection. In a struggle with Katrina, Montoya is bitten, but keeps the wound a secret from Crow. Katrina's telepathy tips the slayers to Valek's whereabouts. Crow, figuring that Father Guiteau knows more than he lets on, brutally extracts from the priest the information that Valek is indeed the original vampire, inadvertently created by the Church in a 14th-century "reverse exorcism" that went terribly wrong. Ever since, the Church has sought to undo the evil it has created, to which end it has hired teams of professional slayers like Crow's to root out and destroy vampires. Father Guiteau also tells Crow that Valek is seeking the fabled Berget Cross, the key instrument needed for Valek's completion of a ritual that will make him finally fully powerful—able to walk and wreak evil by day as well as by night.
     By the time the story is fleshed out, Valek has already located the Cross and wrested it from the Church in an assault on a desert monastery in which he and seven accompanying Masters slaughter the monks and capture the Cross. Montoya feels vampirism—and fondness for Katrina—growing within him, but continues to keep his secret from Crow, although the distance begins to strain their relationship. In a desperate effort to destroy Valek, the three-slayer team attack a small town jail where Valek and his Masters have holed up. The assault is only partly successful, however, and Crow is caught by Valek after sunset. While Montoya struggles against the evil growing within him, believing that it will be destroyed if Valek is killed, Crow becomes the centerpiece of Valek's ritual—the crucified crusader whose blood

energizes the vampire. The "reverse exorcism" is performed by none other than Cardinal Alba, who reveals that fear of death and loss of faith have made the vampires' immortality attractive to him. But at the crucial moment, Father Guiteau comes out of hiding to prove himself by killing the Cardinal and interrupting the ceremony, giving Montoya time to pull Crow out of harm's way. Because the ceremony was timed to climax at the first rays of sunrise, it is now the vampires who are trapped outside at the wrong time. All succumb to either sunlight or the vampire slayers, except for Valek, who makes it back inside. Crow follows him for a titanic confrontation, which Crow wins by exposing the vampire to sunlight. Understanding at last that Montoya and Katrina have the infection, and may be the start of a new race of vampires, Crow nevertheless lets his old friend escape to Mexico, after promising to follow them and kill them if the evil remains. He and Father Guiteau cement their new-found friendship and become the core of a new team of slayers.

MELTDOWN

In production, 1999

Direction: Ate de Jong. *Screenplay*: John Dahl & Rick Dahl, based on a story by **John Carpenter**. *Executive Production*: Harmon Kaslow. *Production*: George G. Braunstein and Ron Hamady.
(107 minutes)

Featured Player   Casper Van Dien

Notes

1. Son of dance director Nick Castle, the younger Castle portrayed The Shape in *Halloween* and also worked on *The Fog*, before becoming a director in his own right. His directorial credits include *The Last Starfighter*, *The Boy Who Could Fly*, and *Tap*—a dance film tribute to the memory of his father.
2. *Dark Star* was subsequently distributed by Bryanston, and later by Atlantic Releasing.
3. The dialogue of the film specifically sets the action in "Precinct 9, *Division* 13" of the Los Angeles Police Department. The working title of the film was *Anderson's Alamo*, which was changed to the stronger but more generic *The Siege*. The film's

present title was given it by distributors who felt that title better conveyed the topic and mood of the film, and would give it a better box office. They may have been right about the more compelling nature of the new title, but they got the number of the station wrong.

4. Subsequently distributed by Samuel Goldwyn Releasing.

5. John T. Chance, the name of the sheriff played by John Wayne in *Rio Bravo*, an influence on *Assault on Precinct 13*, is a pseudonym John Carpenter has used for some of his work as a film editor.

6. So read the credits. The film's dialogue establishes that Michael was 6 at the time of the murder, in 1963, so 15 years later, in 1978, he should be 21.

7. Uncredited cameo.

8. Evans and Gideon won sole screenplay credit following a Writers Guild arbitration. By John Carpenter's account, *Starman* was written by Dean Reisner—to whom Carpenter dedicated the published version of the screenplay. A British fan magazine, *The John Carpenter File*, reports that Carpenter's USC classmates Nick Castle and W. D. "Rick" Richter also had a hand in an early version of the script.

9. Based on a screenplay by John Carpenter.

10. Martin Quatermass, brother of Dr. Bernard Quatermass, invented by Nigel Kneale for a series of science fiction films and television programs, is a pseudonym for John Carpenter.

11. Frank Armitage, a relative of the haunted Dr. Henry Armitage in H. P. Lovecraft's "The Dunwich Horror," is a pseudonym for John Carpenter.

Index

About the Author

Robert C. Cumbow is a lawyer, teacher, and writer. He works in Seattle, where he practices intellectual property law, teaches law to film and video producers, and writes on film, culture, and lifestyle topics. He is also the author of *Once upon a Time: The Films of Sergio Leone*, also published by Scarecrow Press, the only book in English wholly devoted to critical analysis of the work of the director of the most famous "spaghetti westerns." Cumbow holds three degrees from Seattle University, where he teaches a Great Books course, courses in intellectual property law, and clinical internships in art and entertainment law. He lives in Bellevue, Washington, with his wife, Grace, and their daughters, Rachel and Irena. He is a frequent writer and lecturer on film and legal topics.

Lightning Source UK Ltd.
Milton Keynes UK
UKOW05n0617040417
298289UK00012B/169/P

9 780810 837195